THE ULTIMATE BOOK OF
PAINT EFFECTS

THE ULTIMATE BOOK OF
PAINT EFFECTS

MURDOCH BOOKS®
Sydney • London • Vancouver • New York

Published by Murdoch Books®, a division of Murdoch
Magazines Pty Ltd, GPO Box 1203, Sydney NSW 1045
This edition published 2000
First published in 2000 by Merehurst Limited

National Library of Australia Cataloguing-in-Publication data
The ultimate book of paint effects. Includes index.
ISBN 0 86411 998 4. 1. House painting - Amateurs' manuals.
2. Interior decoration - Amateurs' manuals. 3. Painting - Technique. 747.3

Project Editor: Anna Nicholas
Commissioning Editor: Iain Macgregor
Senior Designer: Helen Taylor
Designers: Laura Jackson and Cathy Layzell
Design & Editorial Assistance: Axis Design
CEO & Publisher: Anne Wilson

Colour separation by Colourscan in Singapore
Printed in Singapore by Imago

SAFETY GUIDELINES

Children's rooms

When working on projects for children's rooms, make sure that all materials, especially paints and varnishes, are non-toxic, and do not put anything that has small or loose parts within the reach of a baby. Always keep DIY equipment and materials, together with any unfinished projects, in a locked cupboard and out of the reach of children.

Cutting equipment

When working with a scalpel or craft knife, use a cutting mat or piece of thick card to protect the work surface. Always cut away from your body in case the knife slips, and do not place your other hand in the path of the scalpel blade.

Protective gloves

Wear protective gloves when using paint and varnish strippers, because both are caustic and should not be allowed in contact with the skin. If you find ordinary household rubber gloves cumbersome, try lightweight surgical gloves. However, do not wear rubber gloves when working with a heat source.

Step ladders

When using a step ladder, make sure that the base is secure and stable so that it will not slide or move when you are on it. Never stand on the top platform. Rather than leaning or stretching to reach difficult areas, adjust the ladder. Remove any paint or tools from the platform before moving the ladder.

Heat strippers

When using a hot air paint stripper protect your eyes with safety goggles and consider using cotton gloves. Do not wear loose fitting clothing, which could get in the way of the heat source, and tie back long hair. Make sure that the work area is clear of anything that could catch alight, such as bedding or curtains, and never cover the floor with newspaper. Protect glass and plastic with a deflector when working near them with a heat stripper.

Ventilation

When using oil- and solvent-based adhesives, paints and varnishes, work in a well-ventilated area and do not allow naked flames or cigarettes nearby. Always wear a face mask to protect you from fumes and dust, even when working outdoors.

Safety goggles

Always wear safety goggles when you are doing any job that could produce dust or flying debris, such as paint stripping, sanding, sawing or hammering.

Electricity

If you have problems with an electrical tool, always unplug it before making any investigations or attempting to fix it. Keep power tools away from water. Before working on an electrical fitting or appliance, cut off the electricity supply either by unplugging the appliance or cutting off the power at the main fuse box.

ACKNOWLEDGEMENTS

Authors: Salli Brand, Julie Collins, Catherine Cumming, Tricia Greening, Katrina Hall, Frances Halliday, Clare Louise Hunt, Joanna Jones, Laurence Llewelyn Bowen, Julie London, Merópe Mills, Maggie Philo, Fiona Robinson, Frances Robinson, Tony Robinson.

Photographers: Graeme Ainscough, Dominic Blackmore, Jon Bouchier, Anna Hodgson, Tim Imrie, Andre Martin, Lucinda Symons, Dai Williams.

Illustrator: Stephen Pollitt.

Contents

8   Introduction

10   Getting Started

12   Preparing the surface

22   Basic Paint Effects

24   Using paint and colour
       26 Paints and their uses chart
34   Paint and glaze effects

42   Advanced Paint Effects

44   Metal and stone finish effects
50   Wood finish effects
52   Painting tricks
56   Specialist paints and techniques
60   Stencilling
68   Gilding
72   Stamping

74   Sourcing Inspiration

76   Architectural features
78   Stone, wood and metal
80   The past
82   Flowers and leaves
84   Textiles
86   Art, design and form

88   Dining Room Projects

90   Geometric starburst floor

92   Painted decanter and
       glasses
94   Chequered walls
98   Colour-washed oak
       sideboard
100 Tartan-band dining table
102 Decorative chairs
       102 Gilded chair
       102 Stamped artichoke chair
104 Antiqued table
106 Porphyry picture frame

108 Living Room Projects

110 Freehand painted tables
113 Old oak woodgrained floor
116 Craquelure lamp base
       and shade
119 Gilded mirror frame
122 Scumble-glazed table
124 Colourwashed wall
126 Granite effect fireplace
128 Sponge-stamped floor
130 Stencilled balustrade
133 Painted panels

136 Kitchen Projects

138 Kitchen accessories
       138 Pine shelf
       139 Pine spice rack
       140 Pine spoon holder
       140 Key holder
142 Lined clock cupboard

144 Painted chairs

   144 Stencilled pigs chair

   144 Crackled effect chair

146 Cups and saucers chair

148 A kitchen frieze

150 Ivy-stamped chair

152 Painted china

155 Brilliant painted glass

158 Bedroom Projects

160 Stencilled cane chair

162 Marbled dressing table

164 Hand-painted blanket box

167 Frottaged and stencilled screen

170 Stencilled headboard

172 A bedroom frieze

175 Stencilled animal prints

178 Antiqued iron bed frame

180 Cherub wardrobe

184 Children's balloon stencils

186 Bathroom Projects

188 Verdigris mirror and door handles

190 Mexican-style bathroom

193 Fish stencil shower glass

196 Limewashed bath panels

198 Decorative bathroom chests

   198 Distressed chest

   198 Stencilled chest

200 Marble bathroom

202 Garden & Conservatory Projects

204 Spray-painted table and chairs

206 Hand-painted chest

208 Repeating border and dragged stripes

212 Aged rustic chair

214 Decorated pots

   214 Marbled pots

   214 Sponged pots

216 Brightly coloured pots

218 Painted tablecloth

222 Gift & Accessory Projects

224 Tortoiseshell lamp

226 Malachite painted box

230 Limed picture frame

232 Painted frames

   232 Chequered frame

   232 Periwinkle frame and box

234 Golden pear picture frame

236 Poppies picture frame

238 Newspaper rack

240 Ethnic stamped CD box

242 Stencilled mirror frame

244 Monogrammed box

246 **Templates**

250 **Suppliers**

252 **Glossary**

255 **Index**

Introduction

PAINT EFFECTS ARE NOT A MODERN DISCOVERY. As long ago as prehistoric times, cave dwellers used natural pigments on rock faces to record their activities. For many centuries, paint effect techniques were the secret of craftsmen but recently this information has become available to all. Today, painting is one of the simplest and most versatile ways of decorating your house. Not restricted just to variations in colours, paint can be manipulated and textured to produce a host of different finishes. A 'paint effect' is any technique that goes beyond simple solid colour painting. It may involve painting a base of solid colour and then applying a glaze – a slippery medium that enables you to move paint around on the surface. Or it may involve using some other piece of equipment such as a stencil or a stamp to enhance your design.

With the help of this book, you will soon be able to fill your home with a variety of paint finishes to suit any room or any object, large or small. 'Getting Started' outlines the essential preparatory work and 'Basic Paint Effects' introduces you to paint and its uses. With the chart on pages 26–9, you will be able to select the best paint for your purpose and the useful tips on choosing tools and using colour will help you to put your plans into practice. The introduction to paint and glaze techniques will give you a grounding in the fundamental principles of basic paint effects. Once you have mastered these you can move onto more complicated skills covered in 'Advanced Paint Effects'. Broken colour techniques are the key to many faux finishes – the imitation of a substance other than that on which you are painting. You could, for example, make plaster look like mahogany or wood look like marble. These methods are illustrated and explained in a clear and easy to understand way. Similarly, specialist paint techniques such as stencilling, gilding and stamping are covered in detail.

The 'Inspirations' chapter will fuel your imagination and enable you to plan and design your decorative scheme. The special photography will show you how you can source ideas from subjects as various as architecture, stone, wood, flowers, foliage and fabrics.

Once you are equipped with the skills and have found the inspiration for your design, you will be ready to put your skills into practice. The rest of the book is devoted to step-by-step projects, which will give you the chance to do just that. Each is given a difficulty rating of one to five (indicated by the paintbrushes next to the title), which will act as a quick reference for helping you to decide which projects you might like to attempt. A difficulty rating of one means that you will be able to have a go, achieve great results and exert the minimum amount of effort while a rating of five means that your skills will be more tested and that perfect results may take time and patience.

With the techniques, inspiration and practical ideas in this book, you will be ready to take on any paint challenge. Once you have had a go, you may find that paint effects become a lifelong hobby and you will be able to use them singly or together to give your home a truly unique and individual decorative scheme.

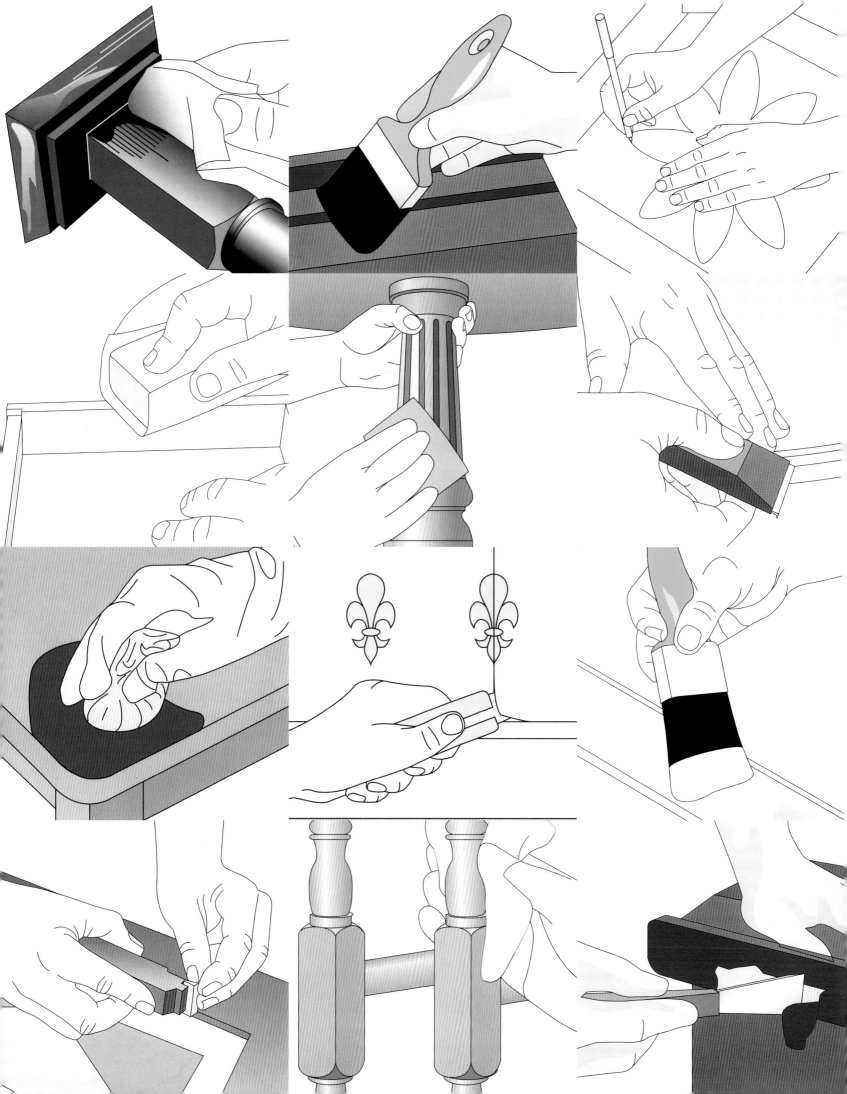

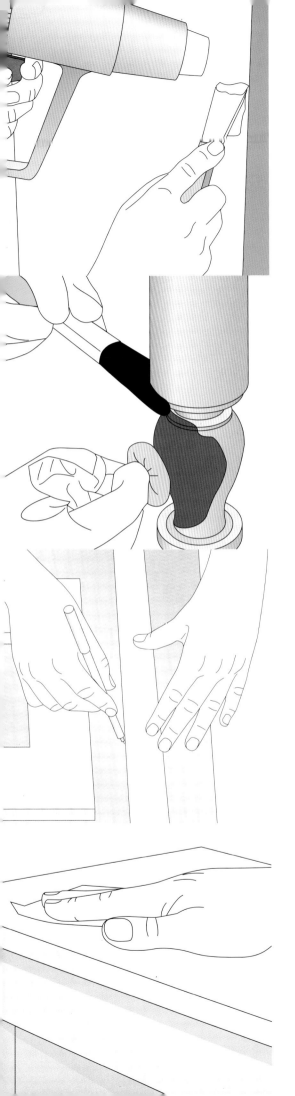

PAINT EFFECTS CAN BE CARRIED OUT ON ALMOST ANY SURFACE BUT EACH NEEDS TO BE PREPARED BEFORE YOU CAN START. THE SUCCESS OF ANY PROJECT DEPENDS ON HOW MUCH THOUGHT, PLANNING AND PREPARATION HAS GONE INTO IT BEFOREHAND. IT MAY SEEM THE MOST TEDIOUS PART OF THE PROCESS BUT IT IS WELL WORTH THE EFFORT.

Getting Started

Preparing the surface

ALL PAINT EFFECTS, no matter how simple or complicated they are, require a well-prepared surface. Although it is sometimes boring and labour-intensive, ensuring that your wall or piece of furniture is thoroughly prepared will help to avoid unwanted peeling and cracking, and prevent careful, dedicated work from going to waste. The next few pages provide a basic list of equipment that you might need, with some guidance on how to perform these simple tasks to best effect. Many are ordinary household items although others, such as masks and goggles, are vital investments for achieving the right finish – both successfully and safely. Remember that the value of good preparation can never be over-estimated.

CLEANING

CLEANING IS ESSENTIAL before you start to create your paint effects. Unwanted dust or grease could potentially ruin the finish and threaten to destroy all your hard work.

WASHING EQUIPMENT

If possible, it is best to perform this task outside where making a mess will not be so much of a problem. Always have plenty of rinsing water to hand and make sure that you protect your clothes with a water-proof apron. Use a spare bowl, household sponge and/or scourer, together with a detergent or sugar soap solution for greasy surfaces. Some items will need more time and perseverance than others, but revealing the true surface beneath the dirt can be rewarding.

CLOTHS

Always keep old cotton shirts and sheets aside for use as spare lint-free rags. It is amazing how quickly rags and cloths need replacing so before embarking on a cleaning project, make sure that there are plenty to hand. It is also sometimes worthwhile investing in a few specialist rags, particularly those that can be used while performing decorative skills and techniques.

- STOCKINET: This is available from large craft stores and is used for polishing or general mopping up. This type of cloth can also be handy for decorative techniques, creating stipple-like textures on painted surfaces or helping to eliminate brush marks from a paint finish.

- TACK RAGS: Small, versatile and long-lasting, these oily cloths are ideal for cleaning wood, metal, plaster or any other surface (except glass). They will pick up and hold dust and dirt, leaving a completely clean surface to work on. Tack rags are used in most projects in this book.

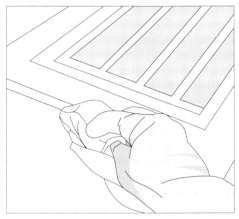

▲ Wear rubber gloves when applying chemicals.

DETERGENTS

A range of commercially available detergents and similar products are good for cutting through dirt and grease deposits, when applied with steel wool or cloths. Check with the chart on p21 to find out what type of product is effective for the surface that you are using and always wear protective rubber gloves. Methylated spirit can also be used to remove grease and grime, but always follow the manufacturer's guidelines with regard to storage and use.

SAFETY ADVICE: Equipment

Always wear goggles and a mask whenever you are rubbing down surfaces. Gloves and protective clothes are especially important when using chemical products such as paint strippers or methylated spirit. Ear plugs are also a good idea for work with electrical equipment such as sanders. Protect all nearby surfaces with suitable covering and always provide plenty of ventilation for dust and fumes.

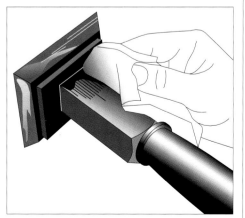

▲ Wipe all surfaces, edges and corners.

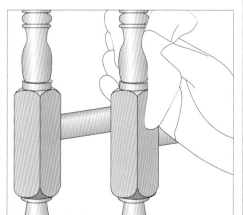

▲ Use a tack rag to remove dust and dirt.

RUBBING DOWN

SOME ITEMS will require more rubbing down than others. In some cases you may have to get rid of a few loose flakes of paint, and in others you might have to remove several layers of varnish or paint in order to get back to the original surface. Metal, in particular, needs a thorough rubbing down because any rust left will invariably recur, spoiling the finished effect. The size of the piece, the type of surface and the desired finish will help to determine what equipment should be used for the project.

ABRASIVE PAPERS

Available in hardware stores, abrasive papers can be used to sand down a surface, distress paint, and smooth and varnish finishes. Most are graded either coarse, medium or fine, depending on the amount and spacing of the grit used – the higher the number, the finer and more compact the grit. Some can be fitted to electric drills or sanding machines, while others are designed to be hand held. Many people wrap the paper around a block of cork or wood for easy handling.

Also, bear in mind that some surfaces suit different types of paper more than others. For example, softwoods tend to fur up more than hardwoods.

Sanding down a surface takes patience and will often require two or more different types of paper. Use a coarse or medium coarse (depending on the roughness of the surface) grade paper to remove most of the jaggedness before finishing off the surface with a fine grade paper.

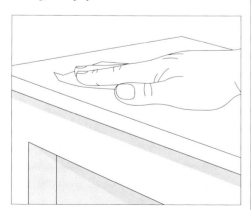

▲ Use abrasive paper for rubbing down.

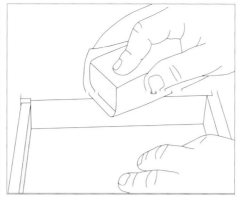

▲ Abrasive paper can be wrapped around cork.

Remember always to wear a mask when using an abrasive paper, in order to avoid inhaling dust particles. It is also a good idea to follow the grain of the wood to help prevent surface damage and scratches.

• GLASSPAPER: A soft abrasive paper containing small particles of glass that is suitable for the first stages of sanding.

• GARNET PAPER: Often reddish in colour, this paper is quite rough. However, it is more hardwearing than glasspaper, making it ideal for hardwood furniture.

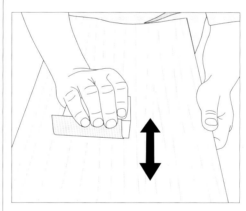

▲ Follow the direction of the grain.

• WET-AND-DRY OR SILICON CARBIDE PAPER: As its title suggests, this paper can be used wet or dry, and is good for fine-smoothing painted surfaces. It is also particularly good for distressing stencils or hand-painted designs, although in these cases the grade should be very fine. For best results, keep the paper dry, which will prevent black smudges on the decorative finish.

• A SANDING STICK: There is a very helpful product on the market known as a 'sanding stick' on which you attach a piece of sandpaper. The stick has a swivel joint on the end of it, which means that you can reach up to sand and turn the sandpaper as you go without the aid of a ladder. A brisk run over any roller-painted wall with a sanding stick before painting will eliminate the orange-peel effect and create a quick, smooth surface on which to begin.

WIRE BRUSHES & STEEL WOOL

Relatively inexpensive and available from hardware stores, wire brushes are particularly good for large pieces of metal with flaking paint or rust. Although intricate areas are best treated with handheld brushes, it is possible to get electric drills with wire brush fittings for large surfaces.

Steel wool comes in various grades of coarseness and can be used for rubbing down wood, metal and glass, as well as applying wax and distressing painted surfaces. It can also be used to apply paint and varnish removers, or be soaked in turpentine for cleaning wooden furniture. If it is used gently, fine steel wool does not scratch or mark surfaces and helps to create a very clean, smooth finish. However, the wool is made of fine steel filaments, which become loose and can be inhaled, so always wear a mask.

SCRAPERS

There is a variety of scrapers available that can be used to remove surface coatings, either alone or in conjunction with a paint stripper or hot air gun. The main types are:

• BROAD SCRAPER: Wooden handled with a wide metal blade, this is designed to glide between the surface and coating.

• SHAVEHOOK: This is either completely triangular or has a combination of curved and straight blades, designed to scrape in awkward surfaces such as curves and grooves.

• SKARSTEN SCRAPER: A scraper with disposable, hooked blades that clip into a wooden handle. Use on flat surfaces, curves and difficult grooves.

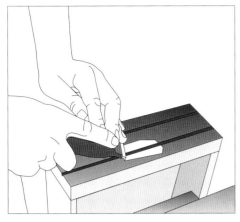

▲ Pull the scraper in the direction of the grain.

USING A SKARSTEN SCRAPER

1 Starting with the flat areas, hold the scraper firmly and pull it towards you, following as closely to the grain of the wood as possible. If the surface becomes a little bumpy, turn the scraper 45 degrees and continue scraping in the direction of the grain.

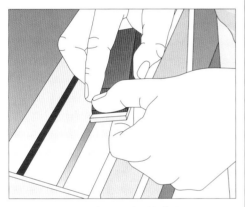

▲ Apply pressure close to the blade for grooves.

2 Only push the scraper away from you in exceptional cases, such as when cleaning out grooves, as this can gouge the wood. In these instances, hold the skarsten scraper firmly and close to the blade, so that you can control the pressure.

3 Fit a serrated blade into the scraper if you are tackling a particularly stubborn surface. However, this will scratch flat surfaces so be sure to remove it after use.

HOT AIR GUNS

Paint can be softened prior to scraping by using a hot air gun. Much safer than a conventional blow torch that has a naked flame, the air gun produces blasts of warm air, similar to that produced by a hairdryer. This causes the paint

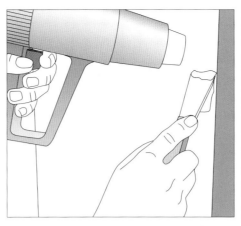

▲ Scrape away the paint as it peels under heat.

to soften and bubble, making it easy for you to insert a scraper underneath and gently lift it off. Hot air guns can also be fitted with various attachments that either disperse or concentrate the heat emitted.

1 Hold the nozzle approximately 5–10cm (2–4in) away from the surface so that the paint starts to bubble and blister, without actually burning.

2 As the paint layer begins to rise, insert a paint scraper underneath and lift it away carefully. Continue in this way until most of the paint has been removed.

3 Sand down the surface with medium, then fine, grade abrasive papers and wipe it over with a tack rag in order to remove any paint or dust residue.

SAFETY ADVICE: Lead paint

• Many old pieces of furniture will have been painted with primers, undercoats or top coats containing lead. Stripping these layers causes exposure to the lead, which is particularly harmful to pregnant women, children and pets. If you are concerned that the piece you want to strip is coated in a lead paint, invest in a special testing kit, available from most hardware stores.

• Blasting, burning, scraping or sanding paint that contains lead should be avoided. The best technique for removing leaded paint is to use a chemical stripper, scraping the removed paint straight into a container for disposal. If the paint is very thick, use a hot air gun to soften the coating but do not allow it to burn as this will cause harmful fumes. After removing the paint, rinse the surface well to remove any residual dust.

• Always wear protective clothing, including a face mask, when removing paint that may contain lead. Ensure that children, pregnant women and pets keep away from the area and avoid working on windy days when loose particles are likely to be blown about.

PAINT STRIPPERS

There are numerous paint strippers readily available for removing both paint and varnish. However, chemical strippers can burn if they touch the skin so always wear protective clothes and gloves. Also, ensure there is plenty of ventilation for unpleasant fumes. If the task of completely removing old paint is too daunting then rub

BASIC EQUIPMENT

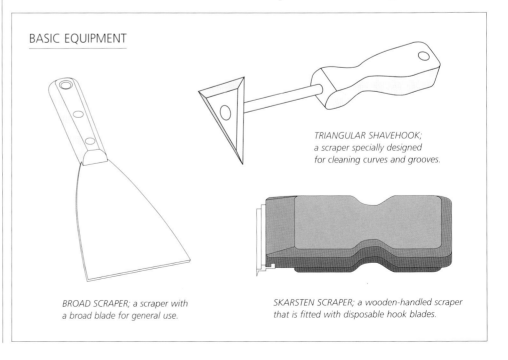

BROAD SCRAPER; a scraper with a broad blade for general use.

TRIANGULAR SHAVEHOOK; a scraper specially designed for cleaning curves and grooves.

SKARSTEN SCRAPER; a wooden-handled scraper that is fitted with disposable hook blades.

it down as well as possible and fill any deep indents where the paint has completely come away with jointing compound (filler) using a damp cloth to wipe it over the edge of the old paint, thus smoothing out the ridges.

STRIPPING PAINT

1 Remove any handles or hinges that are on the object. Then scrape off loose paint and wipe down the whole surface.

2 Using an old paintbrush, apply paint stripper to the piece, a section at a time. Wear waterproof gloves and work with the window open.

▲ Apply stripper with an old paintbrush.

3 Scrape off any loose and soft paint with a scraper. Use a skarsten scraper for grooves and tight areas. As instructed, remove excess stripper with turpentine. (Avoid using water on timber as this may cause damage.)

4 When the bare surface is dry, use medium and then fine grade abrasive papers to sand it down. Finally, wipe the surface with a tack rag to remove any residue.

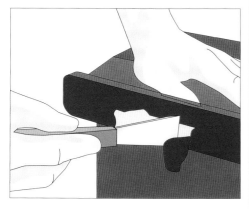

▲ Lift the softened paint with the scraper.

STRIPPING SHELLAC FINISHES

1 To remove shellac finishes, including french polish, apply methylated spirit to a small section of the surface with steel wool or a nylon scourer. (Strong liquid ammonia can also be used but the fumes from these are extremely unpleasant.) Wearing rubber gloves and a face mask, rub the scourer backwards and forwards, following the grain as closely as possible.

2 As you finish scrubbing the small area, use a rag soaked with methylated spirit to rub off all excess shellac. Then move on to another area, making sure that you work on small sections at a time.

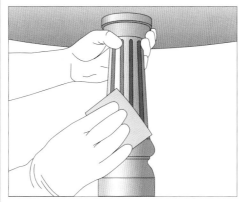

▲ Use a scourer to apply methylated spirit.

3 Clean tight areas, such as grooves and curves, with a skarsten scraper. Then sand the entire surface with medium and fine grade abrasive papers.

4 If you will be using a solvent-based finish, leave the object aside for a while so that the moisture in the air can raise the grain. If you are using a water-based finish, the same effect can be achieved by wiping the surface with a dampened cloth.

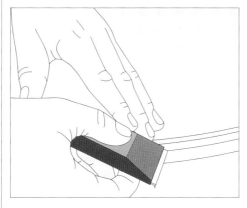

▲ Clean tight grooves with a skarsten scraper.

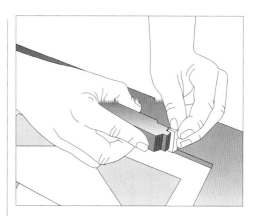

▲ Be sure to scrape out tight corners and edges.

STRIPPING VARNISH

1 Sand the surface roughly with a medium grade abrasive paper. This will help the paint stripper to penetrate the waterproof coating. Then liberally apply paint (or varnish) stripper with an old brush.

2 Leave the surface until the varnish begins to bubble and lift – a process that can take 1–4 hours. Scrape off the softened varnish with a paint scraper and use a triangular shavehook for corners and grooves. Any areas where the varnish doesn't scrape off will need a second application of stripper.

3 Sand down the surface with medium and fine grade abrasive papers. Then wipe down with a tack rag to remove any residue.

HINTS & TIPS: Stripping

• If you have a large piece of furniture, it may be worth using a commercial stripping company. Some businesses use non-caustic methods which, although invariably more expensive than caustic techniques, are safer for delicate objects. Chunky pine items or pieces that are not that valuable can be treated with caustic chemicals. However, when the object is returned, wash it down with vinegar to neutralize any remaining caustic soda solution. Allow the piece to dry and sand it before applying the new finish.

• If you are unsure if the surface you want to strip is coated in shellac or varnish, try rubbing a small corner with some fine steel wool soaked in methylated spirit. If the wool becomes clogged with a brown, sticky 'gravy', the surface is coated in shellac and can be stripped by continuing the procedure. However, if the surface has been varnished, only surface dirt will cling to the wool and so paint stripper will be required.

STRIPPING WALLPAPER

Until you start to strip wallpaper, you will not know if the task ahead is going to be easy or time-consuming. Some paper comes away without the aid of scrapers or soaking. In some cases though, you will need to soak wallpaper off by washing the wall with hot water and a sponge again and again until the old glue dissolves – you may also need to use a flat scraper or filling knife.

When all the paper is off, wash the wall with hot water again to remove old glue residue completely and then sand the entire surface with medium grade paper.

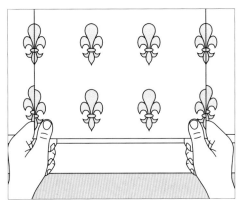

▲ Lift the unstuck edges with both hands.

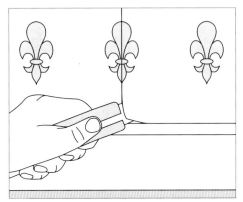

▲ Use a sharp blade to work up the edges.

FILLING

GAPS, HOLES AND DENTS are common defects. By filling these pits, it is possible to create a beautifully smooth finish, ready for decoration. There is a range of different fillers available.

When you buy a filler check whether it is sandable – those that tell you on the label to smooth before leaving to dry are probably not sandable and are more difficult to work with. Powder filler, mixed on a board with water and a filling knife is beyond compare and is used by all the professionals. With sandable fillers, you can safely over fill the crack or hole, and then rub it back to a smooth finish when it is dry. The little holes that appear in plasterboard where the screw attaches it to the wall are best filled with a flexible sandable wood filler, which will move to expand and contract, and may prevent the hole from reappearing. Knock out any areas that look as though they will eventually need filling before starting and re-fill them. It is worth the extra few minutes.

• CELLULOSE FILLER: Popularly used for most small dents and holes around the home, this filler can be used on wood as well as plaster. Although it is not ideal for large cracks, the filler helps provide a smooth surface for rough-grained pieces of wood, and for the rough ends of manufactured 'wood' surfaces such as chipboard.

• WOOD FILLER: There are many types of specialist wood fillers available. Water-based, ready-mixed varieties are the easiest to use and are suitable for filling small holes and cracks, and sealing around bad joins in wood. They come in a variety of wood colours, as well as plain, and sand down well to a very fine, hard finish. Some fillers are bought in powder form, then mixed with water to form a smooth paste.

• CHINA FILLER: A special china filler can be bought at craft suppliers and sometimes at antique centres. Use it to build up missing areas on china edges, and to fill any cracks and chips. It takes on the appearance of china and gives a fine finish when smoothed off and hardened.

HINTS & TIPS: Filling with pumice

Surfaces that are to be given a clear coating (such as shellac) can be filled with powdered pumice. Moisten a clean cotton pad with methylated spirit and dip it into sifted pumice. Coat the entire surface of the object using a circular motion, applying a gentle, even pressure. When the grain is completely covered, wipe away the excess with a clean rag.

HINTS & TIPS: Tinted wood filler

If you plan to leave the wood partly showing for any reason, such as liming or colourwashing, it may be a good idea to use a tinted wood filler for filling holes and cracks.

• PUTTY/FILLER KNIFE: This is a broad blade for forcing different fillers into difficult cavities. Although these knives are very similar to paint scrapers, their blades tend to be more flexible, helping to make the action of pushing filler into cracks, and levelling off flat against the surface, much easier.

FILLING GAPS AND HOLES

1 Sand around the outside of the hole and remove any dust. Apply some filler with a filler or a putty knife. Spread the blade over the hole, pressing the paste deeply into the recess. Scrape away any excess paste and allow to dry. If the filler shrinks slightly as it dries, apply another layer as before. Then sand with a fine grade abrasive paper.

2 If areas of the wooden surface have been compressed, rather than actually gauged or pitted, try removing the dent by putting a thick, damp cloth over the area and then placing a hot domestic iron over it. The steam should help to raise the compacted wood, without needing to use filler.

PRIMING

PREPARATION OF THE SURFACE includes ensuring that any decorative technique finish will be applied to a receptive base.

A range of preparatory primers and sealers is available. Check at a hardware store for a primer that is specially designed for the surface that you are treating. MDF, for example, can be safely primed with two thinned coats of the paint that you intend using. Oil-based paint is highly recommended for this. There are also primers for shiny surfaces such as plastic, tiles and melamine, which have been formulated to grip firmly to the surface. Thin the primer and apply two coats for a smooth finish.

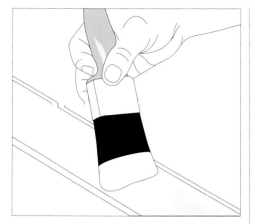

▲ Apply primer to bare wood before painting.

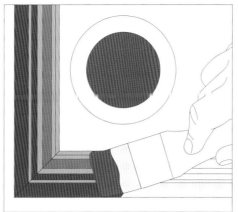

▲ Use rust-inhibiting primer on metalwork.

VARNISHES

Unlike transparent stains that are simply absorbed into a wooden surface and require further sealing, varnishes form a clear, protective layer. Most varnishes are made with polyurethane resins which provide a heat-resistant, scratchproof and waterproof finish. They can be used on painted surfaces, or wood that has been carefully rubbed down and wiped clean with a tack rag.

The range of varnishes is enormous. They can be water- or oil-based and come in a range of finishes including matt, gloss and satin. Some tinted or stained varnishes are also available but these do not sink into the wood like ordinary stains. This means that additional coats of clear, protective varnish should be used as a sealant.

- ACRYLIC PRIMER: This quick-drying primer is generally used for sealing wood, although some brands are also suitable for metal, masonry and other materials. It is usually white in colour and very quick drying. However, if it is applied to bare wood, a further coat (or alternatively a layer of undercoat) may be required.

- OIL BASED PRIMER: A slow-drying, durable primer that is useful for surfaces that do not easily accept or grip acrylic primers, such as some metal and plastic surfaces. Oil-based primers are rarely needed if you are dealing with wooden furniture. The fumes emitted by oil paints are particularly strong so ensure that there is plenty of ventilation while you are working.

- RABBIT SKIN GLUE: This can be used as a preparation for gesso or as a base for gilding (see p68). The sealer can also be applied to paper to prevent the penetration of varnish or water.

- RUST-INHIBITING PRIMER: Sometimes known as red oxide paint, it is helpful to apply rust-inhibiting primer to any metalwork that you have rubbed down. This should kill any remaining rust and prevent further development. Although the primer should not be needed for new galvanized metal or tin, do apply the coating to any surfaces that are likely to rust or that are to be decorated using water-based paints. It is also a good idea to use it as a base for objects that are to be gilded. Normal primer can be used on items that will definitely not have contact with water.

- SANDING SEALER: This spirit-based sealer is ideal for applying to new, stripped, dark or heavily knotted wood. (Knotting fluid, an oil-based solvent, can be used on individual knots, although it should not be used for surfaces that are to be coated in water-based paints.) Sanding sealer provides an excellent base for waxing.

▲ Use sanding sealer on wood for varnishing.

FINISHING SEALANTS

MANY SURFACES, particularly wood, are porous and need sealing before final coats of paint or varnish are applied. Similarly, when a decorative paint technique has been used, it is often necessary to use a further sealant to protect the surface and prevent it from damage or ageing. This is particularly important with objects that are subject to the weather in the garden.

Most finishing sealants consist of either varnish or wax. They work by sealing the painted, stained or natural surface so that the decorative finish is not damaged by general wear and tear, or chemicals that may come into contact with it.

- OIL-BASED VARNISH: There are numerous types of oil-based varnish, all of which are generally slow-drying. Polyurethane types are the easiest to use and are available in matt (almost no shine), satin (semi-gloss), and gloss (high sheen) finishes. To obtain the protection of a gloss finish without the increasing shine, try applying coats of matt or satin varnish over one coat of gloss.

Sometimes available in spray cans to avoid brush marks, oil based varnishes are usually re-coatable between 8 and 24 hours. These varnishes are generally more durable and heat-resistant than water-based varnishes (see below) but they can yellow with time, possibly spoiling the decorative effect. Oil-based varnishes are ideal for sealing water-soluble crackle varnish.

- WATER-BASED VARNISH: Increasingly popular, water-based acrylic varnishes are widely available in gloss, satin or matt finishes. A dead flat varnish is also available, which provides even less sheen than a matt coating. Acrylic varnishes

---

HINTS & TIPS: Oil-based varnish

Several thin layers of varnish always provide more protection than a couple of thick coats. Whenever you apply a second coat of varnish, rub down the surface lightly with a very fine abrasive paper and dust off – this will ensure that the next coat adheres well.

are milky in appearance but dry to a clear finish and are non-yellowing. However, the matt and dead flat versions contain chalk that gives them a cloudy appearance when a number of coats are applied. This makes them unsuitable as a sealant for techniques that require many layers. These finishes are also softer and less durable than satin or gloss varnish.

Some brands of acrylic varnish contain polyurethane for extra toughness, but most offer an average level of resistance, which should be suitable for most home furniture. (Items that receive a lot of wear, such as children's toys or furniture may need stronger types – try using a varnish designed for outdoor use.) Water-based varnish is usually dry to the touch in about 20 minutes and re-coatable after 2 hours.

• SHELLAC: Shellac is the naturally occurring resin of the lac beetle and is mixed with methylated spirit to form a quick-drying varnish. This traditional product is widely used for furniture restoration and French polishing. It should be applied to small areas of the surface by brush and then rubbed in using a round ball of lint-free cloth.

Shellac comes in a variety of grades and colours and is sold under many different names. Use clear shellac sanding sealer, white French polish and white button polish for sealing wood,

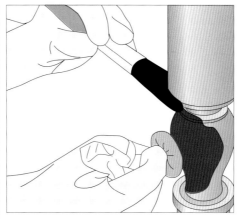

▲ Wear rubber gloves when applying shellac.

paper and paint. Use brown french polish or garnet polish for staining and ageing, in addition to sealing. French enamel varnish is transparent shellac with added dye and can also be used.

• CELLULOSE LACQUER: Usually available in a spray can, cellulose lacquer gives a high sheen protective finish for water-based decorated surfaces. However, it

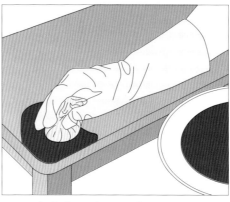

▲ Apply shellac to large surfaces by cloth.

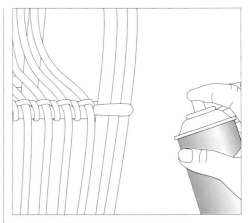

▲ Spray cellulose lacquer in a light, even coat.

should not be used with oil-based mediums as cellulose thinners, which are used to dilute the lacquer, act like paint stripper on the oil.

HINTS & TIPS: Shellac

Although it is possible to apply varnish with any soft household paintbrush, specialist varnish brushes hold more liquid and so are better for covering large surfaces. Flat hog's-hair brushes are the best, usually available from specialist craft and decorating shops.

APPLYING VARNISH

1 Prepare the surface of the object by sanding firstly with medium, and then fine grade abrasive papers. Wipe thoroughly with a tack rag, ensuring that there is no dust remaining on any part of the surface, including any grooves.

❖ VARNISHES & WAXES ❖

TYPE	SOLVENT	SHEEN	TIP
ACRYLIC VARNISH (BRUSH)			
• FLAT	Water	Low	Non-yellowing and quite durable.
• MATT	Water	None	Non-yellowing and quite durable.
• SATIN	Water	Medium	Non-yellowing and quite durable.
ACRYLIC VARNISH (SPRAY)	Water	Medium	Non-yellowing and very durable.
ACRYLIC VARNISHING WAX	Water	Medium	Non-yellowing and very durable.
BEESWAX POLISH	Mineral turpentine	Medium	Can yellow with age, quite durable.
FURNITURE WAX	Mineral turpentine	Medium	Non-yellowing and quite durable.
LACQUER VARNISH (SPRAY)	Mineral turpentine	High	Non-yellowing and very durable.
SHELLAC	Methylated spirit	High	Non-yellowing and very durable.

2 Dip a thoroughly clean brush in the varnish and, without removing the excess, work the brush over a sheet of brown paper. This will expel the air from the bristles and encourage loose hairs out, preventing them from sticking to your intended surface.

3 Apply the varnish with gentle strokes, taking the brush right around the lip of drawers or doors. Try to avoid overloading the surface with varnish as this will cause runs or sags.

4 Leave the varnish to dry completely hard (possibly taking 1–3 days) before lightly sanding, dusting and applying further coats.

WAXES

Wax finishes are usually applied over a varnish coating, and help to provide a soft sheen. The greater the number of coats you apply, the better the sheen that will be produced.

• BLACK BISON WAX: A blend of several waxes, Black Bison wax has a good resistance to water and fingermarks. It can be applied to painted furniture and creates a seal for crackled, aged and peeled-paint techniques. The wax is available in different colours, but beware because some will cause yellowing.

• CLEAR WAX: Clear furniture wax is also effective and can be used for creating an aged appearance on furniture. Use it over paint or wood where you do not want a colour to adhere, such as areas of wear. Clear liquid wax is particularly good for this but coloured versions are also widely available.

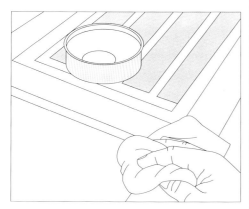

▲ Apply several coats of wax for a good sheen.

APPLYING A WAX FINISH

1 To create a protective sheen on a surface, lightly sand it down with fine grade abrasive paper and then wipe off with a tack rag.

2 Apply the wax with steel wool or a nylon scourer, rubbing the length of the surface with long, straight strokes. Make sure the wax is rubbed right into the grain and try not to leave any build-up of wax on the surface.

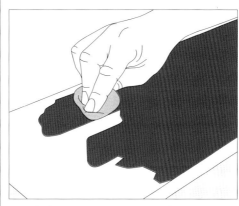

▲ Rub the wax into the grain with a scourer.

3 Within a couple of minutes of application, rub the surface with a lint-free cloth to even out the coating. The surface will feel sticky but continue to rub, changing to a clean section of cloth whenever it clogs.

4 Rub the surface for as long as possible – this will help to create a polished finish. Hold the object firmly while you polish, grasping it through a clean cloth so as to prevent grease from your hand transferring to the timber.

5 Repeat the process at least once more. The greater the number of coats, the more enhanced and refined the final finish will be.

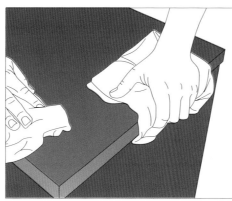

▲ Hold the item with a cloth while polishing.

TRACING & CUTTING

BASIC DRAWING and cutting techniques are often essential to complete the projects in this book. Instructions for detailed work are given in the 'Advanced Paint Effects' section, but simple procedures to help make basic tasks easier are listed below.

PLANNING TOOLS

• RULER: Essential for measuring and marking out designs, rulers should be sturdy and long. Centring rulers of 45cm (18in), available from graphic art suppliers, are very good. Invest in a metal-edged ruler for cutting out – plastic and wooden edges get sliced by the blade.

• SET SQUARE: This is useful for keeping corners accurate, though a frame, book or other rectangular object can also be used for drawing edges. Transparent set squares are most useful as you can see guidelines beneath.

• WATER-SOLUBLE PENCIL: This is ideal for marking wood as any unwanted lines or smudges can be wiped off later.

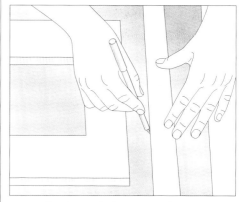

▲ Use drawing tools for accurate lines.

PLANNING A DESIGN

1 Always plan your task in advance. If you are making alterations to a piece of furniture, take measurements of all the dimensions and draw on a rough piece of paper where fixings will be required. Make sure that if the item is to be functional, any alterations you make will be of sufficient strength and adaptability. For example, if you are adding shelves to an old cupboard, think about the size of the items to be stored and maximize the room available.

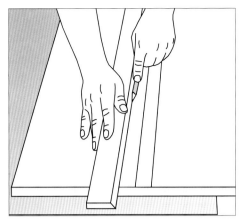

▲ Measure and mark out all dimensions.

However, remember to allow enough space for access. Similarly, decide whether the original positions of hinges or screws really are the most useful, or whether alterations are needed.

2 For large items that need matching shapes, such as two pieces of wooden scroll trim, create a template out of paper and draw around it on to your wood. This will ensure symmetry in the shapes and will help to minimize wood wastage.

TRACING

Always be patient when you are tracing and spend some time on preparation. For example, make sure that your stencil and tracing material are securely fixed – the slightest wobble, and inaccuracies begin. If the material you want to trace on to is semi-opaque, use a light box to help you see the design more clearly. Alternatively, stick the design on a window, position your medium on top, and then trace over it.

TRACING A DESIGN

1 Position a sheet of tracing paper securely over the design. Slowly follow the design with a pencil. For intricate patterns, rotate the design and paper, rather than your body.

2 Follow the outline on the reverse side of the tracing paper with a heavy (2B) pencil. Then put the tracing over your chosen surface, right side up, and follow the outline again. The heavy lead on the reverse side should transfer to the surface. Then cut out the design.

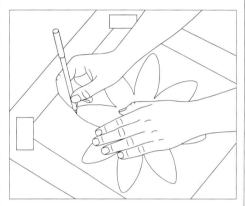

▲ Trace around the fastened design.

CUTTING TOOLS

The secret to effective cutting is sharp equipment – blunt blades cause untidy edges and slips. The projects in this book involve cutting out a variety of items including wood, paper and tin.

• SAWS: There are numerous types of saw available, both for heavy-duty work and intricate cutting. It is best to use a fretsaw for tight curves in

wood or plastic and a hacksaw or heavy-duty tin snips for cutting metal. To cut out detailed shapes, cut away most of the surrounding excess material before trying to follow the intricate outline.

• SCISSORS: Use sharp scissors and keep them aside solely for craft work, rather than odd tasks around the home that might cause them to become blunt. Ordinary scissors can be used for removing excess paper or card before using a craft or trimming knife.

• CRAFT KNIVES: Generally, craft knives and scalpels offer more flexibility and accuracy than scissors when it comes to cutting out intricate designs. Trimming knives are good for cutting straight lines, particularly on semi-thick materials such as cardboard, but knives that can be held like a pen are better for getting to grips with difficult shapes.

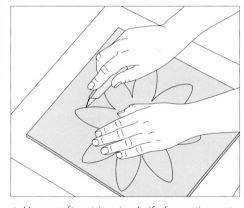

▲ Use a craft or trimming knife for cutting out.

Scalpels that have replaceable blades are particularly useful and, once mastered, can provide crisp edges. Change the blade as soon as the cutting becomes heavy or difficult – going over a slice twice leads to rough and inaccurate edges.

• CUTTING MAT: A cutting mat is essential for protecting work surfaces. Although thick pieces of cardboard make a temporary alternative, scalpels will soon penetrate the board, blunting the blade and making a clean first cut difficult. Self-healing mats are best because they last for years and have guide lines.

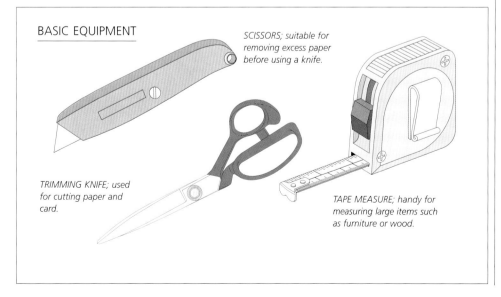

BASIC EQUIPMENT

SCISSORS; suitable for removing excess paper before using a knife.

TRIMMING KNIFE; used for cutting paper and card.

TAPE MEASURE; handy for measuring large items such as furniture or wood.

❖ SURFACE PREPARATION ❖

SURFACE	CLEANING	SANDING	BASE COATS
CHIPBOARD			
• WOOD VENEERED	Wipe with damp, but not wet, lint-free rag.	Fine grade abrasive paper.	If necessary, apply acrylic wood primer or undercoat.
• MELAMINE-COATED	Wash with sugar soap solution, using a lint-free rag and allow to dry.	Wet and dry paper.	Specialist primers available.
HARDBOARD			
• PAINTED	Wash with sugar soap solution, using a lint-free rag and allow to dry.	Fine grade abrasive paper.	Use oil-based primer on oil-based paint and water-based primer on water-based paint.
METAL			
• BARE	Brush off any rust, wipe with mineral turpentine and steel wool.	Wet and dry paper.	Metal primer or rust-inhibiting primer, followed by acrylic primer for water-based paint.
• COATED	Wash with sugar soap solution, remove any coating with an appropriate stripper.	Wet and dry paper.	As above.
MDF			
• PAINTED	Wash with sugar soap solution, using a lint-free rag and allow to dry.	Fine grade abrasive paper.	Use oil-based primer on oil-based paint and water-based primer on water-based paint.
• UNPAINTED	Wipe with damp, but not wet, lint-free rag or tack rag.	Fine grade abrasive paper.	Wood primer or undercoat. Two thin coats are recommended.
PLASTICS	Wash with sugar soap solution, or mineral turpentine.	Wet and dry paper.	Specialist primers available.
PLYWOOD			
• VARNISHED	Brush well with stiff brush then wash with sugar soap solution and a lint-free rag.	Fine grade abrasive paper.	Wood primer and oil-based undercoat where necessary.
• UNPAINTED	Wipe with damp, but not wet, lint-free rag.	As above.	Wood primer and undercoat.
WOOD			
• PAINTED	Wash with sugar soap solution, using a lint-free rag and allow to dry.	Remove loose flakes with a scraper and stripper, then use coarse, medium and fine grade abrasive papers.	Acrylic wood primer, and undercoat where necessary.
• UNPAINTED	Wipe with damp, but not wet, lint-free rag.	Fine grade abrasive paper.	Acrylic wood primer, and undercoat.
• SEALED	Wash with sugar soap solution, using a lint-free rag and allow to dry.	Remove loose flakes with a scraper and stripper, then use coarse, medium and fine grade abrasive papers.	Wood primer and undercoat where necessary.
• VARNISHED	Brush well with stiff brush then wash with sugar soap solution and a lint-free rag.	As above.	As above.
• WAXED	Methylated spirit.	As above.	As above but do not use acrylic primer.

INTERIOR DECORATORS OF ALL
LEVELS OF EXPERIENCE CAN ACHIEVE
SUCCESS WITH BASIC PAINT EFFECTS.
ALL YOU NEED IS SOME PAINT, TOOLS
AND PLENTY OF PATIENCE. THIS
CHAPTER WILL PROVIDE YOU WITH
A BASIC INTRODUCTION TO PAINT
AND ITS USES AND THEN TEACH YOU
THE SKILLS OF BASIC PAINT EFFECTS
THAT YOU WILL USE TIME AND TIME
AGAIN. ONCE YOU HAVE MASTERED
THESE, ALL PAINT EFFECT PROJECTS
WILL BE WITHIN REACH.

Basic Paint Effects

Using paint and colour

Before you can start manipulating paint to achieve paint effects, you must decide on the type of paint that you want to use. The range of paints and painting materials is ever-expanding and it can be difficult to identify the most suitable products for your job. Although there is rarely a right or wrong answer, some products, methods and tools are definitely better suited to some techniques than others. In addition, mixing different types of paint can cause problems – for example, oil-based and water-based products should be kept apart – so plan ahead and think about the finish you want to achieve. Although some paints are designed for specific purposes, most can be adapted or added to other mediums, creating an even greater array of potential results.

▲ There is a wide range of paints available.

CHOOSING PAINT

THE SELECTION OF PAINTS, varnishes and other paint products that are available can be confusing. Listed below are some of the most common types of paint. On the following pages is a paint chart with useful tips about how to use a range of paint products.

PRIMER

Usually oil-based, primers are applied to raw wood to help seal the surface and prepare it for additional paint coverage. Its oil content makes primer ideal for very porous surfaces, but it can be slow-drying.

A different type of primer, rust-inhibiting primer, is used as a base paint for metallic surfaces. It should be applied as soon as any rust has been removed from the item, helping to prevent further corrosion. (See pp16–17 for more information.) Primer not only seals the base but also ensures that the top layers of paint dry and cure properly.

There are other ways of priming wood. MDF can be safely primed with two thinned coats of the paint you intend using. This is particularly successful if you are using oil-based paint. This helps to begin building up the final colour. Thin the paint until it has the consistency of single cream.

Check the hardware store for a primer specially designed for the surface you are treating. There are primers for shiny surfaces such as plastic, tiles and melamine, which have been formulated to grip firmly to the surface. Thin the primer and apply two coats to achieve a smoother finish.

WATER-BASED PAINT

Also known as acrylic, these are relatively inexpensive paints that are available in matt or satin finishes. They are most commonly used for painting walls, but can be used on furniture – 250ml (8fl oz) tester pots are ideal for small items. Acrylic paints can be thinned with water to make a wash or mixed with scumble glaze, or tinted with universal stainers or powder pigments to make a range of unique colours. When you apply a water-based paint, you are effectively applying a skin of coloured plastic and water. The water evaporates and you are left with an even coating of plastic.

Keep windows closed when you are applying the paint, but then open them as soon as the work is finished.

OIL-BASED PAINTS

Oil-based paints come in flat, semi-gloss, and gloss finishes. Gloss paint creates a crisp, clean effect, which is not ideal for making an item look worn and old. For this reason, most people tend to use flat or semi-gloss oil-based paints, both as base coats and to make glazes for decorative finishes.

Oil-based paints give a much tougher finish than water-based paints and are particularly useful in light-coloured glazes where scumble glaze, and the addition of varnish, would be too yellowing. The only drawback to oil-based paints is that they take a long time to dry and need 24 hours between coats. To tint oil-based paints, use artists' oil paints or universal stainers, which are stronger and cheaper than artists' colours but not quite as subtle.

▲ Choose your paint type carefully.

TRADITIONAL PAINTS

A recent development in the production of paints, these paints are a variation on ordinary acrylic. Natural pigments, rather than the synthetic ones used in normal paint production, are used to make the mixture. The paints contain chalk, a traditional ingredient in paint-making, and dry to a completely matt finish, appearing lighter than the colour in the pot.

Most of the paints include modern binders and, although they have the feel and look of those used in the past, they have the advantage of a greater degree of durability. However, they are easily marked so painted surfaces need protecting with wax or varnish. However, applying varnish and waxes over traditional paints will darken them and take away their chalky appearance.

Traditional paints are more expensive than standard acrylic paint but they are definitely worth the investment, if you can afford them. The colours have a wonderful softness and subtlety, which makes them ideal for isolated projects such as furniture or accessories. They can be thinned with water and tinted in the same way as ordinary acrylic paint.

HINTS & TIPS: Professional or trade paints

Most manufacturers also make a special range of paints for the professional painter or for the trade. These tend to be more intensely coloured and dry more quickly. There are just as many colours available, if not more. Thin them and apply two or three coats to achieve a professional finish. Because they dry so quickly and thin so well, the extra time it takes to apply an additional coat is rewarded in the quality of the finish. Unfortunately, trade paints are made with a different formula to domestic paints and so it is not a good idea to mix them. Trade semi-gloss, for example, should not be painted over with ordinary semi-gloss.

GLAZE

Glaze is a medium that can be coloured for use in creating paint effects. It makes the colour slippery and moveable. The glaze is applied with a paintbrush or roller and while it is still wet, it is manipulated with brushes,

▲ Artists' paints come in a range of colours.

rags, plastic or anything you like. See pp34–5 for further information.

ARTISTS' ACRYLIC PAINT

This paint is very quick-drying and durable. Its concentrated colour makes it ideal for many types of surface decoration, including stencilling, printing and general detail painting. It can also be used to colour acrylic glaze, although the paint should be watered down a little first, to avoid getting any lumps.

Acrylics are also ideal paint bases, and can be rubbed back to create an old, distressed look. Although they are less cost-effective for covering large surfaces, they can be used on smaller items or watered down to make general washes. Acrylics are usually available in tubes or jars, and some specialist types, suitable for work such as fabric painting, are now available. Acrylic paint can be quite harsh on brush hairs, so make sure brushes are cleaned thoroughly after use, before they dry out.

ARTISTS' OIL PAINT

Conventionally used for fine art, oil colours can also be used to tint any oil-based paint or glaze. However, they are slow-drying and will slightly delay the drying time of anything with which they are mixed. Paintbrushes must be cleaned with mineral turpentine, before ordinary water and detergent is used.

The most subtle of paints, artists' oil colours can be used for almost any decorative finish, from barge painting to stencilling, although many people prefer to use quicker drying media, such as acrylics. If you want to keep the effect simple and clean, however,

there is often nothing better than simply using oils to paint some scroll work or decorative feature on to an old varnished piece of junk. If you want to speed up drying time, you can add driers to your paint mixture

SPRAY PAINT

Available in easy-to-use cans, spray paint is produced in a large range of colours and finishes. Acrylic water-based spray paint, specifically intended for use in interior decoration, is ideal for almost all surfaces, including wood, metal, plaster, plastic and glass. It can

▲ Spray paints are very easy to use.

be used for small projects such as stencilling, as the main colour for doors and shutters, and is especially suitable for children's trunks and toys because it is non-toxic. You can also buy spray enamels for metals and glass, pearlized finishes and polyurethane varnishes. Apply the paint in several thin coats rather than one heavy one, so as to avoid paint build-up and runs.

GOUACHE COLOURS

Although relatively expensive, these colours are extremely strong and are ideal for tinting water-based glazes or for painting directly on to a surface.

DRIERS

Driers are added to any type of paint in order to speed up the drying process. There is much controversy surrounding their effect on the final finish but they really do make a difference if you are pushed for time and are almost essential if you are using oil-based scumble glaze coloured with artists' oils. The use of driers with water-based paints is not necessary.

Paints and their uses

Product	Quality and finish	Thinners	Use for	Apply with	Number of coats
Primer	Preparation for bare wood. Prevents wood from swelling.	Water or turpentine (check the can).	Bare wood.	Brush or small roller.	1
Undercoat	Matt finish, thin surface preparation and sealer. (check the can).	Water or turpentine.	Walls, woodwork.	Brush.	1
Matt	No shine, general-purpose coverage.	Water.	Walls, new plaster.	Large brush or roller.	2
Low-sheen	Satin sheen, general-purpose coverage.	Water.	Walls, murals and base for glaze work. Not suitable for new plaster.	Large brush or roller.	2
Semi-gloss	Satin sheen, general-purpose coverage.	Turpentine.	Walls, woodwork and metal.	Large brush or roller.	2
Gloss	High shine, durable. (check the can).	Water or turpentine.	Woodwork, doors.	Good-quality brush.	2
Woodstain	Colour without varnish for bare wood.	Water or turpentine.	Bare or unvarnished wood.	Lint-free cloth or brush.	1 or 2
Varnish – polyurethane	Oil-based wood and paintwork protection. Choice of shine.	Turpentine.	Wood and to protect paintwork.	Good-quality brush.	Up to 8
Varnish – acrylic	Fast-drying protection for wood- and paintwork. Choice of sheen. Non-yellowing.	Water.	Wood and to protect paintwork.	Brush or roller.	Up to 8
Wax	Protection and shine for wood.	N/A	Bare or stained wood.	Lint-free cloth.	3
Oil-based glaze	Transparent.	Turpentine.	Mixing with artists' oil colours to make coloured glaze for paint finishes.	Brush or roller.	1 or 2

Washable?	Area per litre (one coat) Square metres	Notes	Drying time before re-coating	Drying time final coat	Undercoat
N/A	12	Thin to a watery consistency. Rub down with sandpaper when dry.	2–4 hours	N/A	No.
N/A	12	Stir well. Rub down with sandpaper when dry.	Oil-based – 8 hours. Water-based – 2 hours.	N/A	N/A
No.	10	Do not stir and avoid frost.	1–2 hours	8 hours	No, but dilute first coat for raw wood.
Yes, soapy water. Do not scrub.	10	Dark colours require 3 or more coats.	1–2 hours	8 hours	Matt.
Yes, household cleaners. Avoid ammonia.	15	Stir well before and during use.	8 hours	24 hours	Primer or commercial undercoat.
Yes, household cleaners. Avoid ammonia.	12	Slow to apply – use good-quality bristle brush. Oil-based is more hardwearing.	4–8 hours	24 hours	Primer.
No.	8	Apply generously with brush. Remove excess with dry cloth. Stainers do not protect wood; wax or varnish when dry.	1–3 hours	1–3 hours	No.
Yes, soapy water.	10	Use thinned and apply several coats for the greatest lustre. May yellow as coats build up.	4 hours	24 hours	No.
Yes, but do not scrub.	10	Difficult to apply as evenly as polyurethane varnishes. Not as durable but quick-drying and crystal clear. Do not use on oil-based paints.	1 hour	8 hours	No.
Yes, with more wax or soapy water.	8	Apply just like shoe polish, buff with a soft cloth between coats. Pure beeswax best for new wood; re-wax often.	3 hours	N/A	Woodstain (optional).
No.	Depends on consistency.	Good workability for ½ hour. Cheap way to extend colour.	6 hours	N/A	Oil-based semi-gloss base.

Paints and their uses (continued)

Product	Quality and finish	Thinners	Use for	Apply with	Number of coats
Craft paint	Intense colours for detailing and small areas.	Various.	Small craft projects.	Soft brush.	1 or 2
Artists' oil, crayons and pastels	Intense, pure colours in stick form.	Oil or turpentine.	Detailing and drawing on walls, furniture or paper.	N/A	N/A
Powdered pigments	Intense colours from natural earth and mineral pigments.	Water.	Making homemade paints for colourwashing.	Brush or roller.	1
Car spray paint	Low or high sheen hardwearing, wide colour range.	Cellulose thinners.	Stencils and basic coverage.	Spray from the can.	1 or 2
Glass paint	Transparent or matt.	Acetone.	Painting glass of all kinds. Transparent detail work.	Soft artists' brush.	1
Blackboard paint	Matt black, very opaque.	Methylated spirit.	Interior matt finishes, chalk boards.	Brush.	1 or 2
PVA glue	General-purpose sealer.	Water.	Walls or woodwork to seal or stick.	Brush.	1
Kitchen and bathroom paint	Moisture and steam resistant paints.	Water.	Kitchens and bathrooms.	Brush or roller.	At least 2
Melamine primer	Primer for shiny plastic surfaces.	Water.	Preparing shiny surfaces for painting.	Brush.	2
Tile primer	Primer for tiles.	Turpentine (best to throw the brush away after use).	Preparing tiles for paint.	Brush or small gloss roller.	2
Textured wall paint	Heavy plaster-like wall and ceiling paint with a textured finish.	Water.	Textured walls.	Range of tools to create different textures.	1

Washable?	Area per litre (one coat) Square metres	Notes	Drying time before re-coating	Drying time final coat	Undercoat
Yes, do not scrub.	N/A	Better quality than poster paints. Widely available in small quantities.	½ hour	N/A	N/A
No.	N/A	Allow to dry for 3 weeks or more before varnishing.	N/A	N/A	N/A
Yes.	N/A	Can be mixed with oil- or water-based products.	N/A	N/A	N/A
Yes.	N/A	Extremely hardwearing; wear a mask when spraying.	1 hour	10 hours	Spray undercoat.
Yes, do not scrub; check label.	N/A	Brushstrokes always show up; vivid colour selection. Use acetone to thin these paints.	1 hour	4 hours	No.
Yes, water only.	10	Fast drying, easy to repair and patch up.	1 hour	4 hours	No.
Yes, soapy water.	12	Dilute 1:1 with water. Apply with brush.	1–2 hours	N/A	No.
Yes.	8	This is really just acrylic semi-gloss paint.	2 hours	8 hours	Save money by undercoating with acrylic.
N/A	5	For best results, sand lightly before priming.	2 hours	16 hours	N/A
N/A	5	Do not over thin.	16 hours	24 hours	Ammonia based, work in ventilated area.
No.	About 10 depending on textures.	Good for hiding cracked or lumpy plaster.	5 hours	N/A	Not needed if applied quickly.

PAINTING TOOLS

ANY VISIT TO A CRAFT shop or hardware store will reveal the vast array of painting tools available. Finding the right tool can be difficult and expensive – many manufacturers will lead you to believe that a different tool is required for every task. In fact, many pieces of equipment are quite adaptable. As long as they are cleaned and well-maintained, brushes should last several years.

PAINTBRUSHES

There is a range of paintbrushes available. Even standard brushes, which are suitable for basic paint application, vary in size and quality. While cheap brushes seem more appealing, they are more likely to lose hairs frequently and may ruin the finished effect.

• BASIC ARTISTS' BRUSHES: These come in a variety of shapes. 'Flats' have a square end, helping to produce thin imprints, whereas 'filberts', which are also flat, gently taper into a conical shape. Round, finely pointed brushes are ideal for painting intricate designs, although these must be stored carefully as they are prone to easy damage.

• HOG-FITCH BRUSHES: All-purpose brushes, hog-fitches are generally used for oil painting and can be round, flat or dome-shaped. Extremely versatile, they may be used for painting narrow bands of colour, applying glue, waxes and gilt creams, touching up paint and tamping down metal leaf.

• STIPPLING BRUSHES: Stippling is the term used for finely lifting on or off very fine speckles of paint. Stippling brushes have stiff, dense bristles in a squared-off shape and come in a variety of sizes. They are useful for many paint techniques and are particularly good for merging paints and getting rid of hard lines and edges. A good quality decorating brush or a round continental brush can be used as a cheaper alternative.

• SWORD LINERS: These long-haired, soft brushes are tapered and angled, so you can produce many widths of line simply by varying the pressure applied to the brushstroke. They hold a lot of paint and are often used by sign writers.

• SOFT-HAIRED MOP: Usually made from squirrel or camel hair, mop brushes are round and are primarily used to apply metallic powder to gold size during gilding. They can also be used to remove surplus gold or metal leaf. Alternatively, a cosmetic blusher brush will do the job of a mop.

• DRAGGING BRUSHES: Sometimes confused with floggers, dragging brushes are used for graining. They have long bristles that are dragged through wet glaze, creating the woodgrain effect.

• FLOGGER: A flogger is used primarily for making the tiny flecks characteristic of oak woodgrain. It is about 5cm (2in) wide and has long bristle and a light, flat handle. After applying a woodgrain with a dragging stroke, tap the end of the bristles gently against the glaze, letting them bounce on the surface. The bristles will flop about and spring from the surface leaving tiny flecks. Work down the grain starting at the top.

• SEA SPONGES: For sponging effects, natural sponges are the most popular tool. This is because their absorbency and irregular natural structure create attractive patterns. Always clean out natural sponges thoroughly after use.

Artists' brushes   Fine artists' brushes   Hog-fitch brush   Hog's hair varnishing brushes   Stippling brushes   Sword liners   Soft-haired mop

- KITCHEN PAPER: This is invaluable for applying shellacs and polishes, for rubbing in and wiping off paint, mopping up spills and buffing waxes.

- PALETTE KNIFE: Flexible-ended palette knives can be used to either apply wood filler or mix oil colours on a palette. Finely shaped varieties can be used to apply paint, producing an interesting texture and style.

- PAINT KETTLE: Although it is possible to paint out of a tin, using a paint kettle or paint tray allows you to use small amounts of paint at a time. This helps to keep the remaining paint in the tin clean and free from air. (Exposure to air will cause a skin to form on the paint.)

- SMALL ROLLER: Suitable for large furniture surfaces, as well as walls and doors, small rollers for gloss paint are ideal for quick coats of paint. Most can be fitted with replaceable roller sleeves.

APPLYING PAINT

The quickest way to apply paint to walls is by roller. However, if you thin the paint until it has the consistency of single cream, you can apply it with a large 10–15cm (4–6in) brush, known as floggers among professionals. The paint will then settle without the brushstrokes showing and the wall will not take on the dimpled orange-peel effect, which is all too familiar these days. It may take three coats of paint but two will be enough if you are using trade paints.

When using oil-based paints, apply slightly thinned paint in 'crows' foot' fashion, which means crisscross in every direction. Lay off the paint by gently stroking the brush in a single direction. You will find that all the brushstokes level out to give a smooth surface. Never apply the paint too thickly because a skin will form on top while the paint underneath will stay soft and eventually peel. A rub between coats with fine grade emery paper is recommended. If you buy a couple of sheets of medium grade emery paper (about grade 180) you can turn it into fine grade by simply rubbing two small pieces together.

CHOOSING AND MIXING COLOURS

THE VARIETY OF COLOURS now available in different paints and mediums can make choosing a final shade difficult. In order to mix colours effectively, it is useful to understand how they interact.

PRIMARY COLOURS

The three primary colours, blue, red and yellow, are the source of all other hues. By mixing one primary colour with another, ie blue with yellow, you create what is known as a secondary colour (in this case, green). The range of subtle shades of green that can be mixed is vast. If blue is mixed with yellow in a ratio of 2:1 (or vice versa), you create an intermediate colour. The same principle applies to the other primary colours. Finally, a tertiary colour is created by mixing the three primary colours together in various different percentages.

As an exercise in trying to find the right colour combinations, you may find it useful to examine a colour wheel (see below). The area between each primary colour provides the secondary colour.

COMPLEMENTARY COLOURS

These are colours that appear opposite each other in the colour wheel; very simply, red is opposite to green, yellow to purple, and blue to orange. These colours react strongly with each other, often becoming more vibrant if they are set side-by-side.

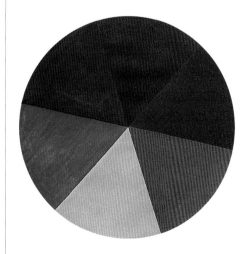

▲ The colour wheel will help you mix colours.

CHOOSING COLOURS

Ultramarine blue

Yellow ochre

Prussian blue

Raw sienna

Cerulean blue

Burnt sienna

Viridian green

Red ochre

Oxide of chromium

Venetian red

Raw umber

Cadmium red

Burnt umber

Alizarin crimson

▲ Useful acrylic pigment colours.

HINTS & TIPS: Shading & tinting colour

- A 'shade' is made by adding raw umber to a paint colour, helping to darken it and reduce its vividness. This will tone down any pigment, even white, immediately giving it an aged appearance.

- A 'tint' is created by adding white to a colour. This reduces the strength of the original hue and tends to make the colour more opaque.

If complementary colours are mixed in equal quantities they become dark grey and muddy, but adding a touch of one to the other will tone it down without making the colour look dead.

COLOUR MIXING

There are no rules about which colours should or should not be mixed together. Many unlikely combinations can produce very interesting shades – it is simply a question of experimenting and developing an eye for colour. With practice, you may find that you come to 'know' immediately how a certain colour will be affected by adding another pigment to it.

NATURAL PIGMENTS

Natural earth pigments, which are warm and soft, tend to be quite easy to live with and are extremely adaptable. These colours have been used in paint-making for centuries; they are literally

▲ Mix coloured pigment with medium gradually.

made of finely ground earth and are very inexpensive. With the addition of white they make very pretty pastel shades. Cooler shades of green and blue can also be chosen, from beautiful mineral colours.

MIXING PIGMENT WITH PAINT & PAINT MEDIUM

One economical way of creating a vast range of hues is to add powdered pigment to a paint medium. It can be added to semi-gloss or traditional paint, but do this gradually and mix it thoroughly to avoid thickening the paint too much. Remember that even if the paint looks adequately mixed in the pot or kettle, it may look less so when painted on to a surface.

▲ Use small amounts of powder pigments.

However, this unevenness of colour can sometimes add to the object's charm and give a more authentic appearance of ageing.

Artists' acrylic colours and universal stainers can be used in place of powdered pigment. Most types of pigment and medium are compatible with each other, so feel free to experiment with different variations. Do, however, make sure that you are using all water-based (or oil-based) products. Also, when you are mixing pigment with paint, work in a room that is well-ventilated and take care not to inhale the pigment powder, as it can be toxic.

For darker or more intense shades, pigment can be mixed with PVA medium or glue and water, or with artists' acrylic medium. This will create a rather plastic paint without texture, but it is good for painting detailed designs.

When diluted, this is also ideal for colourwashing and glazing. If you are using acrylic scumble glaze for a textured effect, you will only need to add a small amount of pigment and it is not necessary to add water.

▲ Artists' colours can be mixed in paint medium.

TROUBLESHOOTING

WRONG COLOUR

If you are not happy with the colour you have applied, you could re-paint the room. Or, if the colour you have applied is fairly pale, consider glazing over it using a simple paint technique, such as colourwashing (see pp36–7) or ragging (see p37). Your base colour will be toned down by doing this but will still glow through the transparent glaze.

If the colour looks too dark, try sponging one or two lighter colours on top. Your base colour will show through but the whole effect will become lighter and mottled. If you are using two or more colours for sponging, use the lightest colour last.

UNEVEN SHEEN

If the paint you have used either does not have as much shine as you would like, or is too shiny, there is a solution.

Buy some acrylic glaze with a gloss, semi-gloss or matt finish, and apply a single coat of this on to the dry paint surface. Acrylic glaze looks like milk when wet but dries clear.

THE PAINT IS WAXY

Careless preparation can often prevent oil-based paint from drying, or cause it to dry with a waxy feel. If you are painting on to a wooden surface you must prime the surface first. Primers provide not only a smooth surface on which to paint, but also a base on which the top colour will cure (dry and set) fully. If you have overlooked priming the surface, wash the troubled paint away with plenty of mineral turpentine and steel wool, and start on a primed surface.

If the paint is drying very slowly with a waxy feel to it, then you have probably applied the coats too thickly. The surface of the paint is beginning to dry and cure and is sealing in the moisture underneath it.

If you can, leave the paint for a week and see if it dries. If the paint does not dry, scrape it off, wash the wood with mineral turpentine and steel wool and start again.

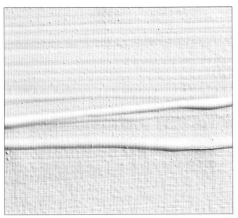

▲ Sagging.

▲ Cracking.

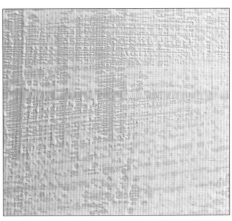

▲ Cissing.

SAGGING

This occurs when the paint has been applied too thickly or each coat has not been allowed to dry fully before the next was applied. To deal with sagging paint you must first allow it to dry fully and then rub the offending areas down with wet-and-dry sandpaper (use it wet for best results) until it is perfectly smooth. Then paint the rubbed-down parts again using the same number of coats as you have used for the top colour.

PAINT HAS BEEN SPILT

Every decorator's nightmare is to spill paint on the carpet. If the paint spill is small, leave it to dry without touching it at all. It can then be removed from the carpet pile with abrasive paper. Water-based paint spills can be removed by washing the area with plenty of water and then blotting with clean rags. Larger oil-based spills will have to be washed with mineral turpentine and then with soapy water.

STAINS SHOWING THROUGH

Even old, dry stains, perhaps from a previous flood or damp patch, may work their way through the new paint. Seal the old stain in well, using a stain blocking solution, and then paint over it. Apply stain block direct from the can and allow it to dry out fully before you start to paint.

BRUSHSTROKES SHOW

This is caused because the paint is so thick that it cannot settle evenly on the wall. A quick rub over with medium grade sandpaper and a further coat of thinned paint will work wonders.

CRACKING

Cracking is caused when paint or varnish is applied over a base layer of paint or varnish of different elasticity before it has been given long enough to cure (which can take up to a month). For example, two separate brands of varnish may react with each other and form cracks. To deal with cracking you must allow the surface to dry fully and then rub it down ready for re-painting. However, you could consider leaving the cracking visible. It is a very popular ageing technique and many people seek this particular decorative effect (see p55).

NOT ENOUGH PAINT

If you notice the potential disaster of your paint running out in good time, you can stretch your paint by diluting it a little with the appropriate thinner. You can also make sure that you use every drop of the paint that you have soaked your rollers and brushes with, rather than washing it away into the sink. Sometimes you can buy a small tester pot of colour to help with that last corner. If you are working with a colour that you mixed for yourself, and which cannot be repeated, then one wall or section of your room will have to be painted in a similar or harmonizing colour.

CISSING

This term is used to describe the appearance of paint that is resisting the surface on to which it is being applied. It usually occurs when water-based paint is being applied on to oil-based paint. For large areas, you will be forced to buy new paint in oil-based form. For smaller areas, try washing the surface with detergent and a light scouring pad to remove any grease that may be sitting on the surface. If the paint still resists, you will have to resort to using oil-based paint.

CHALKING

Prevention is much better than cure for chalking. Sometimes gloss or satin surfaces become dry and powdery, completely lose their shine and give off a chalky powder when rubbed. Using a high quality paint will help to avoid this ageing process because they are more likely to be light resistant. If you do come up against chalking, then wash the surface with a solution of sugar soap and rub it with wet and dry paper until the chalk stops coming off. Then re-paint using a better quality paint.

DRIPPING

Drips or 'nibs' in the dried paint surface are usually oversights. Leave the paint to dry. Rub the dried drip away with fine abrasive paper and re-paint the area. On high-gloss finishes you may need to apply a final coat over the entire area to disguise the patch where you rubbed away a drip.

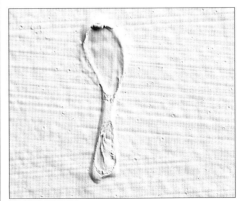

▲ Dripping.

Paint and glaze effects

SOME YEARS AGO the world of decorative effects underwent a dramatic change. For the first time, we began to see interesting mottled effects, which were clearly carried out with paint as opposed to wallpaper, on the interior walls of public buildings. Like most trends in fashion and interiors, the paint effect is of course not new. Back in the nineteen thirties and forties when money was scarce it was a cheap alternative to wallpaper. In those days the effects were achieved using hazardous chemicals. Today, we can access safe formulas of the required ingredients. The scruffy edges of some of the early work were not long tolerated – the paint effect has cleaned up its act and made a firm niche for itself in the world of interior decoration.

EQUIPMENT & PREPARATION

THIS IS GOOD NEWS for any keen amateur because there is little to it except for a special ingredient – glaze. Often called scumble glaze, oil glaze or acrylic glaze but nowadays wearing all sorts of fancy labels, glaze is a slippery feeling medium that makes it possible to move paint around on a slightly shiny surface before leaving it to dry.

So, in very basic terms, add some glaze to a chosen colour and make the paints slippery. Brush this on to a wall that has been painted with vinyl silk and then move it around with a cloth, bag, brush, cork, piece of newspaper and then leave it to dry.

PREPARING THE SURFACE

All paint effects, with the exception of colourwashing, must be worked on a surface that is smooth and at least a little bit shiny. The coloured glaze will move around against this and can be worked until you are happy to leave it to dry. Matt surfaces soak up some of the paint and will leave blotchy marks showing where, for example, the fully loaded brush or cloth first touched the wall and a greater amount of the paint soaked in. You will not be able to slide the coloured glaze around on a matt surface nor lift any of it off in order to expose flashes of the base colour as you would in rag rolling. Even colourwashing will look more professional if worked on a surface with a sheen.

The preparation coat must be good, at least two coats thick. Any misses in the shiny base coat will soak up glaze and appear as a blotch.

You must fill and smooth uneven surfaces prior to painting and remember that the glaze coat will sit firmly in any cracks or dips in the wall and will appear darker. A paint effect is not a way of dealing with lumpy walls unless you are keen to emphasize the irregularities.

GLAZE

Make sure that the glaze you buy is compatible with the paint that was used as a base coat. When the base is vinyl silk or soft sheen, which are water-based, you may use an acrylic or an oil-based glaze. When the base is oil-based paint, you will only achieve a good result by using oil-based glaze (sold as transparent oil glaze). A water-based or acrylic glaze will not grip to an oil-based surface – it would be rather like trying to paint a plastic yoghurt pot with children's poster paints.

Colour the glaze with either artists' paints from tubes or with ready-mixed paint from the hardware store. Use a small can of semi-gloss or satin wood for oil glazes or a small can of silk acrylic for water-based glazes. See 'How to mix a glaze' (opposite) for quantities. You can only colour a glaze with compatible products: water-based into water-based or oil-based into oil-

▲ Once you have applied a glaze, you can manipulate the paint into various decorative finishes.

▲ Use artists' oil paints to colour glaze.

based. You will already be aware of the fact that wall paints dry a little darker than they look in the can. Glaze, however, dries just a tiny bit lighter. Watch out for the words 'student quality' on tubes of artists' paints. They may be cheaper but the colours will fade to brown after a year.

APPLICATORS

You can apply glaze to the surface with a small roller before you begin to manipulate it into the finished effect, but it is much easier to use a household brush. You must work in sections so that the glaze does not begin to dry before you have worked it and, as such, you will only be applying paint to a small area at a time. Rollers also tend to 'drink' about half a litre of moisture before you can use them and so cost more in terms of supplies.

The following examples of paint effects outline the variety of items that can be used to create interesting effects. Anything from old cotton rags to the best department stores' carrier bags can be used. It is easy to experiment because a glaze can be wiped off a prepared wall as long as it has not been left for longer than several minutes. This means that you can sample some of the effects before deciding which one you want to proceed with.

WORKING FAST

Be aware of the fact that once you have chosen your desired paint effects and start working, you will need to move fast because glazes start to dry after several minutes and any overlaps will show up as a 'watermark' or dark line. When you do get to a corner, do not stop until you have brought your painting to a neat edge. That said, with the exception of marbling, paint effects are quick and easy to apply.

Two people working in tandem is a good way of speeding up the process – one person applies the glaze and the other works it into a paint effect. If you do this, it is not advisable to swap jobs because the way in which the first person dabs and manipulates the effect will always be slightly different from the next person and the differences will show up.

ACHIEVING A PROFESSIONAL FINISH

Sometimes when you look at a surface that has decorated with a paint effect, you can see the brushstrokes showing where the coat of glaze was first applied before it was manipulated. You are supposed to be able to see these brush strokes underneath a colourwash and you can leave them to show through beneath any effect if you want. However, if you gently stipple, or jab at the freshly applied coat of wet glaze with the tip of your paintbrush, you can eliminate the brushstrokes and achieve a smoother finish.

Many paint effects require that you move your working hand around in large strokes or that you jab at wet glaze in a back and forth motion and so it can be tricky to continue the effect into hard-to-reach areas, such as behind radiators or around plug sockets. Where possible, remove obstacles. Alternatively, paint right over a plug socket, for example, and wipe it clean immediately with a clean cloth. Glaze will not adhere well to plastic surfaces, such as plug sockets so it is not a good idea to leave the paint there because it will start to chip over time. Getting behind a radiator is always a challenge but you could try putting your tool on the end of a long stick.

COPING WITH YELLOWING

Glazes of all varieties age much faster than normal acrylic paint and will darken considerably in the space of about two years in areas where they do not get any light, such as behind a picture. If they are exposed to light, they will eventually lighten up again.

Many glazes will yellow slightly over time, particularly those with blue in the colour mix. A paint effect on a radiator will tend to age faster than the walls.

HOW TO MIX A GLAZE

2l (64fl oz) will be more than enough to cover a 4m x 4m (13ft x 13ft) room in any of the paint effects shown in this section. Put the glaze into a large paint kettle and then add the colour of your choice, little by little, stirring as you go. Test the mixture on a piece of paper adding glaze until the mixture brushes onto the paper looking glossy and slightly transparent. It should be the same consistency as coffee cream and can be thinned with water or mineral turpentine, depending on whether it is oil-based or water-based. Normally, you will need $\frac{1}{2}$l (16fl oz) of coloured paint for this or a whole 35ml (1fl oz) tube of artists' colours. Artists' oil paint is usually more intense and you will need less if you use this.

Mix thoroughly until the coloured glaze is smooth and even. Get rid of

▲ Mix the scumble glaze in an old dish.

any lumps at this stage. A kitchen balloon whisk is handy for removing lumps if you dare to use your own for mixing paint!

SAFETY OF OIL-BASED GLAZES

When using an oil-based glaze for a technique that involves rags and cloths, be sure to spread them out flat and let them dry fully before throwing them into the dustbin. Oil-based glazes warm up when they are left in screwed up rags and can self combust. It is true and it does happen from time to time especially in warm weather. So be sure to remember to hang your dirty rags on the ladder to dry out overnight or take them away to a cold place where they can dry spread out and not in little balls.

OIL VS WATER-BASED?

In favour of water-based glazes:

- The brushes are easy to wash.
- They do not smell.
- They are cheaper.
- They dry very fast.
- They are less shiny.
- Wet rags are not combustible.

In favour of oil-based glazes:

- They dry slowly and give you longer to work them.
- The lustre of an oil-based glaze is beyond compare.
- They are more hardwearing when fully dry.
- They smell fantastic (if you like the smell of linseed oil!).

WORKING IN SECTIONS

It is important to keep the edges of the work wet while you work in order to avoid drying marks where the overlaps occur. Work in 1m (3ft) sections and remember which section is the oldest (albeit only minutes older). So, work the first section on the left-hand, top corner of a wall and then move on to the next section, just to the right of it. After this, move down and work a section just below the first and then back up to the top. Then move to

both sides of the second row which you just started; one to the right and one just below it. Continue in this way. You will find that you are building up a broad diagonal design of squarish blocks with more blocks on the top. In this way, you will not be leaving a wet edge for too long and will avoid making unsightly watermarks.

PAINT EFFECTS FOR SMALL ITEMS

All paint effects can be miniaturized for use on boxes or items of furniture. You will not have to work in sections as described above and will be able to cover whole sides with glaze in one go. Use a smaller cloth or brush than you would for a wall to achieve a tighter effect.

REPAIRS

If you need to make a repair to a paint effect, it is best to try and patch the smallest area possible because overlaps on the rest of the wall will show up as a dark patch or line. Better still, re-paint the whole wall, working neatly in the corners.

COLOURWASHING

THIS IS A BRUSHY or swirly finish, depending on how it is applied. Colourwashing is just what the name describes – the washing of a colour over a pre-prepared wall.

Using a large, 8–10cm (3–4in), brush, apply the glaze in random backward and forward brushstrokes in every direction. Leave a few patches of the base coat showing through and always apply the glaze thinly.

▲ Colourwashing gives a lovely mottled finish.

Do not overload the brush but just dip the tips of the bristles into the glaze.

If you are working on a matt surface, you can expect to see darker areas of glaze where the new brush load of glaze first touches the wall and then paler areas where it begins to run out of paint. On a silk or semi-gloss surface, you will be able to move the glaze by brushing over it until it is more even.

Work in long bold stokes, using the brush from your shoulder and be prepared to touch up the ceiling after you have finished the walls so that your big strokes look even over the whole wall. It is better to paint onto the ceiling than to have noticeably smaller brush strokes around the top of the room.

If you choose to use a cloth for colourwashing, all you have to do is dip it into the glaze mixture and wring it

▲ Colourwashing with a brush.

▲ Colourwashing with a cloth.

out well. Then wipe the colour onto the wall in swirls, just as if you were washing the walls down with soapy water. The result on a matt finish will be random circles of glaze in a mottled effect. If you have painted the base coat with silk or semi-gloss, you will again be able to move the wipe marks and rub them in until they are softer and more even. One of the added advantages of a shiny base coat is that there is no need to dip and wring the cloth – just dip it gently against the surface of the glaze in the paint kettle and get it to the wall as quickly as possible so that it does not drip everywhere. Thereafter, the excess blob from the first touch can be blended beautifully onto the wall.

Colourwashing is an ideal effect for kitchens and can be built up in layers from light to darker tones to produce beautiful Tuscan effects. The basic technique of colourwashing by cloth is also ideal for ageing and shading around the corners and edges of any paint effect once it is fully dry. Just rub the glaze in completely so as not to leave too many marks from the cloth.

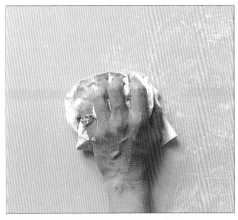

▲ Ragging or ragging off.

RAGGING OR RAGGING OFF

PROBABLY THE MOST common paint effect, ragging is more textured than colourwashing. The most common mistake is to assume that the coloured glaze is applied to the wall using a cloth. As there are no rules in paint effects, it can indeed be dabbed onto the wall from a screwed up cloth. True ragging, and probably the one which you have seen most often is actually the removal of coloured glaze from the wall with a dry cloth. The subtle difference

in technique makes a world of difference. Apply glaze to the wall and then stipple out the brushstrokes by jabbing all over the wet surface of the glaze with the tips of the bristles. Take a screwed up ball of cotton rag in the palm of your hand, about as big as a large orange, making sure that any threads are tucked into the palm side of the cloth. Now dab the rag at random over the wet surface. The glaze will lift away from the wall onto the rag and will reveal some of the base coat from beneath. Twist your hand around so that you do not create a repeated image of the imprint of the rag.

Ragging is often used with colours close to each other such as dark yellow glaze over a pale yellow base coat. It is a good step forward for those who have favoured plain paints and are beginning to experiment with textured surfaces.

RAG ROLLING

THE NATURAL PROGRESSION from ragging is rag rolling, which is slightly more even and shows evidence of

▲ Rag rolling.

repeats in the pattern. Once again, it is best to remove the original brush strokes with stippling but this is not essential. Apply the glaze thinly in sections about 1m square (11ft square). The glaze should cover the wall but should not be applied so thickly that it runs or dribbles. Jab out the brushstrokes with the tip of the brush and then screw up a ball of cotton rag into the size of a large orange. This time, make sure that any loose threads are buried firmly into the core of the ball.

▲ Ragging produces soft terracotta tones that are reminiscent of the Mediterranean.

▲ Rag rolling produces a soft texture on this wall.

Now simply roll the ball of rag quite firmly over the section of wet glaze. The glaze will again lift off onto the rag. Work in random directions for a soft finish or, alternatively, work up in straight lines if you want to see the repeats more clearly. Move on immediately to the next section and do not stop until you have reached a neat edge in the corner of the room. Working at random is more effective and professional than in rows. You will need a good supply of clean rags for this technique as they tend to become soaked, at which point they stop lifting the glaze from the wall.

BAGGING

THIS IS NOT the most elegant name for a paint effect but surely one of the most elegant to look at. Bagging is even more simple than ragging because there is no need to remove initial brushstrokes. It has the appearance of coarse leather and is very effective in situations where a heavier finish is required.

Brush the glaze onto the wall, again working in sections about 1m square (11ft square) and keeping the edges wet as you work. Turn a plastic carrier bag inside out (to stop the print from adding to the wall decor) and scrunch it up in your hand. Now dab the bag all over the wet glaze and watch as magically the glaze begins to take on a thick texture. Move onto the next section immediately.

The technique is really simple and the results are truly stunning. Bagging is even better if you work on an oil-based glaze that is as thick as jam because it takes on an actual three-dimensional texture as well as the flat texture of the paint effect. You will need to use neat oil glaze and artists' oils from tubes to mix a really thick glaze. It is advisable

▲ Bagging.

to add about a teaspoon of dryers to this kind of glaze mix or else it will take at least a week to dry. It is worth the effort though, because oil-based bagging shines deeply. It is just perfect for the area below a dado rail if you are using, say ragging, above the rail. Try painting the wall in bright red and then bagging over the top of this with a deep crimson.

Ordinary supermarket bags produce a neat, tight texture while more coarse and heavy bags produce results that are more like ragging and a little more wild. Try a few before you start so that you can decide which you like best. You will need a few bags of the same type to cover a whole room.

DRAGGING

THE MOST UNIFORM of paint, the effect of dragging is so popular that it is even available as wallpaper. One quick go at dragging will make you realize

▲ Dragging.

that it is foolish to pay for this effect as a wallpaper.

You need the glaze to be fairly thin for dragging, certainly no thicker than coffee cream. It is more successful if you use a dark colour over a pale base than the other way around.

You will need a specialist dragging brush for this, which is a brush about 8cm (3in) wide and only about 1cm (¹/₂in) thick with long coarse bristles, about 10cm (4in). Do not use a bristled flogging brush with 15cm (6in) long bristles because it will surely drive you mad before you get halfway through the job. You can use an ordinary household brush for dragging but you will find the process slower.

Happily, dragging does not have to be worked as quickly as other paint effects so you can safely answer the telephone between sections. This is because of the uniformity of the effect and the fact that you will work in 15cm (6in) wide sections around the room from ceiling to floor. Use a plumb line that falls from the ceiling to the floor in order to keep the lines as straight as possible.

Apply a strip of glaze all the way up the wall and about 15cm (6in) wide. As you become more competent, you will be able to apply wider sections.

Hold a dragging brush flat against the wall at the very top of the strip of wet glaze with the handle pointing toward the floor and, as the name suggests, drag it all the way down the wall. The brush will lift away the glaze where the bristles touch the wall and leave fine stripes of glaze behind. Try not to stop and lift the brush off halfway down because it will leave an uneven mark. For a lighter and more delicate effect, re-drag the same strip and lift even more glaze away.

Wipe the brush regularly to keep it from becoming clogged with old glaze. You will need to trot up and down a ladder a lot for this technique and should, where possible, work from the top of the room to the bottom. Move down the ladder with the brush pressed firmly against the wall and keep it moving as evenly as you can.

▲ Dragging produces a subtle effect.

You may already be aware of the fact that the stripes in dragging are made by the bristles at the point where they meet with the ferule, into which they are rooted, and not by the tips. This is why it is important to press quite firmly and ensure the brush contacts the wall along its entire length. The bristles will bend into a curve under the pressure. The length of the bristles and tips serve to feather and soften the stripes. If the strips of glaze do not drag evenly into fine stripes then the glaze is too thick.

STIPPLING

TIMELESS AND CLASSICAL, stippling in its purest form is one of the most difficult effects to perfect and it takes some practice and energy to master it fully. Yet it looks so very undaunting and so

▲ Stippling.

understated. If you ever find yourself looking at a large wall space that has been perfectly and evenly stippled, stop awhile to appreciate it.

You may be forgiven for not noticing that a stippled paint effect has been added to a wall because it needs close inspection before you can see the tiny pin-prick texture in the glaze. Working with oils is recommended because they dry slowly and allow you more working time, thus minimizing clouding and patches. Oils also take on a gentle texture that is not evident when working with water-based glazes.

For a classical stipple, you will need a glaze mixture that is not too runny; coffee cream and no thinner. Apply to the wall in sections of about 1m square (11ft square) as evenly as possible.

Immediately take a stippling brush

and tap the flat bristles onto the glaze in soft jabbing motions. A brush that is about 8cm square (3in square) will prevent you from tiring too quickly. Keep moving over the wet glaze and wipe the tips of the bristles whenever they stop lifting the wet colour. After you have moved over the whole wet square, look for dark patches and jab the stippling brush directly into their centres. From the centre of the dark patch, work gently out towards a lighter patch using exactly the same jabbing motion. What you are doing here is evening the paint out by moving excesses from the dark patches into the lighter areas.

Work the next square and 'share out' the paint that overlaps the previous square to prevent a mark from showing.

Most stippling has a gentle cloudy effect. This is much easier to achieve and you will not need to concentrate on moving the paint around to ensure an even finish. You may also use a stippling tool that looks as though it is made of astro-turf-type plastic for a more obvious stippled look.

Follow the same principles for this technique as for classical stippling but pay less attention to the even finish. If your overlaps begin to show as obvious squares then it may be worth changing the shape in which you apply the wet glaze to the wall. Try using oval shapes or very wide diagonal strips. Incidentally, quick stippling makes a good sky effect if worked in pale blue over white and you can add some quick and convincing clouds following the sponging technique on p53.

FROTTAGE

THE FRENCH SPEAKERS among you will realise that this is the French word for 'rubbing'. As with most of the basic paint effects, it describes the technique accurately because it is nothing more than a layer of glaze that has been rubbed over with a sheet of paper.

That said, the effect is bold and random, it will create a more radical finish than those of the aforementioned techniques, especially if worked up in layers changing from light to dark. Frottage can be shaded dramatically into corners or highlighted to bring feature areas forward into a room.

Because this technique is 'big', it is not suitable for very small items. A large tea tray is about as small as you can go to creating good effect without making your finished item look dreadfully scruffy.

Frottage is also the basic technique for making the effect of old cracked plaster so is worth mastering if you are interested in developing your skills to include trompe l'oeil – another French word, this time meaning 'trick of the eye' but better described as realistic painting.

Once again the base must be soft sheen or shiny. For very basic frottage, apply the glaze in large, very scruffy sections, as big as you can comfortably reach from your ladder or standing position. Don't panic at the idea of big sections because frottage is very quick to manipulate. You must however, be able to access the whole glazed section safely with both hands so do not over reach from the top of a ladder.

When the scruffy section has been applied to the wall, immediately press a large torn piece of newspaper flat onto the wet glaze and pat it onto the surface all over. Now, pull the paper off carefully so that it does not tear, revealing a blotchy, wet and somewhat rippled texture. Move over and reapply in this way until the whole section has been frottaged. Continue across the entire wall using the same colour. The same piece of newspaper will go a long way.

That is all there is to frottage. You will find that some of the newsprint ink comes off on the wall, leaving effective smudges and shading. Sometimes though, the newsprint is so cheap that

▲ Frottage.

you may see an exact mirror image of the text appearing on your wall. The better dailies seem to work better than the cheap tabloids! If you prefer not to have these marks, then use large torn sheets of greaseproof paper. Use a torn-edged piece of paper to prevent any straight lines from showing up.

Frottage is one of the effects that really benefits from being worked in layers of differing shades. Let the first layer dry fully and then start again with a deeper tone, perhaps leaving some areas and patches of the first layer unpainted. A third layer can be applied more heavily into corners to produce an aged and tarnished effect and a final much lighter coat over areas that naturally catch the sunlight such as the chimney breast can work to make the room look very three-dimensional.

Just like a wallpaper with a really big pattern, frottage works best in larger spaces and can look too tatty in tiny rooms such as cloakrooms and toilets. When the tool used for a paint effect is as big as a sheet of newspaper you really need a large flat space for it to work fully.

You could try using a base coat of primrose yellow and then adding three layers of frottage, firstly matching the colours of pale dried bricks, then of terracotta flowerpots and finally of dried earth. To take frottage a step further, look at the mock plaster effect on p49.

With the exception of sponging, the techniques outlined above are the basis for all basic paint effects. Sponging does not require a glaze medium and is covered opposite. Once you have mastered these basic paint effects you will be ready to move onto some of the more adventurous finishes such as softening techniques. These in turn lead to the very satisfying effects such as mock stones and marbles.

COLOUR TONING

TWO TONE EFFECTS

Any of the above paint effects can be two-toned by using two different colour glazes and applying the glaze to the wall or item in random patches. Remember that the two colours will mix together in places as you

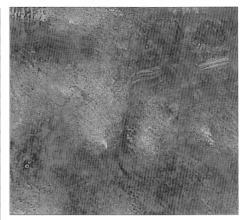

▲ First, rag a yellow glaze to the wall.

▲ Add cream glaze to produce a mottled effect.

manipulate the glaze. This means, for example, that blue and yellow used together will result in some green patches here and there. If you would like the two colours to be unblended then apply the first, leaving lots of spaces for the second and allow it to dry before adding the second colour.

SHADING

Once the first coat of a paint effect is fully dry, shade into the corners of a room or item for a well used and aged appearance by rubbing on some darker glaze.

Mix a weak glaze in a darker colour by using less colour than usual and additional clear glaze. Then rub it into the first coat around the corners and the top of the room, perhaps also along the bottom of the room. Curve around the corners. Use the technique for cloth colourwashing as outlined on p36. Raw umber is the best colour for ageing most paints but try yellow ochre for very pale yellows. The finished result is stunning for something so simple and shows an attention to detail that is easy to miss in our hurry to get the job done.

BLENDING COLOURS

As long as you are prepared to work fast, you can successfully use two or more colours to create a blended effect such as sunset colours graduating from dark at the top to light at the bottom of the wall. For effects such as these, you need to work as before except in bands along the wall, working from the darkest colour up to the lightest or the other way around.

Do not be tempted to work a single band of colour all the way around the top of the room before moving onto the lighter shade. Instead, work one wall at a time in order that the colours remain wet and easy to blend. An oil-based medium will be more successful because of its slow drying time. Overlapping the colours by 30cm (1ft) or more will save you from having to mix lots of graduating shades as they will blend in when they are in place. It is a good idea to have two people on the job for blending because speed is of the essence.

▲ Work quickly when blending colours.

SOFTENING COLOURS

Softening is probably the most important technique for those who would like to develop a full range of decorative painting skills. It is worth practising until you get the hang of it because the results are very satisfying. Softening removes brushstrokes and gently smudges and blends a finish. For example, a brushy colourwash can be softened while wet to produce a quite different finish in the form of gentle clouds of colour. Softening is essential for marble finishes and helpful in most mock stone or wood looks.

Unfortunately the essential tool, a badger-hair softener, does not come

▲ Soften the finish with a badger-hair softener.

cheap. They are readily available from many art stores and some hardware stores or a professional trade supplier of paints and papers will certainly be able to help. You can expect to pay at least five times as much as you would for a half decent household brush of the same size. Badger-hair softeners, as with other expensive brushes, benefit from being washed carefully and left to soak for a day now and then in good hair conditioner. An 8cm (3in) badger-hair softener will serve well for most techniques. At a push, you can use a hog's-hair softener but the finished result will not be as smooth as that achieved with a badger-hair brush.

The bristles are long, soft and floppy and, by flicking them gently across the wet surface of oil- or water-based paints, you will see the edges of the brushstrokes begin to go out of focus before blending softly into the background. Tickle the brush in one direction and then the opposite direction. Repeat this until no brushstrokes are visible. It is possible to eliminate your painting marks completely but this tends to take time and practice.

Of course, if you are working on an area that will not be subject to close inspection, such as the wall above a picture rail, you will not need to achieve a completely immaculate finish. For furniture and smaller items, it is really worth the effort though.

ADJUSTING THE SHEEN OF THE FINISH

Once your paint effect is complete you may wish to make it more or less shiny. While today's glazes are hardwearing

enough to survive without a coat of varnish, you may like to coat the wall with a product called acrylic glaze coat. This product can also be used on wallpaper and is available in matt, sheen or gloss finish. It can be applied by brush, or very slowly by roller (so as to avoid foaming and unsightly bubbles). It goes onto the wall looking like milk but will dry clear. As most paint effects are slightly shiny, this is a good way of making a matt finish. Acrylic glaze coat is unfortunately not suitable for use in kitchens and bathrooms where you would be advised to use a varnish.

Varnish often contains a degree of yellow stain because it is designed to make wood look more beautiful. Look out for perfectly clear varnish if you want to keep the colour exact. Acrylic varnishes are best for a clear finish but, of course, cannot be used on an oil glaze. If in doubt, test a small area first.

HINTS & TIPS:
Paint effects that do not require glaze.

Some paint effects do not require that the paint be movable once you have applied it to the wall; the position in which you apply the paint is the position in which the paint will be left to dry.

• Sponging: First wet and squeeze out the sponge in warm water so that it is soft and pliable. Any paint can be used for sponging but water-based acrylics are particularly easy to work with. Dip the sponge into a shallow tray of your chosen colour and then apply two or more gentle dabs of the paint onto some scrap paper to dab off any excess paint. Then gently begin to tap it against the wall. The hairs and protruding pieces of the sponge should make contact with the wall, not the entire sponge. Repeat the tapping of the sponge and keep your hand moving around so that you do not sponge the same area twice.

• Stippling on: Stippling takes on an entirely different effect if the paint is stippled onto the wall and not worked with a glaze. All you need are three shades of paint, one very light, one medium and one dark. Gently dip the tips of a wide stippling brush into the medium colour first. Apply the paint to the wall in patches or long squiggly lines using a gentle jabbing of the brush so that it goes on in little dots with no brushstrokes. When the brush runs out of paint dip it into another of the three shades and repeat against the first area of paint while it is still wet. The two colours will blend where they meet to make a third shade. Repeat with the third colour.

ONCE YOU HAVE MASTERED THE BASIC TECHNIQUES, YOU WILL BE READY TO MOVE ON TO MORE CHALLENGING PROJECTS. THIS CHAPTER WILL SHOW YOU HOW TO CREATE EYE-CATCHING AND EXCITING FAUX FINISH EFFECTS INCLUDING METAL, STONE AND WOOD AS WELL AS LETTING YOU IN ON A NUMBER OF PAINTING TRICKS. IT ALSO SHOWS YOU THE DECORATIVE PAINT FINISHES THAT YOU CAN ACHIEVE WITH THE AID OF A STENCIL OR A STAMP.

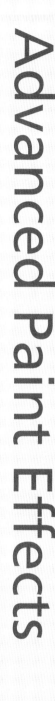

Advanced Paint Effects

Metal and stone finish effects

Metal and stone can add a unique touch to your decorative scheme, from the weathered surface of verdigris to semi-precious stones such as lapis lazuli. However, the genuine article can be expensive to buy and cumbersome to handle. As such, the aim of many paint effects is to recreate the finish of a particular type of stone. The following techniques will enable you to take the first steps towards achieving the stone finish you desire. Before you start, think about the style that would suit the object you intend to decorate. Tortoiseshell, malachite, verdigris, porphyry and lapis lazuli work particularly well on small items, while granite, marbling, faux stone and mock plaster are effective ways of covering entire walls or large areas, such as a fireplace.

VERDIGRIS

VERDIGRIS IS ONE OF the most popular paint finishes and is a very useful treatment for any items that are supposed to be made of metal but are in fact made of something else. When brass and copper are left out in the weather, they corrode and age, producing a greenish powder. This corrosion is very easily imitated in paint and can therefore be used to make any item look like it is a really old piece of brass or copper. There is a wonderful secret ingredient in the form of 'rottenstone' – a grey powder pigment made from crushed rocks, which will give you a more realistic appearance than plain paints. Although it is not essential, you will be able to find some in a good art suppliers' shop and will be more pleased with the results of your verdigris.

All you need to bear in mind when working mock verdigris is the fact that it is a fairly dry and powdery looking

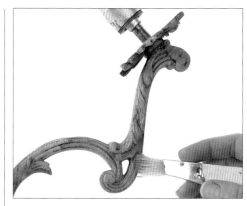

▲ Apply two shades of verdigris green.

finish. Work with the paint as dry as you can, forcing as much whiting into the mixture as it will take, and dab the colours on randomly. When painting verdigris, it is acceptable to cake your brush with powdery paint mixture.

Gilding the item in patches with copper leaf (see on pp69–70) will also allow you to leave a few little spaces here and there through which the copper leaf shines. It will help to make the article look as though it is indeed genuine copper underneath. Or you could add in some gold highlighting after applying the green base colour.

Using two shades of verdigris green or a mixture of pthalocyanine green, white and raw umber artists' acrylics paints, mix up a cake-type mixture of each colour in separate jars by forcing as much whiting powder into the mix as you can. If you have no whiting powder, use acrylics only and apply the paint in lots of sparse layers.

Jab the two colours at random all over the surface, allowing them to overlap and blend with each other here

▲ A verdigris finish is a very effective way of ageing an object.

▲ Highlight the edges with gold.

and there. If you want to go the one step further, then apply some rottenstone when the paint is still a tiny bit wet by jabbing on the powder using a dry brush. It will stick to any wet paint and make the item look extremely old and dirty.

To protect a verdigris finish use a flat matt varnish rather than oil-based paints because it is not supposed to have any shine.

TORTOISESHELL

A GOOD STARTING POINT for stone effects is tortoiseshell because it does not require too much intricate detail and it is so rarely seen in its genuine form these days that no one will notice if your attempt is realistic or not!

Work on a base of pale yellow so that it shows through the paint that you are about to apply.

You will need to make three shades of brown paint. Mix some scumble glaze with a good squirt of artists' colour in raw sienna, raw umber and, if you can get it, transparent yellow ochre, which is great for tortoiseshell.

▲ Varnish tortoiseshell to a high shine.

If not, then use another burnt-type colour. This technique requires a much more concentrated, colour intense mixture than is used in the basic wall effects.

Using a square-ended artists' fitch (a grand word for a cheap artists' brush, made of hog hair with a long pale wood handle) about 1cm (½in) wide, apply patches of the various colours in small oblong shapes, the same shape as the end of the paintbrush. Apply a random selection of the three colours and leave some spaces for the background colour to shine through.

It is best to work diagonally across the surface of the item you are painting rather than from side to side. Imagine a chequer board or crossword puzzle grid, with all the black squares replaced with a variety of the three browns and then turn it diagonally.

Now take a badger-hair softener and gently brush the wet paint in the direction of the painted oblongs, back and forth a few times. Then prepare for the magic as you brush the opposite way using the same light motion. Suddenly the regular oblongs of colour begin to merge into the background. Wipe the badger-hair softener from time to time and repeat this over and over until all of the brush strokes disappear. Immediately wipe away everything you have just done, all the way back to the pale yellow background and do the whole thing again but this time make it a bit more irregular. You will soon see that a few variations in the size of the dashes of coloured glaze make a significant difference.

Tortoiseshell looks great if it is varnished four or five times with thinned gloss varnish when it is completely dry. You will find that a thinned varnish is easier to apply evenly to the object.

MALACHITE

THIS IS A VERY MESSY technique so prepare to be covered up to your elbows in green glaze. It is very simple though and unlike most of the mock stone techniques this one does not require any softening.

▲ A malachite finish is very striking.

Work on a base of aqua or pale turquoise. Mix a scumble glaze using about a tablespoon of glaze and a teaspoon of artists' colour in pthalocyanine green, which is a deep bluish green. If you ask for fallo green, they will know what you mean. You will also need to make a glaze mixture using a dash of raw umber. Now apply the green all over one side of the item on which you are working, using a stippling or jabbing motion so that you do not make brushstrokes. Incorporate a tiny dash or patch of the brown here and there.

Now take a small piece of cardboard, about 8cm square (3in square) torn from a larger sheet and draw it across the surface just as if it were a paintbrush you were dragging. Move slowly and in broadly recognizable circles. The irregular edges of the card will scrape awaysome of the paint leaving the familiar trace marks of malachite. You will soon find that giving the card a little wiggle here and there helps to make the malachite look more natural. Some pure dots of the brown about the diameter of the end of a pencil will also help. If you overlap the circles you will end up with something very like the real thing.

Once again you will need to varnish this finish and may like to build up a number of coats so that the slight ridges in the finish are eventually buried deep into the layers of varnish.

GRANITE

WITH SUCH AN immense variety of granite paint on the market, it is easy to trick the eye into believing that a speckled granite paint effect is the real thing. One simple method is to mix a granite-coloured paint using various shades of green and adding dark green, silver and black glitter for the speckle effect. Apply over a pale base coat for best results.

Another possibility is to stipple the base with a mixture of cream, light brown and fawn paints (which will blend into a myriad of browny shades) and then spatter first with white and then very sparingly with burgundy or caramel. But of course there are no rules on the colours.

Another method is to begin by stippling on some of the colours you have chosen for your granite using the same technique as verdigris (see p44) or stippling on (see p39), that is to say, use a very dry, cake-mix-like paint or a lightly loaded brush. Make sure that the

▲ Apply the granite and glitter mix.

paint is not caked onto the item though because while this will work for verdigris, it is not effective for mock granite. Add some rottenstone if you have it, but go easy at this stage.

When the base is completely dry, you can start on the speckles of granite, which you create by spattering the object with three shades of paint in tiny droplets. Using an old toothbrush, dip the bristles gently into a thinner mix of paint. Tap the brush gently on the edge of a pot to get rid of excess paint and then, holding the toothbrush about 30mm (1in) away from the surface, gently rub your fingers along the bristles. Watch out for travelling droplets of paint that can flick quite a long way.

MARBLING

MARBLING, the paint effect that everyone wants to learn first, is a separate art form in itself. You will find that some expert help and practice will really make a difference to the results you achieve if you are trying a complicated marble. That said, some are quite simple to copy – all you need is a bit of patience and a badger-hair softener, which is so important for marbling that it is really not worth doing unless you have one.

Likewise, although marbling can be carried out in acrylics, the lustre and depth of real marble is only achieved when working with oils – artists' oils, straight from the tube and thinned down with a drop of oil-based scumble glaze. As oil paints dry extremely slowly, adding a tiny dash of driers will help to speed up the process.

The first rule of marbling is not to rush. Work gently and you will be amazed at what you can turn out. Prepare the surface with two coats of oil-based semi-gloss paint in the base colour, which is usually white or cream.

FANTASY MARBLE EFFECT

It is best to start with a fantasy marble effect so that you will see some fairly speedy results, which have the air of marble without actually imitating a stone.

Squirt a couple of inches of two paint colours (for example, yellow ochre and raw sienna) in two colours onto a palette or mixing tray. Take a paintbrush no more than 2.5cm (1in) wide, dip it lightly into one of the colours and then dab it into a small dish of scumble glaze (with some driers mixed into it if you have decided to use them). Scrummage the brush around on the palette until the paint mixture is really smooth and there is not much left on the paintbrush.

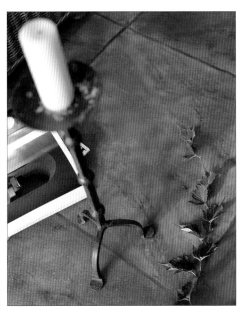

▲ Create a fantasy marble effect.

Now apply this first colour onto the painted surface in soft squiggly lines, which are roughly diagonal and all going in the same direction. It is very important that the paint is thin and that you are not applying it so thick as to make a textured surface. Leave quite a lot of the background unpainted. You may join the squiggles in 'y' shapes in places. Immediately repeat this with the next colour, filling more of the background and yet still leaving a little of the background unpainted.

▲ A granite fireplace.

Now immediately stroke a badger-hair softener backwards and forwards in the same direction as you have painted. You will see the colours begin to move and smudge. Brush again in the other diagonal direction – the paint will begin to blur around the edges and the squiggles you applied will widen and spread out, with some blending into each other. Continue brushing in both directions until all the brushstrokes have disappeared completely. Now you should have the base of a marble finish, without any veins.

For a more realistic finish, dip a tiny brush into some turpentine and run it lightly in the same diagonal direction as before. Perhaps dot it lightly against the paint here and there or spatter a fine spray of turpentine. You will see the paint open up, revealing the base colour as soon as you touch it to the surface. Try dabbing a crumpled piece of cloth onto the surface just here and there and then re-softening but remember that this is marbling, not ragging (see p37).

If you are happy with the marble base at this stage, then let it dry fully before continuing. By doing this, you will be able to wipe off any mistakes in the veining without destroying the base.

Apply the veins in one of the colours already used but this time use thicker paint. Use the thinnest artists' brush you can find for this with bristles about 1cm (½in) long. Hold the brush as lightly as you can and gently pull it down the diagonal flow of the marble base. Look at a real piece of marble and copy the vein structure – this will make life easy as you build up a network of veins. Don't make right angles to join the veins, but join them up to each other in the way a slip road joins the motorway in a 'v' shape. You should be able to trace all the veins to the edge of the piece so that they never appear out of nowhere. You can soften these veins to make it look like soft marble.

When this is completely dry, apply a second vein structure. Use the thinnest brushstrokes and a very weak paint mix to apply the secondary veins. This will produce the almost invisible veins that close inspection of the real thing reveals. Varnish the completed marble several times using thinned gloss varnish.

▲ Realistic marble is convincing.

REALISTIC MARBLE EFFECT

Having come to grips with how softening oil paints can produce a marble effect, try imitating one of the popular white marbles, which actually exists and can often be seen as cafe table tops.

Begin by making the surface slippery so that you can smudge the effect – wipe it all over with a drop of neat scumble glaze, like greasing a cake tin before baking. As you did before, dip a paintbrush approximately 2.5cm (1in) wide into a squirt of paynes grey oil paint on a palette and then into glaze and driers. Dab any excess paint off onto the palette until the brush is almost empty of paint.

This time, don't paint the colour onto the surface, but jab it on very lightly

▲ Paint roughly diagonal lines.

with gentle stippling strokes. Again aim for broadly diagonal but not clear stripes. Leave most of the background unpainted. When stippling the paint onto the surface, tap over and over each bit until you cannot see the imprint of the shape of the brush. Repeat this with a slightly darker application of paynes grey with a touch of raw umber in it.

The next thing that you need to do is soften the overall effect with a badger-hair softener. Gently allow the colours to smudge into the unpainted background. Most of the background should remain white and you can wipe off any paint you want to remove at this stage and re-soften. The secret of this marble finish is sparsity of paint. In fact, you only really need a hint of colour on your brush. Apply the veins in a thicker paynes grey as before.

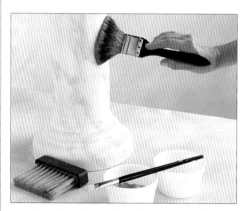

▲ Soften the effect with a badger-hair softener.

These two techniques – painting on the background of the marble and stippling on a tiny amount of colour – form the basis for nearly every type of marble effect. Soon you will have the confidence to copy those you see on buildings and floors.

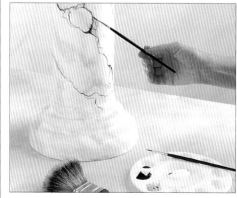

▲ Apply the veins using paynes grey.

FAUX STONE BLOCKS

HAVING SUCCESSFULLY turned out a mock marble you are well on the road to more serious trickery of the eye. The best starting place for murals and theme painting is a stone wall, which is so very easy to recreate. If anything, stone blocks are more laborious than they are difficult.

Use a very pale base coat of matt acrylic paint and divide the wall up into a brick pattern using a spirit level and a plumb line to keep you straight. Keep the blocks as big as possible because this will make for less work.

Make a mucky stone paint colour by mixing grey glaze with small quantities of black or white colourizer or artists' acrylics paints. Mix the colour slowly because these hues are very powerful.

▲ Sponge the paint on the wall randomly.

Sponge the paint on the wall so that it is thicker in some places than others. Work each block separately and try not to go over the edges. Some painters prefer to use a grid of thin masking tape but this method is quicker and looks more like a dry stone wall.

Now darken the paint a little with a dash of raw umber and add a second

layer of gentle sponging. Make sure that you apply thicker paint in the corners of the blocks and sponge a few patchy areas on each brick.

Add a tiny hint of a darker colour to each block of stone. You should already be seeing the effect of stone as long as you are remembering to work each block individually and are not being lazy by going over the edges! Remember to keep that sponging gentle.

▲ Use a dark crayon to add the shadows.

When this is dry you are ready to work some magic with oil crayons from the art store. Outline the top and right-hand sides of each brick by drawing along it by hand in white – don't use a ruler. Smudge each line by running your finger along the crayon line. Now outline the bottom and left-hand side of each brick with a crayon darker than the colour of your blocks. Use a dark brown for sandstone colours and very dark grey for grey stones. Again, smudge the lines by running your finger firmly along them to produce a feeling of light and shade. Now tidy up the corners and draw in the odd crack with sharpened crayons. Soften the effect with a fine brush.

▲ Blend in any obvious drawing lines.

▲ Use a dark-coloured glaze to produce a Gothic end result.

MOCK PLASTER

THIS IS A STEP FORWARD from frottage (see pp39–40) and an intriguing way of creating cracks that can be used when painting mock stone walls. It takes longer to execute than straightforward frottage but the finished effect is very rewarding.

Use the same technique as that used for frottage for the first coat of paint – apply a light terracotta to create a deep red plaster or a muted pink for a lighter finish. When the first application is completely dry, apply a darker glaze to fill an area about 1m square (10ft square) and press a piece of torn paper against the wet glaze. Pat it into place and then, before removing the paper, jab a paintbrush over the torn side of the paper in stippling motions from the wall and onto the paper and back again. Lift off the paper carefully and you will see that the stippling has made the image of a crack in the paintwork.

Instead of working along the wall in a uniform fashion, apply the next piece of paper so that you continue the crack line. Build up more layers of deeper tones for greater effect.

Apply a dead flat (very matt) varnish to mock plaster so that it looks really dry and powdery.

PORPHYRY AND RED LEATHER

LIKE GRANITE, porphyry relies on the spattering of paint to bring it to life. Real porphyry is deep red and very rewarding to paint. Oil-based paints are recommended because of the resulting depth and lustre. This means that you will have to allow plenty of drying time between the steps.

Using a glaze made of oil scumble and Alizarin crimson oil paint – dip a cloth into the glaze and wipe the prepared object (which has been painted with silk or semi-gloss paint) in swishy circular motions. This will look like a tight colourwash. Cover up the rest of the glaze to stop it from drying out while the background dries.

Next, add an extra squirt of Alizarin crimson to the glaze so that it becomes

▲ Spatter paint on to create a porphyry effect.

very intense in colour and as thick as jam. Make another glaze in the same way but add some paynes grey to give a very dark red. A few drops of driers will help here because oil paints can take weeks to dry. It is best to use two round brushes (domed sash brushes). First, dip one into the red glaze and stipple the paint all over the surface, making it fairly even. Then add some of the darker red glaze in patches here and there and stipple the two colours into each other so that they blend. The darker patches should not look like blobs. Keep it thick and colour intense.

If you prefer, you can adapt your effect at this stage to look like faux red leather. While the paint is still wet, press a piece of plastic sandwich bag flat onto the surface (as you did with frottage) and gently peel it away to create a wonderful leather effect. Experimentation and keeping the paint thick are the key factors in this effect.

For a perfect deep red porphyry finish, allow the stippled surface to dry and then spatter it with white, paynes grey and dark red paint. If deep red does not fit with your colour scheme, you can use a terracotta base colour instead (see 'Porphyry picture frame' project on pp106–7).

Neither of these effects need to be softened and both benefit from a couple of coats of gloss or satin varnish.

LAPIS LAZULI

LAPIS LAZULI is one of the most important semi precious gems in the world of painting and art because it is the purest form of ultramarine blue.

The stone itself has tiny flecks of gold and sometimes even marble-like veins.

It is best to paint onto a background of gold so that any gaps or spaces in the paintwork will glint through, looking like the flecks of gold in genuine lapis lazuli. Spray the item all over with gold spray paint and let it dry completely. Mix some artists' oil paint in ultramarine blue with a touch of oil-based scumble glaze or linseed oil and a drop of the all important driers. Stipple this all over the surface using tiny sharp jabbing motions at random. Occasionally, just touch the tip of your brush into some darker blue,

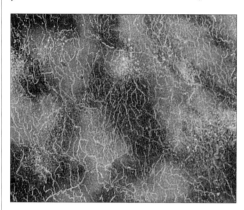

▲ Use a deep ultramarine blue for lapis lazuli.

such as Prussian blue and continue the stippling. This deeper colour will liven up the effect and provide some realistic variation.

Once you have covered the whole area, check for any brushstrokes and stipple them out carefully. The surface should have the tiny indents of your paintbrush tips all over it. Now soften the effect carefully using a badger-hair softener, creating a soft smudged surface so that no brushstrokes show through. Use the softener in all directions – remember that this is not a marble effect and so the brushstrokes should not all follow a definite diagonal direction.

Finally, while the surface is still wet, gently scratch through the surface in tiny squiggles, perhaps using the sharpened point of a feather or a kitchen skewer. The gold base will be revealed through these scratches. Lapis lazuli is so often seen in its highly polished form that the paint effect looks even better if given a few coats of high gloss varnish as soon as it is completely dry.

Wood finish effects

THE TEXTURE AND FINISH of wood has long been admired by interior decorators. If you do not have much wood in your home and want to recreate its effect, then use a woodgraining technique to produce a faux mahogany or oak finish. If on the other hand, your house is full of different types of woodwork, then use a paint technique such as woodstaining or liming to use the wood to best effect. Woodstains come in a wide range of colours that will enable you to experiment with different hues. Liming is an traditional technique best suited to open-grained timbers such as oak, maple and pine. In the past, floors and furniture were treated with limewash to prevent damage by insects. Today, there is a paint effect that simulates this finish.

WOODGRAINING

SIMPLE WOODGRAINING

Woodgraining, like marbling, can be as simple or difficult as you choose to make it. In its most basic form the imitation of a woodgrain is no more than a form of dragging (see p38). Try dragging an earthy brown glaze over a terracotta base and letting your dragging brush wiggle slightly here and there. Even this will look convincingly like wood and the addition of a few strokes with a softening brush or some fine, intense, deep brown dashes will further enhance the effect.

Once you have achieved this finish, add knots in the wood by dotting a single blob of glaze, about 0.5cm (¼in) in diameter, onto the dragged surface and then re-dragging around this dot. Move the brush around it as you come down the grain and you will develop little 'heart grains' as if there was once a branch attached at that point.

MAHOGANY FINISH

For those who are aiming to achieve even more intricate woodgrains, a base of smooth vinyl silk or semi-gloss is essential for the best results.

You will need to get hold of some pure crystals of pigment from an art supplier in Van Dyke brown or raw umber. Mix a good teaspoon of these in a shallow dish with some vinegar. The crystals will not all dissolve but most of them should. Now dip the tips of a flat household paintbrush, varnishing brush or a

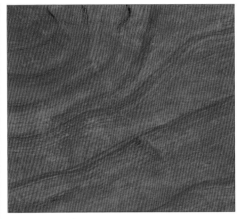

▲ Classic mahogany is easy to recreate.

mottler into the mixture and brush it up and down all over the surface that you plan to paint. Do not use too much, just a thin layer of colour. Drag this as before but let your hand fidget and wiggle as you drag through the vinegar mixture. The effect you achieve will be amazing.

Drag a badger-hair brush through the grain in places to soften the finish. You can experiment with all sorts of different brushes to find which open up and which close the grain. Make knots by painting a dot and dragging around it. When the vinegar starts to dry out, you only need to re-dip the tips of your brush in the mixture to get it going again.

When you are happy with your graining, let it dry for a few minutes and then repeat the process using a mixture of oil-based scumble glaze and a dot of raw umber oil colour. This time though, do not coat the entire area but run some lines of the dark glaze down the lines of your existing piece as enhancements to the depth of colour.

You may find that you need to wipe the whole board clean and start again several times before you finally achieve a perfect woodgrain finish.

OAK FINISH

To achieve an oak grain finish, use a pale yellow base and a raw sienna pigment. Drag the grain in the same way as you would for mahogany and then, when the paint is still wet, flick the end of the long bristles of a flogger brush gently onto the surface. This produces the tiny light streaks that are characteristic to oak.

▲ An oak floor finish is ideal for a study.

STAINING WOOD

STAINING REAL WOOD does not have to be limited to just one colour. You can experiment to produce intricate designs by using a few different colours of woodstain. The key principle is to prevent one colour of the stain from spreading along the grain of the wood and blurring into the next. Just as a trench will stop cattle or animals from straying from their designated area, a groove in the wood will prevent wet stain from straying beyond where it is meant to go. So, if you plan to stain untreated wood in a number of different colours, you must carve the outlines of your design into the wood.

▲ Apply woodstain direct from the can.

First, draw the design lightly in pencil onto the wood. Complete the design before you start to cut the wood or apply the colours so that you can be sure that it fits in properly.

Now score deeply into the wood along the outlines using a good quality worker's knife and plenty of blades. A ruler with a handle on it is a highly recommended investment because it will keep you hands away from the blade. Pay particular attention when scoring along lines that go across the grain because this is where the stain will spread most rapidly.

Using soft artists' brushes (about size 6 or 8), apply the woodstain, working from the middle of each section towards the edges. Hesitate for a moment or two before you paint right up to the edges because the stain will be soaking in and may do this last bit for itself.

▲ Apply at least three coats of varnish.

If the stain does go into the next section you might be able to scrape it away lightly with the blade of the knife. Re-score this line because it was obviously not deep enough to prevent soaking through.

When the entire design has been coloured and has dried, wipe the surface with clean dry rags to pick up any excess stain before varnishing the area with at least three coats of clear varnish.

LIMING

As the name suggests, liming is a technique that was once only achieved using lime powder. The grain of wood is highlighted and filled with a pale paste while the main body of the wood remains visible. A very popular effect in kitchens, liming lightens a wood and has the effect of gently softening the usual hard lines associated with plain

▲ Apply liming wax with steel wool.

dark wood. Liming works particularly well on deep grained hardwoods such as oak and will not be as successful on smoother woods such as pine because there is nowhere for the pale paste to sink in.

There is a variety of liming pastes on the market but you may choose to make your own by mixing whiting powder into wax.

First rub away any old sealant from the wood with sandpaper and remove any old paint that might remain. Now open up the grain of the wood by stroking a stiff wire brush fairly hard only along the grain of the wood. If you want to achieve a very limed look, brush more brutally to scratch some new grain into the wood.

The first thing that you need to do is to brush away any dust from the wood. Then rub the wax or liming paste into the grain, always going in the direction of the grain first, then briefly across it, then along the grain again. You will be filling the grooves with the paste. There will be quite a lot of overspill and so wipe this off with a soft cloth just like buffing polish. Some brands of paste are buffed off while wet and others while dry, so read the instructions before starting.

There is no need to varnish limed wood because varnish may lift the liming paste out of the grain, but a coat of clear wax polish applied a couple of days after the liming process will add a lustre to the surface and help to protect it against moisture. Be sure that the liming is fully dry before you start wax polishing.

▲ Gently buff the finished effect with a cloth.

Painting tricks

THERE ARE A NUMBER OF painting tricks that every interior decorator should have up their sleeve to make life easier. Trompe l'oeil is one of the most difficult paint effects to get right but the tips offered in this chapter will help you to recreate stunning lifelike images on your walls and furniture. Ageing is a common paint trick that will enable you to make brand new objects look like antiques. There are also two types of crackled finish that can transform any uninspiring pieces of furniture. Crackle is, in fact, an ageing paint effect that simulates what happens when an incompatible paint type is painted over another. Craquelure, on the other hand, produces a glazed crazy paving effect on your item.

TROMPE L'OEIL

KEEN PAINT EFFECTS fans often ask for books on the subject of trompe l'oeil. The French phrase for 'trick of the eye' describes a painted object or mural that looks so very real that you are mistaken into believing it is.

Think about this and you will soon realize that art galleries are filled with amazing paintings that look like photographs of the real thing. We wonder at the painters' skill and marvel at how anyone finds the time for such attention to detail. And yet we expect to be taught a quick way of painting trompe l'oeil, just because it is going straight onto the wall. Trompe l'oeil is a genuine skill that should be admired and appreciated. It is the skill of the

▲ Project the image that you want to recreate onto the object and fill in the orginal lines.

fine artist using all of his or her know–how and equipment but no canvas.

If you have been successful with some of the paint effects outlined earlier such as woodgraining (see p50) and mock stones (see p48), then you are well on the way to a satisfying mural in basic trompe l'oeil.

PAINTING FROM PICTURES

Here are some tricks to get you started. The ultimate trick of trompe l'oeil, which is used by set painters in film and theatre, is to project a slide photograph of your subject onto the wall. This will help you to get the outline shape perfect. Take the photograph up close, especially if you are working in a small room and won't be able to pull the projector back a long way. Keep the projector in exactly the same position and check your work from time to time. Using this method, you really can copy every brushstroke in an old master direct onto your walls. It does take time but it is quite the most enjoyable way of learning how to paint and the results are stunning.

The next best thing is to use a drawing or painting as your inspiration rather than a photo from a book, which will enable you to see where to

▲ The finished project is eye-catching.

put the shadows and highlights because the original artist will already have done it for you. This is particularly helpful when painting murals of nature – use gardening books with drawings as opposed to photographs of the plants.

PAINTING SKIES

Once you have tried basic sponging (see p41) and are comfortable with the technique of delicately dabbing paint with a natural sea sponge, you will be surprised at how realistic a summer sky you can now paint. Suitable as the background for murals and much used for ceilings and childrens' rooms, a basic sky can be painted onto a matt surface and takes very little time to complete.

Start with a weak white paint and increase the intensity of the paint as you build up layers. First, tear a large sponge in half or quarters until it is the size of a satsuma. Dampen the sponge in water so that it is soft and dip it into the weak mix of paint on a palette or tray. Tap the excess paint from the sponge by dabbing it a couple of times on scrap paper, so that it is not too soaked in paint. Dab the sponge gently onto the wall making the shape of a goldfish bowl – a circle with a flat bottom. Then make another of these shapes, just overlapping the first but with the flat bottom at the same level. Repeat, but this time make more of an oval shape with the same flat, level bottom.

Every time you re-load the sponge or overlap onto existing sponged paint, you will add new depths of colour. In some parts of the wall, increase the amount of paint on your sponge and in others, let the sponge almost run out

▲ You can also use a sponge to paint trees.

of paint. You will by now be seeing the puffiness of white clouds appear.

Take a look out of the window on a lightly clouded day and you will see that clouds often have a flat bottom. Although not all do, it is an easy way of tricking the brain into thinking it sees 'clouds'. You will also notice that clouds are not entirely white and so a gentle addition of some very pale grey just along the bottom of the clouds and around the same side of each puff will make them look even more realistic. Add a few highlights in pale yellow to create the effect of summer sunshine.

PAINTING SCENES

For scenic trompe l'oeil, paint the whole wall as a sky (see above) and then put the details over the top so that any spaces you leave look intentional.

▲ Use a wide paintbrush for the background.

Block out the base of each piece of the mural in a pale colour first. You could, for example, use various shades of green to draw the background to a landscape or a pale yellow for stone columns and statues. Apply obvious shading over the blocking mentioned above using a dilute wash of the next deepest shade. Highlight really light areas, such as where the sun catches a statue with a dilute wash of white.

Remember to keep the light source relative to the room so make the highlights fall on the side of pieces where the sun really will come through the windows. Do not worry if the effect looks terrible at this stage because it is supposed to and will soon be transformed.

The level of detail that you wish to draw is up to you. Trees are a good place to start – use a very fine

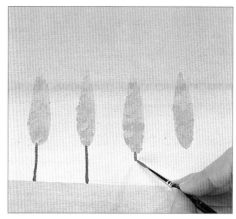
▲ Use a thin paintbrush to add detail.

paintbrush to draw thin trunks and a sponge to add the foliage.

Trace, copy, enlarge a design on a photocopier, use carbon paper and add textures such as sand to your paint. You can use sharpened crayons instead of tiny brushes and marker pens for outlines. Gold pens are easier to work with than gold paint. Shade with pencils and use chalk first because it washes off. Remember that impressionist painting is just as widely admired as realistic painting.

SHADING TRICKS

Build up shading with layers of a dilute wash and blend shadows into the main body of the subject with a softening brush. You can buy these long-handled, fan-shaped brushes in art shops.

One way of deciding where shadows and highlights will fall on a painting is to imagine that it is snowing furiously through the window and that the wind is blowing so hard that the snow is coming in sideways. The places where the snow will hit your subject are the places to highlight with whites and the places the snow would have a hard time getting to are for shadows.

▲ This country scene is ideal for a nursery.

AGEING

GLAZE AGEING

Any paint effect can be given an ageing treatment to make it look as though it has been in place for many years. The most obvious way to age an item is to make it look as though it has had several years of dust and grime using a technique that only takes a few minutes. And then you could add in mock cracks and woodworm holes or perhaps wear away some of the paint.

First, you must add the years' of dirt to your item. Make a glaze in acrylic or oils in a colour that is darker than the wall surface, such as yellow ochre for very pale walls or the famous raw umber for deep-coloured walls. This glaze should be quite weak but not thin. Aim for a consistency as thick as coffee cream using about one teaspoon of artists' colour per 0.5l (16fl oz).

Rub the glaze into the corners of the wall or item, making sure that it goes right into cracks and corners and then, as the cloth begins to run out of paint, work towards the middle slightly. Do not rub glaze all over though because you will change the colour completely instead of just ageing it. Try to imagine where dirt would normally settle and apply more of the coloured glaze to these areas. It is best to build up the appearance of dirt and the passage of time by applying more layers of paint rather than increasing the amount of

▲ Rub down any edges with steel wool.

dark colour that you add to the glaze.

Another popular method for ageing painted work is to rub some of it away with fine grade sandpaper or steel wool and then perhaps to add some ageing glaze as outlined above. This removal of new paint can be heartbreaking, especially on mural work but it is dramatically effective. Use only fine grade paper because scratches from coarser papers look very artificial.

If you want to add woodworm holes, drill them using a tiny drill bit or just paint them on as little dots. To create cracks, run a tiny brush loaded with a dark brown paint along the item always in the direction of a a corner or edge from where a crack might naturally have come from. A touch of shading with white or a pale colour where the sun might catch the edges of the crack can be very effective.

▲ Rub the ageing glaze into the object.

TINTED WAX

A large variety of brown or antiquing furniture waxes are available, which can be used on their own or in combination with the varnishes and glazes already decribed. Walnut shades are particularly good for ageing paint surfaces, both because of their antique colour, and by the feel and subtle sheen they impart. Bear in mind that antiquing waxes may have a yellowing effect on the painted surface beneath.

▲ Dark tinted wax.

If the wax is to be applied to a varnish finish, make sure the base is a matt varnish, so that the wax can adhere properly. Alternatively, rub a satin finished surface with fine steel wool to help remove the shine, before applying the wax. Apply the wax evenly with a rag or kitchen paper and leave it for about half an hour before buffing to a good sheen.

CRACKING

THERE ARE TWO TYPES of cracked finish, both of which are popular decorative treatments – crackle and craquelure. They are fundamentally different from each other so the first thing you need to decide is which of the two effects is most suitable for the object or item that you are decorating. If the label of the product you are buying does not show a picture of the effect then ask for details because the two names do often get confused. Craquelure tends to be more popular than crackle but neither effects are suitable for covering very large areas such as walls or doors because they require speedy working and are difficult to control.

CRACKLE

This is where the top layer of paint is cracked and split just like an old painted gate that has been subjected to extremes of cold, hot, wet and dry weather. Before the paint actually begins to peel off, it cracks along the lines where the painter applied the paint. Crackle is suitable for areas as large as columns or pillars, as long as you work it in vertical or horizontal sections and do not try to cover more than 24cm square (9in square) or a 30cm (12in) vertical strip at a time.

Apply a base coat of water-based acrylic paint and allow it to dry completely. This is the colour that will peep through the cracks and splits in the paint. Using a brush, paint a good coat of crackle glaze in one direction only – the direction in which you want it to crack mostly. You may use a roller instead of a brush but it will make the end result more scruffy. Crackle glaze will dry clear.

▲ Apply the crackle glaze to the base coat.

When the coat of crackle glaze has dried fully, apply the top colour – again, use a water-based acrylic paint and brush, and paint in the direction that you wish to see the bulk of the

▲ Apply the top coat of acrylic paint.

▲ A crackle finish makes an object look old.

cracks appear. Load your brush fully and apply confident single strokes of paint. Do not re-brush over any of the initial brushstrokes. In minutes you will see the cracks begin to appear as the top coat dries and shrinks. Protect with two coats of varnish.

CRAQUELURE

Remember what happened to that non-oven plate that you once put under the grill? The glazed surface cracked into a pattern of tiny squares and irregular shapes, all joined together to form a close network of almost straight lines. As time has gone by the cracks have stained and now the surface of the plate is a darker pattern than it was originally.

Craquelure is perfect for boxes, chairs and any article that can be treated in smaller sections such as one side of a box at a time. Water-based craquelure paints are the most reliable and easiest to control. Oil-based craquelure is not for the faint-hearted.

First, paint your object until you have achieved a perfectly smooth finish in the main colour – water-based semi-gloss is superb for this. Craquelure is supplied in two parts, step one and step two. When the base paint is dry, apply a layer of step one craquelure all over the item and also to a small test piece that you can touch to test if it is dry. Use

two coats if you are looking for smaller crackles. Let this dry fully before painting a coat of step two onto the item and then leave it to dry for fifteen minutes or so before studying the item very closely for tiny cracks in the surface of the top coat. Touch the spare piece of paintwork and, if it is beginning to feel dry, you should start to see the cracks. These are caused by the fact that the top coat has a different elasticity to the bottom coats and it splits as it stretches.

Finally, when the item is fully dry and you can see the network of cracks on the surface, wipe the surface all over with a cloth dipped in a tiny dot or two of artists' acrylic in an ageing colour such as raw umber and then wipe the surface clean. The dark paint will now be sitting in the cracks and they will be easily visible.

Protect both types of cracking with two coats of varnish.

HINTS & TIPS: Helping craquelure to dry

If you are finding that your craquelure is taking a long time to dry, you can help it along by heating it very gently with a hairdrier – be sure to use it on a gentle setting though. It is best to leave your decorated piece to dry on its own, perhaps under a warm lamp, near a radiator or in an airing cupboard. Try to avoid using this technique on a rainy or humid day because the cracks will need a considerable amount of encouragement to appear!

▲ Craquelure gives a crazy paving effect.

Specialist paints and techniques

SOME SURFACES AND FINISHES require specialist paints and techniques. Be sure to check if you need a special type of paint in order to complete your project successfully. There are specially formulated paints available for most surfaces such as glass, ceramics and fabrics, which will enable you to be more versatile in your painting.

Freehand painting and variations of this such as barge painting and Scandinavian painting are specialist techniques that are easy to master and produce exquisite and unique paint finishes. It is best to begin with a small project that will enable you to see good, speedy results. The success of this will fuel your confidence to have a go at something larger.

GLASS AND CERAMIC PAINTING

THERE ARE A WIDE RANGE of glass and ceramic paints available for the keen amateur. Most are acetone-based and hard-wearing enough to withstand gentle washing with soapy water (but, do not use in the dishwasher or oven). Acetone is the primary ingredient of nail polish remover and so you will not stumble if you simply imagine that you are painting with nail polish! You can thin the paints (with acetone) until they are as light and gentle as water-colours, which can be blended together or dribbled onto the glass. Remember that they will dry quite fast and can only be changed by removing the paint completely with acetone once it is dry.

For a stained glass window effect, look out for imitation lead when buying the paints. It is supplied in tubes with a long thin nozzle and can be squeezed directly onto the glass from the tube to outline areas of different colours.

Use soft brushes for glass and ceramic painting so as to avoid any scratchy looking brushstrokes and clean brushes immediately after use with acetone or nail polish remover.

Decorative ceramics can also be painted using glass paints but will not be suitable for everyday dining. If you want to achieve a permanent design, look out for shops where you can sit and paint your own design onto a plate and then leave it to be fired in a special kiln.

HINTS & TIPS: Spray painting glass

Glass paint looks particularly effective when applied with a spray can. It produces a light, misting effect, rather like frosted glass. See the 'Fish stencil shower glass' project on pp193–5.

FABRIC PAINTING

WHEN PAINTING FABRICS, always use paints specially designed for the purpose so that your handiwork will last. You will also be able to wash them, as long as you keep them apart from the rest of your washing. Most fabric paints have a liquid consistency and soak into the weave of the fabric like coloured inks. Some are thicker though and these will make the fabric appear slightly hard when the paint has dried.

It is best to stretch the fabric that you want to paint over a frame and pin it into position while you work. Secure it as tightly as a drum to achieve the best

▲ Glass painting can instantly transform uninspiring pieces of kitchenware.

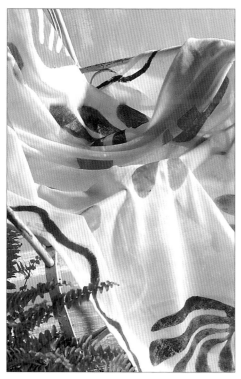

▲ Bright colours look great on white fabric.

results. If you are painting a design with the liquid paints, then the paint will soak along the weave of the fabric and may travel beyond the areas you wish it to fill. Outline the shapes with a product called 'gutta' to prevent this from happening. Gutta is a type of liquid rubber that impregnates into the fabric and provides a blocking point beyond which the liquid paint will not

▲ Specialist fabric paints are widely available.

be able to soak. Apply it through a nozzle – it is rather like cake icing, only much finer. It washes off to leave the painting perfectly smooth and is available in a range of colours.

All fabric paints must be sealed when dry, either with a hot iron or by steaming them over boiling water for a few minutes. The product you select will outline the recommended method.

For interesting mottled effects, try painting a wash of various colours onto a large square of silk and then immediately, while it is still very wet, sprinkle rock salt granules onto the silk and leave it to dry. The salt absorbs the colour and pulls the paint into fascinating starburst shapes.

Fabric can be stamped, masked and painted or freehand painted with both types of paint, though the thicker paints and fabric pens are recommended for stamping.

FREEHAND PAINTING

THERE ARE SOME decorative techniques that do not require any equipment except a small artists' brush and a palette loaded with colours. Freehand painting a small embellishment is often quicker than making a stencil or stamp.

See trompe l'oeil (pp52–3) for a brief outline of some of the tricks you can bring into play such as slide photography and carbon paper. Of course, for small-scale projects, you can always use tracing paper.

A good way of building up your confidence is to start by stencilling a design onto a wall and then using a small artists' paintbrush to shade in and embellish the stencilled background. You can then use the stencil as a guideline, just as if you are painting by numbers.

Of course, freehand work does not necessarily have to be carried out with paints and brushes – you can use crayons, coloured pencils or can sprays. If you know exactly what finish you wish to achieve, ask for some advice from the art store because they will be able to tell you which paints

or products are specific to your project. Otherwise, experimenting is the key to success.

You only need a limited palette of colours to get started – red, blue, yellow, white and raw umber mix to make most of the basic colours, though you may like to add a deep green to the selection. Black is rarely used, except on its own. Add raw umber to colours to make them darker. Artists' paint from a tube goes a long way and is very economical. You will only need a little dot of colour on a palette for most of the hand painted ideas in this book. Avoid 'student quality' paints because they will not keep their colour.

When selecting brushes, the middle of the range soft ones, which come to a point when moistened, are a good starting point. Shorter bristles are easier to control but do not hold as much paint as longer bristles. Imitation sable is almost as good as the real thing and half the price. If you intend to paint any long strokes, such as a branch or flower stem, then a no. 4 'rigger' will be invaluable to you. It has long soft bristles and flows paint onto the surface allowing you to paint a long stroke without having to re-load your brush. These brushes, as their name suggests, are used by painters of boats to add the rigging and ropes. Instead of buying a palette, you could always cover an old dinner plate with foil or cling film, which saves washing up.

Keep brushes wet and wash them as soon as you have finished; dry paint is very difficult to get off the brushes without spoiling their shape. Do not allow brushes to stand on their tips in water for long periods of time because they will bend into a curve.

▲ Use tracing paper to transfer the outline.

▲ Freehand paint in the detailed colour.

▲ Barge painting is ideal for kitchen containers.

BARGE PAINTING

BARGE PAINTING decoration is the term used to describe the decorative finish traditionally associated with narrow boats. Like any folk art, however, the decorative effect can be achieved on a range of furniture. Traditionally, the themes for canal boat decorations are limited to scenes with castles and groups of roses and daisies. Yet there is plenty of scope for variation, both in terms of the designs and methods of painting. Although the roses shown here might not suit the item you wish to decorate, the method of painting can be used to create other designs or variations. Remember that traditional background colours for barge painting are dark, providing a base for striking colours.

TYPES OF PAINT STROKES

1. ROSE PETAL STROKES

Paint the rose petals in this order: first the two central petals then, working from left to right, the three large outer petals, followed by the three smaller ones. Apply the stamens last of all, when the roses are completely dry.

Hold the brush upright and press it down so that half of it is flat on the surface. Then pull the brush towards you, lifting and curving it so that you finish the stroke with only the point touching.

2. USEFUL DECORATIVE STROKES

Hold your brush upright so that just the tip touches the surface. Then, moving from left to right and curving the line, dip the brush down and back up to finish on the tip again.

3. DAISY AND BORDER STROKES

Press the first quarter of the paintbrush on to the surface that you are painting and move it back, lifting it at the same time. As you gently pull the brushstroke across, you should finish on the tip.

4. THIN STROKES FOR STAMENS

Press the first quarter of the brush on to the surface and move it back, lifting it at the same time, so that you finish on the tip.

5. SMALL ROSE PETAL STROKES

These are made by using the same technique as that described in step one, but by using less brush and curving upwards.

6. LEAVES

Starting and finishing on the point of the paintbrush, pull it towards you, flattening it while curving it outwards and inwards. Start at the same point and make the second paint stroke in exactly the same way, but this time curve out in the opposite direction. Then finally fill in the centre of the leaf.

7. LONG & CURVED STROKES

These are made in just the same way as the decorative strokes described earlier in step two, only this time your brush must be well charged with paint and you should lift the paintbrush gradually as you move towards the point.

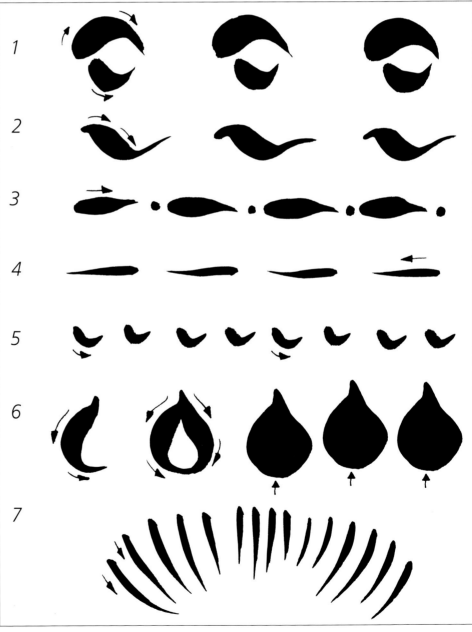

▲ Barge painting paint strokes.

ROSES

- YELLOW ROSE: Start the rose with an orange circle and paint the shadows with crimson paint. Using a clean brush, paint the top petals and the stamens in yellow.

- WHITE ROSE: Start the rose with a pink circle, made by mixing bright red and white together. Make the shadows with bright red and the top petals with white. The stamens are painted yellow.

- RED ROSE: Start the rose with a crimson circle and add a little black to this to make the colour for the shadows. Paint the top petals with bright red and the stamens in yellow.

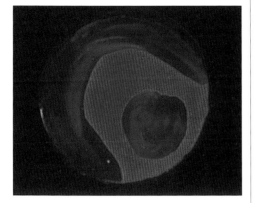

▲ Paint an orange and deep red centre.

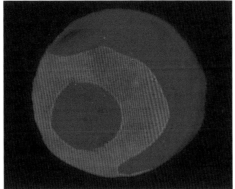

▲ Start with a red and pink centre.

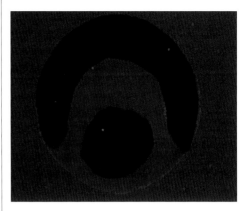

▲ Create a crimson and black centre.

▲ Add yellow top petals.

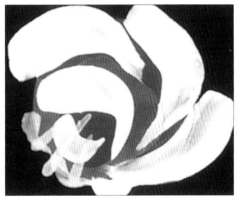

▲ Add white top petals and yellow stamen.

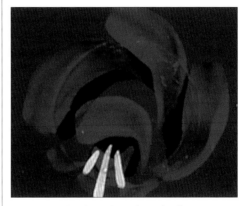

▲ Paint on bright red petals and yellow stamen.

DAISIES

Daisies are begun by painting a circle of white petals. The yellow centre has a small bright red brushstroke flicked around one side. These flowers are ideal motifs for connecting other decorative features.

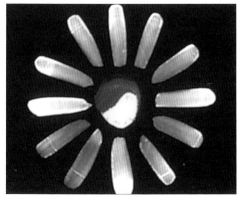

▲ Add a yellow and red centre.

LEAVES

The leaves are painted in lime green with a small smudge of tan paint at the base. The veins are painted in yellow. All the filling lines and trimmings are usually painted in yellow, but you can intersperse another colour around them.

▲ Add yellow veins to the lime green leaf.

SCANDINAVIAN PAINTING

JUST AS WITH BARGE painting, there is a definite style about Scandinavian hand painting and the two are similar. Tiny swathes of painted flowers on a background of muted green or bright red and blue are the most common design in Scandinavian painting. All you need to do to emulate this style is to keep the painting very simple. Instead of painting a flower petal by pulling the brush, just lay it flat and lift the brush off immediately. The shape made by a small artists' brush (a circle with the tip of the brush mark toward the centre) is used repeatedly to make flowers such as daisies. A little yellow dot in the centre will complete the image. Use the barge painting technique to paint leaves.

Stencilling

STENCILLING IS A SIMPLE DECORATIVE paint technique that can give a totally different look to your room or piece of furniture. It is an inexpensive way to create great paint effects. All you need is a little paint, a few pieces of equipment and plenty of imagination. There is no end to its uses, whether for unifying the design scheme in an entire room, or adding that extra finishing touch to the most ordinary of objects in your home. You can use it on anything, ranging from the tiniest of boxes to a cushion or lampshade – even a window. If you are a first-time stenciller, start small and have a clear plan in mind. Time spent developing your stencil design and analyzing its shape, scale, repeat and colour scheme will dramatically increase your chances of success.

DESIGNING YOUR STENCIL

Hardware and craft stores are full of designs that are cut and ready to use and the array can provide ideas for entire themes in any room of the home. You may, however, like to take the more original approach of designing your own image. Anything can become the basis for a stencil from intricate Chinese dragons to simple pictures of childrens' toys. For many people, ideas for repeating patterns spring from existing home decoration, such as wallpaper or upholstery, or from various soft furnishings around the home. If this is the case, the simplest technique may be to trace the pattern direct.

Try focusing on the more dominant elements in the room and remove them from surrounding shapes to see how they work alone. Remember, also, that single motifs are likely to need less reworking than a stencil that is to repeat continuously. For border patterns, leaves or scrolls are very useful as connecting links.

Flatten out the design, then trace it accurately line for line, using a soft fibre-tip pen or soft pencil. Take out any small or complicated shapes that

▲ Carefully trace the design.

might prove impossible to reproduce – the idea is to create a design that is derived, rather than directly copied, from the existing decor. If necessary, take another sheet of tracing paper and make a new tracing, which uses the main design elements.

Remember that stencils use 'negative space' – that is to say, it is the area you cut out that creates the pattern. So negative space should always be completely surrounded by positive space (the uncut remainder of the stencil). There should be a constant

HINTS & TIPS: Reversing the design

If you come across a design element that is perfect in size and shape for the stencil but is pointing in the wrong direction, trace it and reverse the paper, creating a mirror image. Remember that although stencil cards can be reversed, the first side will be coated in paint and may ruin the surface. It is therefore advisable to cut out two stencil cards, marking one as the correct position, the other as the reverse, and then use each accordingly.

▲ Choose a design for your stencil.

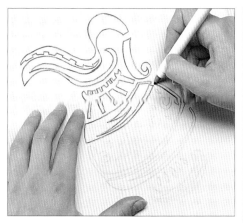

▲ Draw around the areas to be cut.

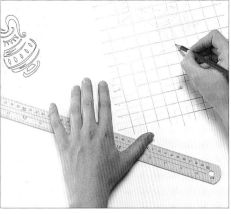

▲ Use a grid to enlarge or reduce designs.

border that is not cut or broken by the intrusion of another shape.

In some cases, it will be necessary to create your own borders or 'filaments'. For example, a bunch of grapes gains its original form through shape and colour. To convey the shape of grapes, it will be necessary to create filaments that define the outline of the bunch and, within that, a few odd grapes. The same principle applies to more complicated flower or leaf shapes. For your stencil to work properly, you will need a space of around 5mm ($^1/_{10}$in) between each cut. Smaller filaments are liable to break and may allow paint to seep behind the stencil, causing the picture to 'bleed'. For this reason, try not to leave too many 'floating' or unsupported filaments. Isolated bridges (gaps) tend to make weak joins, which will move or break as paint is applied through the stencil.

SCALING UP AND DOWN

Some designs need to be enlarged or downsized from their original trace. You can do this in a number of ways.

• PHOTOCOPYING: After measuring the desired size, photocopy the design to the nearest possible setting, keeping any intermediate-sized copies because they may prove useful later. It is also a good idea to take a few copies at the correct size, ensuring that there will be sufficient versions to adapt for the final stencil.

• GRIDS: These can also be used for scaling designs up or down. If the original design is 20cm (8in) high and the required size is 40cm (16in), draw a grid over the pattern using squares measuring 1 x 1cm (approximately $^1/_2$ x $^1/_2$in). On a separate sheet of paper draw another grid, each of whose squares is exactly double, that is 2 x 2cm (approximately 1 x 1in). Draw the grid in ink so that as the design is transferred in pencil by freehand, mistakes can be erased without affecting the grid markings. Then, either by eye or using a ruler, assess the position of each line within the squares on the smaller grid. Sketch the overall shape onto the larger grid, enlarging the lines to the correct size.

• PANTOGRAPHS: These can also be used for enlarging or downsizing images. Although using one of these gadgets effectively takes practice, the result can be a very accurate, refined enlargement of the original design. As you follow the outline of the smaller image, a pencil, rested in the pivoted levers draws the same outline but to a specified scale. Once mastered, the device can be used for basic outline positioning, before the remaining image is drawn freehand. Interestingly, many people

▲ Pantographs can be used for enlargements.

find that using a pantograph has actually helped them to improve their hand and eye co-ordination.

MAKING THE FINAL COPY

Once the design is at the correct size, make a fresh trace so that the lines are completely clean and refined. Use fluid motions on the tracing paper with a soft pencil or small watercolour brush dipped in ink – remember that making a trace will not damage the original underneath so be as relaxed and loose as possible.

The original, disjointed pencil marks should eventually be replaced with elegant lines, as you become increasingly familiar with both the tracing technique, and the shape of the design itself. With confidence, your lines will become more constant and the design should start to flow a little more freely. This final version was known during the Italian Renaissance as a 'cartoon'.

▲ Put the design together to check for gaps.

To check the symmetry of the design, and to identify any mistakes, unwanted marks or poor proportions, try turning the picture over and viewing it from the back.

▲ Make a final trace of the refined design.

MAKING YOUR STENCIL

STENCIL CARD

The next thing you need to do is decide what sort of stencil card to use. The type of card (or transparent sheet) that is used is important because it will influence how quick and easy the pattern is to create. There are three main types to choose from.

• OILED MANILA CARD: The traditional choice for stencilling, oiled manila card is tough, durable and easy to cut. However, it tends only to be available in A2 and A3 sheets, which can be restrictive if you wish to make large repeats. Symmetrical patterns require careful tracing onto the card, using a reverse tracing technique. This is because the card is opaque and can not be laid over the design on a light box, as other transparent materials can.

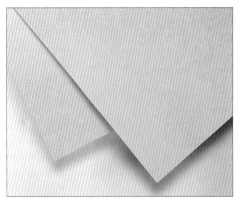

▲ Oiled manila card is opaque but easy to cut.

• ACETATE SHEETS: One of the most durable of stencilling materials, acetate sheets are often used for commercial stencilling projects. Its transparency enables you to see exactly what you are doing, and assists with positioning on the object.

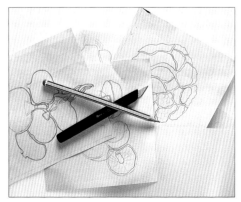

▲ Acetate makes strong, long-lasting stencils.

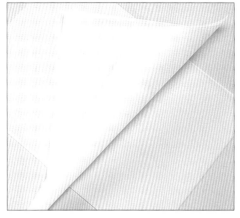

▲ Plan trace is both durable and easy to cut.

However, acetate is extremely smooth, and so it can be common for blades to slip on the surface. Always take care when cutting out a pattern and apply even pressure to the knife at all times.

• PLAN TRACE: A tracing paper that combines the best properties of both acetate and manila card, plan trace can be easily cut, is translucent and extremely tough. It may also be used in photocopiers, making copying, enlarging or reducing of designs much simpler, and its fine density ensures that cut outlines are neat, clean and crisp. Plan trace can be tricky to find but large art shops and graphic suppliers should stock it.

TRANSFERRING THE DESIGN

If possible, photocopy the final design on to a sheet of plan trace. This will ensure that there is a back-up copy of the design, just in case anything should go wrong during the cutting stage. For transparent stencil cards, such as plan trace or acetate, the design can be immediately cut out (see p52) but for manila stencil cards, there are four different methods for transferring the design, each described here.

CREATING A GRID

The least reliable of methods, the design can be transferred to card by drawing a grid on the card and copying the pattern. Use the same technique as that for scaling up and down, but, this does require freehand skills and leads to fuzzy lines, which can be a hindrance for accurate cutting. Going over the pencil lines with a felt tip pen may help.

▲ Follow the outline with a series of pin-pricks.

MAPPING PIN

Although it is quite labour-intensive, this method can be fun and was favoured by stencillers in the Renaissance. Position the design on top of the card and push through the lines with a series of pin-pricks. Judge the distance between the holes carefully – too far apart and they will leave only the barest of impressions; too close and the card could end up becoming excessively perforated.

Ordinary needles and pins tend to produce holes that are too fine for this exercise. However, mapping pins, with their stout heads and long sharp points, generally make neatly rounded holes and are ideal for transferring designs through to the stencil card beneath. Ensure that the design and card are adequately anchored together, so that the original picture does not slip and alter the accuracy of the pin-pricks.

CHARCOAL

A more faithful transfer can be achieved by rubbing charcoal through the pin-pricks on to the card beneath. (Use a piece of cotton wool to force the powdery charcoal through gently.)

▲ Rub charcoal through the pin-pricks.

▲ Carbon paper can be used for transferring.

This method is ideal for repeating designs because the pin pricks only need to be made once – any number of transfers can be made simply by reapplying the charcoal.

PENCIL OR CARBON PAPER

One of the simplest techniques involves liberally shading the back of the pattern with a very soft pencil. Then the design is positioned, right-side-up on the card, and the lines are retraced using a harder pencil or ball-point pen. The pressure of this nib should transfer the graphite from the other side. However, the transfer may be difficult to see particularly on dark manila cards. In these cases, position carbon paper between the design and the card, and trace around the lines. The carbon will be transferred from its backing, onto the card surface. Remember that typewriter carbon paper, as opposed to plain carbon paper, is actually more sensitive and therefore most suitable for this kind of work.

CUTTING THE STENCIL

Accurate cutting is vital when making a good stencil so spend plenty of time on creating the right shape. Always use sharp blades in a scalpel and ensure that they fit the handle properly. Use a cutting mat, which will protect the surface and minimize blunting of the blade. Scissors can be useful for large, flowing designs but, with practice, scalpels produce a much cleaner cut.

Start with the more intricate shapes as these tend to pull at the card. Avoid beginning with long or flat areas as these may distort or even tear as smaller, adjacent sections are cut.

It is generally a lot easier to cut towards the body but keep the knife as close to an upright position as possible, in order to reduce the likelihood of slipping and causing injury. Steady the stencil by keeping your free hand behind the cutting blade. Some longer lines are best cut by keeping the knife in a constant position and moving the stencil card. This tends to be less tiring and increases the flow of curved lines. The shapes do not need to be cut exactly as they are drawn – it may help to make a series of short cuts, rather than one or two long ones.

Having cut the design into the stencil, cut the stencil itself down to a more usable size. If the design is to fit a specific area, it's a good idea to cut the stencil to fit exactly. For a repeating border around a room, the top edge of the stencil must be exactly square, in order to stop the design wobbling or running out as you follow the bottom edge of the moulding. Marking the middle line of the stencil will make it easier to position. To do this, draw a square around the motif. By joining each corner diagonally, you will find the exact centre of the design. Using a set square, you can then mark off the vertical and horizontal mid-lines.

If the design is for a repeating border, trace one half of each of the neighbouring motifs either side of the stencil. This will help with lining up the stencil for paint application.

HINTS & TIPS: Accidental cuts

Broken or accidentally cut filaments can be mended using masking tape. Make a rough or oversized splint with the tape and then cut the masking tape down to fit, ensuring that you don't break the outlines.

▲ Mend broken filaments with masking tape.

PREPARING THE SURFACE

CERAMICS

Use special ceramic paints to work directly onto glazed ceramic tiles and unglazed ceramics such as terracotta. Make sure all surfaces are clean so that the stencils can be fixed easily. Apply the paint with a brush, sponge, spray or mini-roller. Ceramic paints are durable and washable, and full manufacturer's instructions are given on the container.

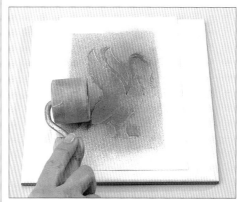

▲ Use a mini-roller to stencil onto ceramics.

PAINTED SURFACES

Stencils can be applied to surfaces painted with matt, satin or vinyl silk acrylic paint, oil scumble glazes, acrylic glazes and varnishes, and to matt wallpaper. If you wish to decorate a gloss surface, stencil first with an acrylic primer, leave to dry and then stencil the colours on top. Surfaces to be stencilled need to be smooth so that the stencil can lay flat.

FABRIC

Use special fabric paint for stencilling on fabric and follow the manufacturer's instructions carefully. Place card or blotting paper behind the fabric while working and keep the material taut.

▲ You can apply stencils to painted surfaces.

63

▲ It is possible to stencil on fabric but you will need specialist fabric paint (see pages 56–7).

If you are painting a dark fabric, best results are achieved by stencilling first with white or a lighter shade. Heat seal the design following the manufacturer's instructions.

BARE WOOD

Rub the wood surface down to a smooth finish. Then fix the stencil in place and paint with a thin base coat of white so that the stencil colours will stand out well when applied. Leave the stencil in place and allow to dry, then apply your stencil colours in the normal way. When completely dry, you can apply a coat of light wax or varnish to protect your stencil.

GLASS

Before applying the stencil make sure the glass is clean, spray on a light coat of adhesive and place the stencil in position. Spray on water-based or ceramic paint, remove the stencil and allow to dry. If you wish to stencil

drinking glasses, use special non-toxic and water-resistant glass paints. An etched-glass look with stencils on windows, doors and mirrors can be achieved with a variety of materials.

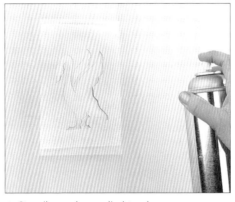

▲ Stencils can be applied to glass.

STAINED WOOD

If you are staining wood or medium-density fibreboard (MDF) prior to stencilling, you have a choice of many different wood shades as well as a wide range of colours. If the base coat is

dark, stencil a thin coat of white paint on top. Apply your stencil and protect with a coat of clear varnish when dry.

POSITIONING THE STENCIL

ACCURATE MEASUREMENTS

There's nothing worse than a stencil that is obviously supposed to be right in the middle of a surface and is quite obviously not. Similarly disconcerting is a crooked motif or border that starts dropping halfway across a surface. To avoid this, identify the middle of the design and mark a straight rule, mid-line. Now, marry up the middle of the stencil with the surface marking. For smaller flat surfaces, use a set square to ensure the centre line is a true right angle.

One of the cardinal rules of stencilling is always to start in the middle and work outwards. This ensures that the design is correctly balanced within

▲ Use a spirit level to get your stencil straight.

the perimeters of the surface – even if the repeating stencil has been designed to fit exactly from corner to corner. By starting from the middle, any small fractions or gaps are kept to the less visible perimeters.

▲ Add colour to white base coat on bare wood.

▲ Use a clear varnish on stained wood stencils.

▲ Use marker lines to position the stencil.

MARKING VERTICAL LINES

If you need to work out the vertical position for a stencil on a wall, hang a plumb line above the area that you plan to stencil and use a ruler to draw a vertical line with a piece of chalk or a soft pencil. You will need to use this method when creating an all-over wallpaper design.

MARKING BASE AND HORIZONTAL LINES

Select your stencil area and take a measure from the ceiling, doorframe, window or edging, bearing in mind the depth of your stencil. Using a spirit level, mark out a horizontal line. You can then extend this by using a chalkline or long ruler with chalk or soft pencil.

FIXING THE STENCIL IN PLACE

Small squares of masking tape can be used at each corner of the stencil in order to hold it in place but do check that the tape will not mark or remove any of the existing surface paint. Avoid drawing pins because they may leave permanent holes, and Blu-Tack because it tends to raise the stencil away from the surface, allowing paint to seep or dribble. However, the best type of adhesive is non-permanent adhesive spray, such as that used for mounting photographs. Avoid overspraying as an excessive layer can work as a paint remover, lifting the paint surface below.

If the stencil needs to be reapplied several times, wipe off the adhesive and apply a new coat – avoid adding continuous layers. In addition, take care when removing the stencil as delicate filaments may tend to stick to the surface and tear on lifting.

▲ Use spray adhesive to fix the stencil in place.

▲ You can use acrylic or artists' acrylic paints.

APPLYING THE PAINT

TYPES OF PAINT

Specialist stencilling paints are available but it can be cheaper and more creative to experiment with other types. Almost any paint can be used for stencilling, although some may have more advantages than others.

ACRYLIC PAINTS: Available in a variety of different colours and also in handy, tester-size tins, acrylic paint is water-based and extremely easy to use. It comes in two different finishes, matt and vinyl silk, which can create their own interesting effects when used in conjunction with each other. For example, stencilling a design in a slightly darker shade of vinyl silk, on to a matt base of the same colour, can simulate rich damasks or brocades. Alternatively, by isolating and stencilling one element in vinyl silk, you can lend a feeling of movement to the overall design, as the light is reflected by the paint's slight sheen.

ARTISTS' ACRYLIC PAINTS: Perhaps the most flexible and manageable of paints for stencilling, these paints are suitably hardwearing yet water-based. They can be used neat or diluted, although very diluted mixtures are more likely to run under the stencil card.

SPRAY PAINTS: Ideal for people who find hand-applied methods hard to master, spray paints are available from art, craft and model shops in an increasing range of colours. Although these are appropriate for most porous surfaces, car sprays should be used for stencilling on surfaces such as glass, ceramics or metal. Always apply spray paints in thin, even layers – almost a dusting – so as to avoid runs and dribbles. To achieve this, hold the can as far from the stencil as possible, using additional paper masking around the main stencil card. Spray colours can be mixed by using successive, very lightly sprayed coats because the paint hits the surface in tiny pin-prick spots, which are easily offset by using different hues. Only use spray paints in well-ventilated conditions and always wear a mask. Spray paint tends to be very fine and can travel into the smallest of areas. For this reason, always provide plenty of

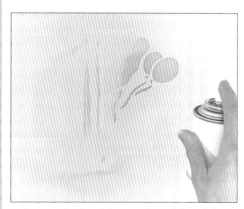

▲ Spray paint is quick to apply and fast drying.

masking around the outside of the stencil, to protect the surrounding areas. This can make using registration or centre marks difficult so avoid using sprays for tight, repeating patterns. As with brushed or sponged stencils, any

▲ Mask off all edges if you use spray paint.

build-up of paint near the edge can lead to drips or dribbles, so keep the spray as fine as possible. Hold the cannister at a sufficient distance from the surface and apply several even coats, rather than one thick layer.

ALKID PAINTS: These provide many of the qualities of oil paints with as fast a drying time as acrylic. The texture is buttery, so they do need to be thinned with mineral turpentine substitute for stencilling.

OIL PAINTS: The choice of purists, oil paints are the trickiest type of paint to use for stencilling and they dry extremely slowly. However, for people who are practised in oil paint application and mixing, these paints can create beautiful transparent effects when mixed with a little varnish or oil painting medium. Extreme care must be taken when you remove the stencil after applying paint. Oil pigments remain unstable for at least four hours, which means that accidental smudging, by lifting the card too soon, is a hazard.

USING A SPONGE

Paint can be applied in a variety of manners for stencilling. For sponging, it is a good idea to use a 'reservoir' – a spare piece of sponge that acts like an ink pad, helping to prevent irregular ink flow. Simply place the reservoir sponge in the bowl of paint and squeeze it firmly until it has taken up most of the mixture.

Then gently dab the reservoir sponge with the applicator sponge, until this too has taken up the paint. Dab the applicator sponge on a clean sheet of newspaper or an uncut part of the stencil, to check that the paint isn't oozing or dribbling. A clean crisp imprint means the sponge is ready for use. Then, starting in the middle of the largest cut, apply the paint with the sponge, working back so that, by the time the sponge reaches the edges, a minimum of paint is being applied. The paint can be built up in layers, but this simple technique is ideal for a first practice run. It not only helps to provide a sense of what a sponged

finish will look like – it also reveals the final shape and image of the cut-out stencilled design. Smudgy edges are caused by a build-up of paint. Avoid this by starting in the middle of the design and gradually working outwards, gently pushing the paint towards the outside edges. If the design begins to look a little insipid around the sides, try applying further, light layers. Always allow each layer to dry, however, and aim for numerous light coverings, rather than one thick coat, which is likely to cause a build-up of paint and smudging.

▲ Dab paint gently using an applicator sponge.

Before deciding on a final method of paint application, it's a good idea to experiment with different techniques. Each method creates a slightly different effect, and it can be useful to try out the whole range of techniques before deciding on the final finish you want to create. Remember that all stencilling methods produce a slight clouding, but this is characteristic of a carefully worked piece and contributes to the three-dimensional charm of the decorating technique.

USING A BRUSH

If you are applying paint by brush, remove excess paint from the bristles on newspaper before working through the stencil. Keep the brush at right angles to the surface, otherwise stray hairs may sneak behind the stencil and mark the surface. Gently stipple the paint through the stencil, working from the centre outwards to help avoid paint build-up and smudges. Keep a small dish or saucer of water and lots of washing up liquid to hand. If small smudges or dribbles occur, a timely wipe with a

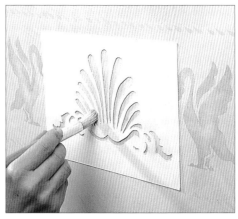

▲ Stipple paint lightly through the stencil.

cotton bud should remove any problems or stray marks. However, most mistakes can be rectified with a fine artists' brush once the paint is dry.

Other variations of brush application include feint oil painting and shadow stencilling. Feint oil application involves using artists' oil bars, rather than conventional paint. The oil bar is rubbed onto a pallette and then a stiff brush is swirled into the colour. Use this brush to press the colour lightly through the cut-out stencil in short

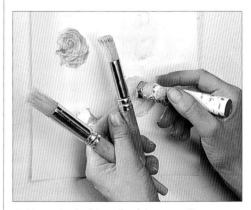

▲ Use artists' oil bars for feint stencilling.

circular motions. The final effect should be a feint finish, softer than usual paint, together with gentle brush marks.

Shadowed stencilling involves applying paint or artists' oil bar colours in the same way. However, after the first application, the stencil is removed and repositioned about 2mm (^{1}/$_{16}$in) over the right- or left-hand edge. A lighter shade of the same colour, or perhaps a subtle shade of grey, is then applied between the edge of the first coat and the border of the stencil. This creates a three-dimensional effect, providing the original stencil shape with a soft, decorative shadow.

▲ Re-position stencil to make shadows.

HIDDEN STENCILLING

The most subtle of stencilling techniques, this method is ideal for very soft finishes and projects that are designed to blend into a room, rather than stand out. It is achieved by coating the base surface in a very lightly coloured glaze. Once this glaze has dried, the stencil is positioned over the surface and the same glaze is applied through the cut-out, using a stippling motion. The stencilled effect is created by the double layer of glaze.

▲ Hidden stencilling is a subtle stencil method.

REVERSE STENCILLING

A very simple version of stencilling, this technique does not require as much planning as other techniques and it is far less time-consuming. This is because the design does not need any filaments – the images are, effectively, cut out silhouettes.

Reverse stencilling is ideal for small projects in which the cut-out will only be used once. Although the stencil can be removed and reused, it must be totally cleaned between applications. This means that acetate or plain trace rather than oiled manila card, are most suitable for the job.

▲ Stick the cut-out in position.

The idea is to cut out the stencil shape as a block – what is known as negative space in other stencilling methods actually becomes positive space. The chosen colour of the stencilled design should then be applied to the object's surface. It is not necessary to coat the whole item, only the areas in which the stencil is to appear.

Once the base paint has dried, position the stencil over the top and stick it temporarily into place. Then use a brush to gently apply the top coat around the cut-out, taking care not to lift the edges. Once these areas have been carefully covered, you can coat the rest of the surface more liberally. If it helps, go over the stencil itself, but make sure that the brush or roller action does not lift or move the cut-out stencil beneath.

While the paint is still wet, carefully remove each cut-out. (It may help to locate and lift the corner with the tip of a scalpel.) Take care not to smudge the wet surface paint, or damage the cut-outs. Then leave the surface to dry. Remember to wash the stencils thoroughly, if you plan to re-use them.

▲ Stipple around the edges of the cut-out.

▲ Carefully lift the cut-out with a knife.

HINTS & TIPS: Storing stencils

If a stencil is to be re-used, make sure that it is stored flat. Fix soggy stencils to a glass or ceramic surface with temporary adhesive spray, as this will hold them flat while they dry. Excess paint should be carefully wiped off before storage.

HINTS & TIPS: Stencilling around corners

• Stencilling borders around corners is particularly difficult, especially when it comes to matching up the design. To avoid mistakes, try the following method: when you have calculated where the stencil is to go and how many times it is to repeat, make a mental note of any halves or fractions of the design that will be needed to fit into corners. Ensure that every section of an area that takes a full repeat has been tackled, before attempting to bend the stencil for fitting into corners. This is because bending stencils reduces their strength and lifespan, and can distort the design.

• Bending the design around a corner is best done in two stages, with time allowed for the first half to dry before applying the stencil to the adjacent surface. You will be surprised how a corner can cover up inconsistencies, as long as the top and bottom edges correspond with the stencil levels on the neighbouring surface.

▲ A corner can hide any inconsistencies.

Gilding

POPULAR THROUGHOUT the world for thousands of years, gilding was even used to decorate the jewellery of the Incas and the ornaments of ancient Egyptians. Although the term is commonly associated with the application of gold, gilding can involve all kinds of metal leaves and powders, including silver, bronze, aluminium and platinum. Gilding often provides the perfect final touch to a room, whether it is used on a picture frame, vase or storage box. Creating the impression of an object made of solid, precious metal, the technique involves applying a very thin layer of gold to any base – even something as flimsy as papier-mâché. There are a variety of different methods for creating this effect, including gold leaf, gilding cream and metallic powders.

MATERIALS & EQUIPMENT

THE EQUIPMENT AND TOOLS you need to create a gold effect will depend on the type of gilding you choose to use. Even so, you should not need to invest too much money in order to produce a stylish, extravagant effect. Before deciding on which technique to use, it may be a good idea to think about how much equipment you want to invest in, how much time you wish to spend on the project, and how intricate you want the final effect to be.

ABRASIVE PAPERS

The variety of abrasive papers needed will depend upon the surface of the item that is to be gilded. However, it is useful to have a range of coarse, medium and fine grade abrasive papers to hand, and to work through the appropriate different levels, always finishing with a fine grade paper. You can also use wet-and-dry paper on a slightly wet surface for a smooth finish.

▲ Abrasive papers and bole for preparation.

CUTTING MATERIALS

Only relevant for gold leaf applications, cutting materials can include scissors or a sharp craft knife. For the best results, however, it is worth investing in a gilder's knife, a long metal bar with a sharp edge. This knife can be used both to lift sheets of gold leaf, and to cut the medium in one sharp pull, rather than in a sawing action which would cause the leaf to tear and damage.

PAINT

Depending on what you are decorating and the desired finish, you may find it useful to apply a coat of bole to the surface prior to gilding. Bole is a special type of background paint that works both as a filler for slightly rough surfaces and as a paint base. It comes ready-mixed and, once applied, is ideal for sanding down to a very smooth finish. Alternatively, a satin-finish paint, not matt or gloss finish, can be used as a base coat. However, make sure that the paint has the same base (either oil or water) as the gilders' size (see below).

ADHESIVES

Ordinary, household varnish can be used to make gilding powder adhere to a surface. However, gold leaf requires a special type of adhesive known as gilders' size. The medium is used both to stick gold leaf into place, and to seal gilded and normal surfaces. It is available as a water- or oil-based product and, depending on the brand, can require drying times ranging from

▲ Gilder's size for gold leaf application.

20 minutes to 24 hours. Gold leaf must be applied before the size is fully dry, but when it is still tacky (much like gold powder to a varnished surface). Too early and the leaf will be marked by the wet size underneath, causing the gold to appear lifeless and dull. If it is applied too late, the leaf may not adhere to the surface properly, causing a poor and untidy finish.

BRUSHES & APPLICATORS

Brushes are needed for both tidying gold leaf, and for applying gold powder. They should be as soft as possible – pony-hair or squirrel brushes are ideal. If possible, keep gilding brushes aside purely for that job. Wash gilding brushes rarely; it is far better to tap them clean where possible. Use cotton buds for gently pressing gold leaf into position, particularly in difficult or intricate areas. Velvet can also be used for pressing gold leaf over large surfaces, and for polishing gilded surfaces to a shiny finish.

▲ Gold transfer leaf.

▲ Gilding cream.

▲ Gold powder.

THE GOLD EFFECT

Gold leaf, gilding cream and gilding powder all have their different advantages. For example, while leaf is more time consuming and complex to apply, it provides a long-term finish which is less likely to lose its lustre than other forms. Gilding cream is a popular choice for small projects or highlights – it is conventionally used for patching up gold work – whereas gilding powder is considerably more messy than the other methods, but it can be carried out with basic metallic powders and household varnish.

• GOLD TRANSFER LEAF: This is available from specialist paint suppliers or gilding shops. Transfer leaf is a very thin layer of gold or brass, supplied in small squares and lightly attached to tissue backing with a layer of wax film (see above). Professional gilders use specially designed cushions for applying leaf transfers, but it is possible to create a good finish simply with a soft brush or even a silk scarf – see the 'Gilded chair' project on pp102–3.

Try not to touch the metallic surface until it is in place on the object, as it will stick to your fingers. Many people find the easiest way to lift the sheets is to use the bristles of a soft brush that has been swept across their cheeks. The light coating of grease should provide just enough adhesive.

• GILDING CREAM: Commonly used by gilders for repair work, gilding cream is particularly handy for patching areas where the size dries and cracks (see above middle). The cream can also be used for small highlighting work.

• GOLD POWDER: This can be used as a quick alternative to leaf transfers (see above right), though it tends to be messier and will definitely require a protective varnish cover. The powder is applied to a surface that has been coated with varnish – the varnish should be allowed to semi-dry so that it feels tacky. Gold powder can also be used to patch up cracks in gold leaf gilding. However, it's important to ensure that the powder is an exact match of the shade of the gold leaf.

APPLYING GOLD LEAF

TAKE SOME TIME to sand down the item to a really smooth finish. Leaf transfer is so thin that any rough patches will show through and mark the gilded surface. Once sanded, remove any dust residue with a tack rag. Wipe ridges and crevices clean with a cotton bud.

If the item is large, or is to be totally covered in gold leaf, it may be worth applying one or two coats of bole, or a paint in the colour of your choice. If the size for the leaf transfer is oil-based,

▲ Apply a coat of gilders' size to the item.

make sure that the paint you use is also oil-based. Once dry, sand the surface with fine grade abrasive paper and fine wet-and-dry paper.

Then use a soft brush to apply a thin layer of gilding size to the surface. Try to avoid leaving brush marks in the coat. Although the size will be milky on inital application, it should dry to a clear, slightly petrol-like colour.

Very carefully cut a single sheet of gold transfer leaf to the required size. Remember to leave some excess on each edge, so that each piece overlaps on the surface and can be trimmed later. However, bear in mind that transfer leaf will adhere to gilding size on contact, so avoid leaving so much excess that unwanted pieces stick to the surrounding wet size.

Press the leaf face down on to the tacky size, keeping the backing paper in place, and rub it with a cotton wool ball, soft brush, or piece of cloth to ensure that it is firmly in position. Then gently peel away the backing paper, taking care not to lift the leaf from the object's surface. Repeat this process until the whole item is covered with gold leaf transfer.

▲ Brush away excess gold leaf with a soft brush.

▲ Apply tiny flakes of gold leaf for this effect.

Gently press the leaf flat with a soft brush. Although wrinkles may appear, these should disappear as the surface is brushed clean. Then, gradually brush away any overlaps and excess pieces of gold that remain. Any large pieces, known as skewings, that you have left can be kept for patching up corners and crevices.

Continue working around the surface, gradually brushing away wrinkles, loose flakes and lumps. As you work around the object, small faults, such as cracks or gaps may become apparent. These can be repaired, using the same technique described above, with the skewings. Alternatively, while the size is still tacky, touch up any cracks or gaps by gently brushing gold powder over the top of them.

Leave the item to dry completely – you will need to follow the guidelines on the size tin – and then polish it very gently using a piece of velvet or a cotton wool bud. However, the gold surface will still be vulnerable to breaks or tears so avoid using rough movements.

HINTS & TIPS: Working environment

Always ensure that the work environment is as dust-free as possible. Remember that wet size will be vulnerable to dust and particles for up to several hours so, if you are worried about dust rising and settling on the piece, try damping the floors with a water spray, or putting down wet towels. Also, make sure that your tools are clean and to hand, to avoid disruption later.

If you prefer the slightly aged effect of the curtain pole shown left, use tiny flakes of gold leaf instead of whole sheets. It is always worth looking at the finish on gilded articles in stores and antique shops. Although the aim is to create as refined a finish as possible, using sheets of leaf will inevitably create some joins and overlaps. Note, however, that these are barely visible when the piece is looked at in its entirety.

Although the object is now gilded, it will not be able to withstand scratching or heavy handling. The surface is also liable to tarnish with time. It is therefore important to protect the surface with a few coats of varnish.

AGEING THE PIECE

To give the gilded finish an appropriately old and time-worn appearance, try adding some stain to the protective varnish. This can be applied all over the item, or simply to areas that would age and wear naturally, such as exposed corners.

First, apply one coat of clear, oil-based varnish to the surface and leave to dry. Then mix a small amount of artists' oil colour – either burnt sienna or raw umber – into a small pot of varnish. Apply two coats of this mixture to the item, allowing each application to dry thoroughly. Then add more artists' colour to the mixture to darken it even further. Apply this to creases or moulded areas of the surface, and to any areas where dirt is likely to have settled over time, such as edges, grooves or handles. Finally, wipe away some of the varnish with a soft cloth. The idea is to leave darkened varnish only where age may have led to tarnishing or grime.

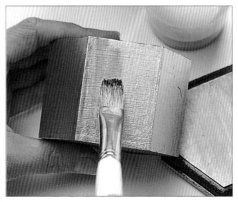

▲ Apply two coats of the stained varnish.

GILDING WITH CREAM

FOR A FASTER gilded effect, or for items that can not be sanded, such as papier-mâché, gilding cream can be used. (The cream is also ideal for creating gold highlights on painted surfaces.) Cheap and easy to obtain, the finish will not polish to as high a sheen as leaf transfer, but it still creates an effective, metallic surface.

The item can be varnished with spray varnish or aged with a stain/varnish mixture as before. In the case of this star, the darkened varnish sits comfortably in various crevices creating natural low-lights and shaded areas.

▲ Use cream to gild unevenly shaped objects.

Begin by painting any raw surface with bole, or the chosen paint colour of your choice. Once this has dried, use your fingers to gently rub gilding cream all over the surface. Be sure to cover all crevices and intricate areas – if necessary, use a cotton bud to insert cream into difficult gaps.

Allow the cream to dry for the recommended time (usually about

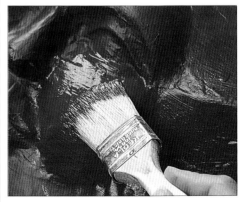

▲ Apply a coat of bole to raw surfaces.

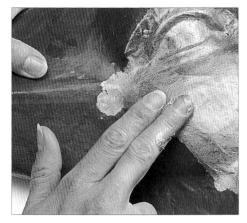

▲ Rub gilding cream over the shape.

2 hours) and then buff the surface gently with a soft cloth. This will help to give it a slight shine and lustre.

GILDING WITH POWDER

ANOTHER QUICK and satisfying way of applying a gold finish, gilding powder is less messy than gilding cream. It is also suitable for items that will have to stand up to quite a lot of wear and tear, such as lamps, handles and doorknobs. However, the actual powdering does create quite a bit of dust so it may be wise to do any projects involving gilding powder outside. As with other gilding methods, apply a base coat of colour, or a couple of coats of bole to

▲ Apply a coat of varnish and leave until tacky.

seal the surface. When the paint is dry, apply a thin layer of gilder's size and leave to dry until it is just tacky.

Dip a clean, dry brush into the gold powder and gently brush it on to the tacky size. Apply the gold powder fairly thickly as it will soak into the size. Brush away the excess until you can handle the item without too much powder coming off.

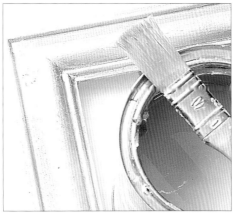

▲ Dust on a generous amount of powder.

If you prefer, use different coloured metallic powders for a varied effect. To do this, simply apply different colours directly to the surface and mix them together as they stick to the size.

Once dry, apply a coat of clear protective varnish to the object. If the item is to receive a lot of handling, use several coats, allowing sufficent drying time between each application.

OBJECTS FOR GILDING

GILDING CAN BE applied to almost any surface, providing the base has been adequately prepared. It tends to be most effective when it is used in small areas, such as for highlighting trims or borders, or on small room accessories such as lamps or frames. Gilding techniques can even be used on natural items such as shells or stones.

Whenever you use gilding as a decorative effect, try to resist the inclination to over-use the colour. Gold, together with silver, bronze and other metallic colours, tends to look its best when it is used sparingly.

HINTS & TIPS: Colour variations

Gilding does not have to be gold. Leaf powders and creams are also available in silver, aluminium and copper, while creams come in a myriad of shades.

▲ Use a gloss varnish to produce this elegant finish.

Stamping

PRINTING DESIGNS on to items of furniture or walls is not a new idea, but it has enjoyed a revival in recent years. It is an excellent technique for creating repeating patterns on flat, painted surfaces, and tends to be less intricate than some other decorative methods such as stencilling. Stamping designs can be simple or complex, and much of their effect comes from a fairly relaxed, random application. This means that you rarely have to worry about achieving symmetrical effects, or measuring accurate spacing for each stamp motif. Although rubber or wood are conventionally used for stamping techniques, it can be interesting to experiment with other mediums such as metal, sponge or even halved vegetables (see below).

STAMPING MATERIALS

A RANGE OF DIFFERENT materials can be used to make printing stamps. The type of material you choose will influence the texture and definition of the print, as well as the durability of the stamp itself. For example, stamps that are to be used consistently should be hardwearing and easy to clean and maintain. Small, one-off projects, however, could be decorated using quick homemade stamps that will be disposed of after use.

▲ Professional rubber stamps can be reused.

• RUBBER STAMPS: The most common type of stamp, rubber print blocks are able to withstand constant use over a length of time. Although ready-made, rubber stamps can be very sophisticated, large objects may need more than one design and this can prove to be quite costly. It is therefore often more economical, (and creative!), to make your own rubber stamp which can be adapted to your personal needs.

▲ Use sponge for a textured finish.

• FIRM SPONGE, CORK AND LEATHER: These are less durable than professional rubber stamps but they should last for a sufficient length of time. Material such as these tend to create a textured finish, creating a more craft-like appearance.

• STAMP PADS: Ink stamp pads are available from most craft or stationery stores and are ideal for quick, simple stamping. Originally designed for fabric decoration, they are quick-drying and leave a good hardwearing finish on wooden surfaces.

• PAINT: Virtually any kind of paint can be used for stamping, although the type of surface on which the stamp is to be applied, will influence the choice.

HINTS & TIPS: Making a mirror image

For a mirror image of the design, make another stamp by simply printing the first one directly on to another piece of rubber. Cut around this image and stick down.

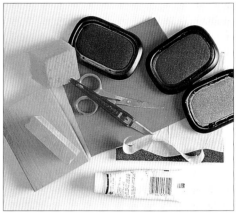
▲ Stamping materials.

MAKING A RUBBER STAMP

TO MAKE YOUR OWN rubber stamp, work out a rough design on paper. Then transfer or copy the design on to a piece of rubber, on the side which will form the top of the stamp.

Make sure that the design is simple and clean. The decorative effect should come from repeating motifs, rather than from complex shapes.

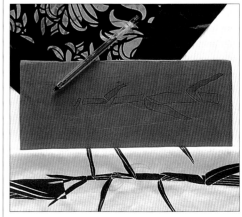
▲ Transfer your design onto a piece of rubber.

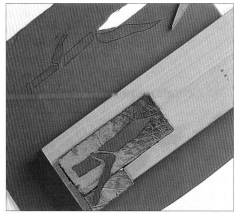

▲ Position the rubber cut-outs on the foam.

▲ Cut away the excess backing foam.

▲ Stamping provides a rustic finished effect.

CUTTING THE STAMP

Use some PVA adhesive to apply a piece of foam to a wooden block. Do not worry about keeping the foam neat – it can even be in several pieces – because it will be positioned behind the actual stamping surface.

Carefully cut out the rubber design using sharp scissors or a craft knife and cutting mat. Using the same adhesive as before, stick the cut-out pieces of the rubber on to the foam. Press firmly and add extra adhesive to any areas or edges where the rubber isn't sticking.

TESTING THE STAMP

Apply an even coat of artists' acrylic paint to the rubber stamp with a chunk of smooth sponge. Then turn the stamp over and press firmly onto a spare piece of paper. This image is how the final pattern will appear, so make any changes to the shape at this stage.

Once satisfied with the rubber design, cut away excess backing foam with a craft knife. This helps the stamp to stand proud of the block and prevents paint straying as the stamp is used and gently rocked on the final surface.

APPLYING THE STAMP

Dab artists' acrylic colours with either a sponge or brush onto the stamp. (Other paints can be used but they should be both opaque and thick – about the consistency of double cream.) Test the stamp on some spare paper to remove any excess paint, before pushing the design down onto the surface of the object.

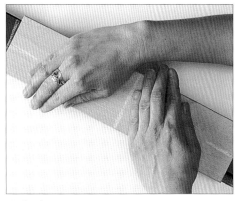

▲ Apply even pressure to your stamp.

Gently rock the stamp to ensure even pressure (it may help to practise this technique on spare paper first). Then, holding the surface steady with your spare hand, carefully lift the stamp in one swift, single movement.

Depending on the type of stamp material, it may be possible to reapply the stamp a few times before more paint is needed. Sponges, for example, absorb considerable amounts of paint and will not need new paint after every application. If this is the case, remember to press lightly for the first print and then gradually apply harder pressure for the following few applications, in order to try and keep the depth of colour even throughout your design.

MAKING A VEGETABLE STAMP

MANY FIRM VEGETABLES, such as potatoes or carrots, can be used for cheap, basic stamps. However, they only work for one-off projects, creating a semi-textured finish. Cut the potato in half and wipe off the moisture. Cut around the template (such as the ivy leaf shown below) with a craft knife on to half a potato. Then cut away the background so that the design to be printed stands proud. (See the 'Ivy stamped chair' project on pp150–1). Remember that vegetables give off a fair amount of water, so you will need to blot the potato with tissue occasionally to prevent the paint from diluting or smudging.

▲ Test your stamp on a spare piece of paper.

▲ Use a scalpel to carve out your design.

The inspiration for your paint project could come from anywhere, from the pattern on an old tablecloth to the texture of an ageing wooden gate. Ideas tend to spring from the most unexpected of places, and the more unusual they are, the more individual the project is likely to be. Always be on the look out for inspiration and follow your instincts. Allow your imagination to run wild and you will find the creative confidence to turn all your inspirational ideas into practice around the home.

Sourcing Inspiration

Architectural features

RCHITECTURE DIFFERS HUGELY from country to country and century to century. As such, there is a vast amount that might inspire you if you look closely at the architecture around you. The best way to find out about different styles of architecture is to get out of the house and visit as many different buildings and locations as you can. And as well as admiring the columns and arches, watch out for details that you might otherwise miss – the brickwork, the iron railings, the timber beams and the small features on a door.

If you are a keen traveller, you will be able to find paint inspiration in architectural styles from all around the globe. When you have seen the classical architecture of Athens or Rome, you may be tempted to recreate the magical world

by using faux marble in your home. Once you have paid a visit to a splendid Gothic cathedral, you may be inspired to mirror the arches on your walls and ceiling using a trompe l'oeil paint technique. After observing the colourwashed charm of painted timber houses, you may wish to add similar tones to your palette to use inside your home. Once you have marvelled at the subtle hues of past centuries in crumbling Mediterranean frescoes, you may wish to paint your home in a combination of distressed ochre, sepia, burnt sienna, rust and deep red, redolent of the long hot summers. Another great source of ideas is to delve into architects' source books. These are ideal, particularly if your design calls for historical influences or structured images. They are copyright free, packed with images and available from the local

library or bookshops. And remember not to overlook the numerous small architectural details that may hold just the inspiration that you are looking for. You may, for example, want to recreate the multi-layered verdigris that has built

up on a door handle, the distressed finish of a weather-beaten wind vale, the marble finish of the tops of pillars and columns, or the timber frame effect of a Tudor-style house.

Stone, wood and metal

THE COLOUR AND TEXTURE of the surfaces of stone, wood and metal have long served as inspiration for paint effects. The essence of the technique is to re-create the look of the surface using paint. From faux marble to wood-graining, malachite to verdigris, liming to tortoiseshell, there is a great deal that can inspire you. Look closely at objects that you may take for granted such as a cobbled garden wall, a woven wooden basket or a rusty metal wheelbarrow and think about how you can mimic their patterns and texture in your own house.

Among the most tactile of surfaces are smooth stone, textured wood and gleaming metal. Inspiration can be sourced from all sorts of modest everyday objects such as freshly polished cutlery in your kitchen, a wooden gate in your garden, the

brickwork in your walls or the rusty surface of old railings in front of your house. Nature too provides a great deal in the way of inspiration - the smooth pebbles on a beach, the woodgrain in a branch fallen from a tree or the glowing surface of gold. The best way to re-create metal, stone or wood is to examine the desired surface extremely closely and carefully note its structure, texture and colour. If you want to try your hand at marbling, for example, inspect the vein structure of the stone carefully: the veins should not criss-cross or branch out like they do in a tree but they should run diagonally to each other. If you want to make your imitation marble look even more realistic, then you can divide your surface into sections to make it look as if it is made out of marble blocks. Another popular paint effect is verdigris, inspired by the

natural weathering of copper, brass and bronze objects - over a long period of time, a layer of copper sulphate will slowly start to build up on their surfaces. Look closely at an example of real verdigris and think about how you can best imitate

it. Observe the areas in which the copper sulphate has started to form and how it spreads. It should be seen to be running vertically down metal objects so bear this factor in mind as you apply your paint.

The past

FROM DISTRESSING to crackle glaze, verdigris to liming, the purpose of many paint effects is to make objects look older than they really are. Inspiration can be sourced from all sorts of different places. Have another look at relics of the past that surround us everyday – objects that are starting to decay and show signs of their age, such as metalwork, stones, natural features or museum artefacts. Think about the ways in which each of these different objects age and the sort of look that you want to recreate in your home.

Looking closely at everyday objects that have been weathered by age is a great source of inspiration for the interior

decorator. This world that once belonged to the past is all around us and the more observant you are, the more you will

notice it. Examine how the rust has formed around the metalwork in your garden and think about how it has affected

the different features. Ageing tends to show first on exposed corners and edges, or on parts of the object that have been handled or used most often, such as the handle of an old water pump. Stones and bricks take on a very different appearance when they start to age. Observe the flaking distressed look of neglected brickwork and the way the colours have subtly changed after years of exposure to rain and sunshine. Go for a walk in the countryside and have another look at natural features that are starting to show signs of age. You may find inspiration in the shape and texture of the twisted, knarled trunks of old trees or the patterns formed by ivy that has grown ravenously over trees and stones.

 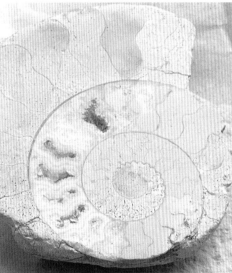 

Perhaps you could visit a museum and examine the exhibits on show. Looking at ancient artefacts and fossils (some of the oldest remaining objects from centuries gone by) will help you to see how time takes its toll on different surfaces and

structures. It is not hard to recreate such finishes. Once you have mastered the paint techniques outlined in this book, you will be able to transform a cheap modern table or a brand new wardrobe into an antique-looking piece of furniture.

Flowers and leaves

FLOWERS AND LEAVES have served as inspiration for artists for many centuries, from William Morris to Van Gogh and Monet to Rousseau. The unique variety of shapes, colours, sizes and textures offers a wealth of potential for the interior decorator. If you are floundering, then get away from your paint and tools for a while and look to nature for ideas and inspiration – a quick trip around the garden or park should be enough. Or pay a visit to your local art gallery and have a look at how great artists have interpreted nature in their work.

The ever-changing colours of leaves and flowers throughout the year are a rich source of inspiration for interior

designers. Choose from the warm, muted tones of autumnal foliage, the delicate, tender aspect of spring's first growths,

the cool, stark colours of winter trees or the vibrant, vivid hues of midsummer blooms. Each of these colour schemes will

have a very different effect on your house – wintery blues will have a cooling effect while summery oranges and yellows will warm even the darkest corner. The varied shapes of flowers and leaves are ideal for making stencils. Draw along the stem to create an outline of the basic shape and flow of a plant. Then break off the leaves and draw around them individually, leaving a bridge where the leaves are separate or where they naturally overlap each other. If you need to change the size of the plant, try drawing around it first and then increasing or reducing the size of your finished drawing on a photocopier. Then transfer your design onto manila card, acetate or plan trace and you will be ready to start.

The leaf, which is often wrongly considered to be the poor relation of the flower, may also inspire you: the veins tructure of a leaf may throw up some interesting ideas for paint patterns while the leathery texture can be recreated

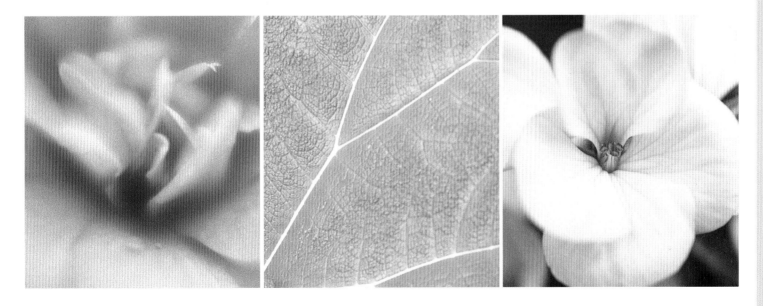

by manipulating paint with a plastic bag. Look also at flowers and leaves from far-flung parts of the globe, such as slipper orchids or peonies, which are becoming widely available, and bring a touch of the exotic into your house.

Textiles

THERE IS A WAY that you can source inspiration for your paint effects without even leaving the house. It is easy for us to get accustomed to the patterns and designs that surround us every day, so much so that we cease to notice them and overlook their inspirational potential. Take a close look at the fabrics that you have around you in the house – the curtains, the carpets, the towels, the cushion covers and the throws. Each will have its own colour, pattern and texture that can serve as inspiration when you come to painting your house.

Start in the bedroom – look at the design on your curtains. Would it be possible to trace or adapt the pattern to use as a stencil? Perhaps the design could be reproduced on your walls to make a matching border. If you don't have any spare

material, you could always photocopy it on a colour copier and use that instead. Next, move to the kitchen and look closely at the design on your tea towel – would you be able to reproduce this freehand on your cabinets? Perhaps you could mimic the tablecloth's checked pattern on your plates or curtains. The texture of many different types of fabric can also be inspiring for the interior designer. You can use a trompe l'oeil technique to make it look as though your surface is covered in fabric – the multi-layering paint technique, frottage will make an MDF screen look as though it is covered in antique damask. Fabric colours can also be incredibly lush and rich. All you have to do is to choose which you like best and then decide how you want to make it work in the colour scheme of your home. Remember to observe how differen

colours change in different lights. Some shades alter dramatically in artificial or evening light, compared to how they look in the day. Lilac can be a prime example of this – it looks much more pink in the evening light than it does in the

morning sunshine. Once you have discovered a colour that you like at all times of day, take a sample along to your hardware store and they will be able to match it to the nearest paint colour.

Art, design and form

I F YOU ARE REALLY STRUGGLING for paint inspiration, why not visit your local art gallery or design exhibition. Looking at other people's work is an excellent way to get ideas for how to use paint. Look at the shapes and forms that artists and designers have used and think about how you can incorporate such elements into your home. But art and design are not restricted to galleries – start to be aware of the forms, shapes and colours that surround you every day. You may find inspiration in something as simple as a bowl of fruit or the cogs of a wheel.

Looking at paintings and designs is particularly useful if you are planning to attempt some freehand. It is always helpful to examine how the work was put together before you start your own design. Look at the direction of the brushstrokes,

the paint type and thickness and how the piece is constructed – what is the central focus point and how does the picture pan out from there. Look at the different techniques used by artists to form trees, flowers or people.

It may be simpler than you think. And take note of the artists' subject matter. Maybe you could pick out a particular feature and incorporate it into a design for your home — cubist blocks would make a stylish border and Art Nouveau motifs could be adapted into an inspirational stencil. Look also at the mood created by different colours — if you were to choose tones from the sombre palette of Rembrandt or Caravaggio, you would give your home a very different feel than if you were to use the vivid hues of Matisse or Kandisky. Take note also of the wonderful colour combinations that

surround you in the course of everyday life. Perhaps you will find insipiration in a chequered floor pattern or the gilded finish of a brass instrument. Watch the way that light falls on objects, for example, the mirror-like effect of the sun

glistening on the surface of water or spilling through a dark tunnel of foliage. Look closely at shapes that you might otherwise neglect to see, such as the sinuous curves of a violin or the delicate structure of an orchid.

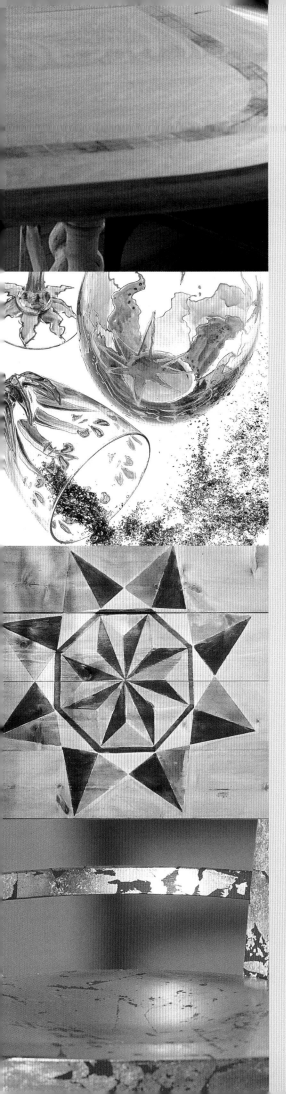

WHETHER IT IS USED FOR FAMILY GET-TOGETHERS, SOCIABLE SUPPERS OR ELABORATE DINNER PARTIES, THE DINING ROOM IS THE PLACE TO INDULGE YOUR SENSE OF THEATRE. ADD STRIKING ACCESSORIES TO CREATE A MOOD OR PLUCK UP COURAGE AND TRANSFORM THE FURNITURE. THIS CHAPTER IS FULL OF INSPIRING IDEAS FOR TRANSFORMATIONS, BOTH GREAT AND SMALL, TO HELP YOU TO CREATE THE PERFECT ENVIRONMENT FOR GOOD FOOD AND COMPANY, MAKING EACH MEAL AN OCCASION TO LINGER OVER.

Dining Room Projects

Geometric starburst floor

THE STARBURST and geometric edges of this floor design are produced using a template. The results can be truly stunning. This stencilled floor, which is about 2m (6ft 6in) square, took only two days to complete, plus time for varnishing. You may find it comfortable to lie on a cushion or use a kneeling pad. Stand up at frequent intervals so that you can check your work. It also pays to walk away from your work for 10 minutes in order to shake off 'artist's blindness' and come back to the design with fresh eyes when you are more likely to notice any errors that might have crept in. The wood was not varnished, polished or treated, so the stain soaked right into the grain. If the floor is varnished, the design will not have the same depth of colour and so it may need to be sanded first to remove any old varnish that might still be present.

❖ YOU WILL NEED ❖

Paper template

Steel rule

Scalpel (or cutting blade) and cutting mat

Woodstain colours of your choice

Household paintbrushes

Plastic cup or glass jam jar

Deep tray

Varnish

1 Pin the paper design in the middle of the floor. Starting at the outside of the design, cut out each section individually using firm and quite deep cuts that go through the paper and into the wood. These cuts form a border within which to paint and they act as a barrier, preventing the stain from seeping into the wood outside the design. If you do not start from the outside of the design, you may have trouble keeping the template together as you gradually cut it into pieces.

2 Decant a small quantity of each of the colours into a plastic cup or glass jam jar and confine them to a deep tray while you work. You can also use this tray to put wet brushes on, which will prevent them from rolling onto the unfinished work. Do not let your brushes dry when you take a break or the woodstain may harden on them.

3 The cuts in the wood prevent the stain from soaking beyond them and they therefore form an invisible outline or the equivalent of the bridges previously mentioned. Using a soft brush, very carefully fill in each section with the colours that you have chosen. You will find that the stain soaks into the wood quite quickly and travels right up to the cuts. Try to work in an area where you will not be disturbed because spills are so difficult to remedy.

HINTS & TIPS

• When the work is finished it must be protected with a hard-wearing varnish to stand the test of time. Varnish your way out of a room before going to bed and then walk barefoot only on the floor for a few days while the varnish cures.

For further floor projects see:
Old oak woodgrained floor pp113–15;
Sponge-stamped floor pp128–9.

▲ Cut out the template with a scalpel.

▲ Use a tray for your stain and paintbrushes.

▲ Carefully fill in your design with a soft brush.

Painted decanter and glasses

STAINED GLASS is a wonderful way of brightening up any uninspiring pieces of glassware that you might have around the house. You do not need to have had any previous experience of glass painting and you will be able to achieve stunning effects extremely quickly and simply. I have stained this decanter and glasses with special glass paints so that they can be used for practical purposes – the paints are non-toxic and water-resistant so the colours do not start to fade after you have washed them a few times. The decanter and glasses would make a great centre piece on the table at a dinner party. However, if you wish to stain glass for display only, you may prefer to use spray enamel paint, gold pens and glitter glue instead.

YOU WILL NEED

Cloth

Methylated spirit

Wet and dry paper

Gold outliner

Special glass paint in rose and blue violet

Design for your stencil (see pp246)

Manila card, acetate or plan trace

Scalpel (or cutting blade) and cutting mat

Squirrel hair art brush

1 Firstly, you will need to prepare the glass and decanter by washing them thoroughly in warm soapy water and drying them well. Wipe them over with a damp cloth and methylated spirit in order to remove any excess dirt and allow to dry. Rub over all the surfaces with wet and dry paper and wipe down with a dry cloth.

2 Squeezing the tube of gold outliner directly onto the glass, make large wiggly shapes around the sides. Use the templates on p246 to cut two stencils out of manila card, acetate or plan trace. Very carefully hold the star shape in place with your fingers and squeeze an outline around this. Use the fleur-de-lys stencil to decorate the top of the glasses. Leave them to dry for at least ten minutes. You do not have to limit yourself solely to using stencil patterns. Feel free to use your imagination and come up with your own ideas and designs.

3 Use a squirrel hair art brush to fill in the colour. Dip the brush into the glass paint and fill in the centres of the shapes that you outlined, alternating the colours each time.

4 Decorate the decanter in the same way as the glasses. The stopper is usually more tricky because it is smaller. Using the gold outliner, squeeze a swirling line on the stopper from bottom to top and then, with the brush and glass paint, create the same pattern as on the decanter.

For further wall projects see:
Brilliant painted glass pp155–7; Fish stencil shower glass pp193–5.

▲ Outline the design on the glass.

▲ Fill in the shapes with glass paint.

Chequered walls

THE COMBINATION OF fresh yellow and green complements the crisp chair covers and creates a neat and airy effect in this bright dining room. Once you have managed to master the basic technique of colour washing, more intricate designs such as chequered or striped patterns are relatively easy to achieve. In this project, the transparency of the glaze work allows the base colour to glow through the pattern, providing an attractive depth and intensity of colour where the stripes cross over each other. Painting these effects does not take long, though it is important to spend some time before you start to apply the paint preparing, measuring and masking the wall, to ensure that you achieve a professional finished result.

❖ YOU WILL NEED ❖

Low sheen base paint

Pencil

Long straightedge

Spirit level or plumb line

Tape measure

Masking tape

1l (35fl oz) acrylic scumble glaze

Artists' acrylic paints for staining glaze or coloured acrylic paint

Household paintbrushes

Acrylic glaze coat

---

1 Carefully plan how the colour scheme will work before you begin, to ensure that the pattern will fit in with the shape of the room. Paint the walls of the room in the yellow base colour, using a paint that has a slight sheen, such as vinyl silk. For the best results, choose a base colour that is paler than the desired colour of the stripes or checks. If you are painting on to a dark base colour, more than one coat of glaze may be required to ensure that the pattern shows up.

2 When the base coat is fully dry, mark out the vertical stripes lightly in pencil with the aid of a long straightedge and a spirit level or plumb line. Then, position lengths of masking tape along the outside edges of the darker stripes, so that the areas you are going to paint are not obstructed. The stripes shown in this project are 25cm (10in) wide.

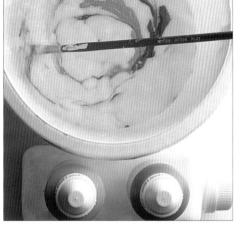
▲ Mix a glaze with the colours of your choice.

3 Mix a glaze, using the acrylic scumble glaze and about a tablespoon of artists' acrylic paint or coloured acrylic paint in the colour of your choice. (Here two different shades of green – sap green and oxide of chromium – were added to produce a more unusual hue.) Add the colour a tiny bit at a time, as it is easy to add more but it is impossible to remove once it has been added. Also, take care not to add too much colour to the glaze because the aim is to maintain its transparent qualities.

4 Apply the glaze in a thin coat to the masked out stripes, using a household paintbrush in a random, crissscross motion. When painting, take care only to overlap areas where the glaze is still wet because wet glaze meeting dry glaze will cause undesirable lines and marks to form in the final coat.

▲ Choose a base lighter than the stripes.

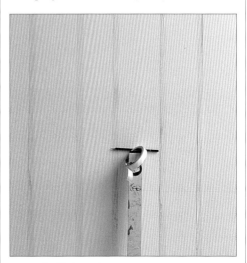
▲ Mask off the stripes.

5 While the glaze is still wet, carefully remove the masking tape along the edges of the stripes. Peel the tape slowly back on itself, making sure that it does not pull the paint base away from the wall.

6 When the vertical lines have completely dried, mark and mask off the horizontal stripes. To save measuring each stripe on the wall, which can be difficult to do accurately, mark a long piece of wood with lines spaced the appropriate distance apart. Then work along the wall with the piece of wood and use the marks as guidelines for marking in the position of the horizontal stripes.

7 In most homes the join between the ceiling and the wall is not perfectly straight. Check this with a spirit level before you begin to mark out the horizontals. If the ceiling is not quite straight, make tiny adjustments of about 1cm (¹/₂in) at a time on each horizontal stripe. These gradual alterations should create a more pleasing finished effect than one large adjustment, which will create a top or bottom stripe that is obviously out of kilter with the others.

▲ Apply glaze to the vertical stripes.

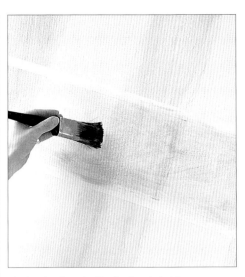

▲ Apply glaze to the horizontal stripes.

▲ Mark the position of the horizontals.

▲ Make adjustments to the horizontal lines if necessary.

▲ Remove the masking tape carefully.

HINTS & TIPS

• Horizontal stripes can only be adjusted if the ceiling is no more than 5cm (2in) out of line. If the ceiling is distorted any more than this, horizontal stripes (no matter how greatly they are adapted) will actually emphasize the problem. A ceiling that is severely uneven dictates that the walls should have only vertical stripes, rather than the chequered effect used here.

• Low-tack or cheap masking tape is ideal because it is less sticky than more expensive brands.

• If you need to mix up more glaze while you are working, try to avoid leaving a stripe half-coated while you do this, because the glaze will begin to dry before more wash can be added.

For further wall projects see:
Colour-washed wall pp124–5; Children's balloon stencils pp184–5; Marble bathroom pp200–1; Repeating border and dragged stripes pp208–11.

8 Mask off the horizontals, checking that there is always a right–angle where the lines meet. Then apply glaze to the horizontal areas, again using the brush in a criss–cross motion. Then carefully remove the masking tape.

9 To give the design extra longevity and durability, give the walls a single coat of acrylic glaze coat, in either a silk or matt finish once the stripes are dry. Although this appears cloudy and milk-like when it is wet, the glaze dries clear to provide an additional protective coat over the walls' decorative finish.

▲ Apply a coat of acrylic glaze.

Colour-washed oak sideboard

WITH PAINT EFFECTS, you can co-ordinate the furniture for one room and ensure that it all matches. The colours in the sideboard match the painting on the table, which picks up the tartan on the chairs, which in turn complements the green bureau.

The sideboard was already very decorative and so any further decoration was kept very low key. A cream colour wash provided just the right note and worked well with the grain of the oak. A little faded colour was added to echo the colours of the tartan on the table and chairs.

❖ YOU WILL NEED ❖

Fine grade abrasive paper

Tack rag

Cream acrylic paint

Old tablespoon

Jam jar

2 x 5cm (2in) household paintbrushes

Clean cloths

Gouache paints in various colours

Artists' paintbrush
(sable or synthetic mixture)

Artists' lining brush (synthetic)

Sanding sealer

Clear matt polyurethane varnish

This old oak sideboard was revamped in subtle colours so that the grain of the wood showed clearly.

1 First, get the sideboard professionally stripped of its coat of varnish. This will ensure that the colour wash penetrates the wood and displays its beautiful grain.

2 Remove the doors. It is often easier to deal with large pieces of furniture in bits. Rub down the sideboard with fine grade abrasive paper and dust with a tack rag.

3 To make the colour wash, spoon some of the cream paint into a jam jar with an old tablespoon and add sufficient water to make a milky consistency. If you intend to treat other pieces of furniture in the same way, note the proportions used.

4 Apply a generous helping of the wash brushing it out in the direction of the grain.

5 Leave for about 15 minutes to allow the paint to sink in and dry a little. With a soft, clean cloth, rub the wash back to expose a little more of the grain. When the paint is dry, lightly sand the sideboard and remove the dust with a tack rag.

6 Mix up the desired colours, diluting them with water to achieve the right tone. Then, using an artists' paintbrush, paint on the carved flowers and leaves.

7 Mark a 2.5cm (1in) wide band around the edge of the top of the sideboard and divide it into 4cm (2in) sections. With an artists' lining brush, paint them alternately in faded green and blue. Run a line of reddish/tan colour through the centre of the band, then paint short lines across the middle of each blue section.

8 When the colours are dry, give the sideboard a coat of sanding sealer and allow it to dry before finally applying a coat of clear, matt polyurethane varnish.

For further freehand projects see:
Tartan-band dining table pp100–1; Freehand painted tables pp110–12; Kitchen accessories pp138–41; Hand-painted chest pp206–7.

▲ Pick out the flower decoration.

Tartan-band dining table

THIS OLD DINING ROOM table had obviously been put to very good use during the last fifty years. It now looked somewhat out of date and there were stains and small areas of missing and lifted veneer to be dealt with before the painting could begin. It was stripped professionally and then defects were repaired with wood glue and wood filler. The light cream colour wash and subtle tartan motif transformed this dark, heavy piece of furniture into a bright more delicate looking item, which would fit well into a modern decorative scheme.

❖ YOU WILL NEED ❖

Small, flexible palette knife

Wood glue

Wood filler

Fine grade abrasive paper

Steel wool or coarse grade abrasive paper

Tack rag

Cream colour wash (see p98)

Clean cloths

2 x 5cm (2in) household paintbrushes

Small pieces of stiff card

Ruler

Pencil

Scissors

Gouache paints in various colours

Artists' paintbrush
(sable or synthetic mixture)

Artists' lining brush (synthetic)

Sanding sealer

Clear, matt polyurethane varnish

This old dining table was badly in need of repair and renovation.

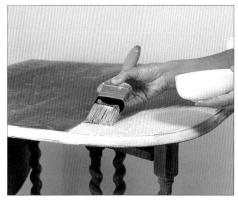

▲ Apply the cream colourwash.

1 Using the thin end of a palette knife, insert wood glue underneath any loose veneer and press the wood back into place. Leave it to dry completely, under the weight of a pile of heavy books.

2 Once the veneer repairs are fully dry, use the same flexible palette knife and neutral coloured wood filler to fill in any indentations that remain. Once the wood filler is dry, give the table a complete rub down with the fine grade abrasive paper.

3 Here and there, especially on any areas of complicated moulding or carving, where there are still traces of varnish, use steel wool or coarser grade abrasive paper to strip back to bare wood. Then, give the table a final rub over with the tack rag to collect up all the dust and debris.

4 Paint the dining table with cream colour wash in the same way as you did for the sideboard (see p98).

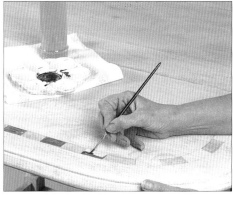

▲ Paint the decorative band.

5 A simple way to mark out a regularly spaced border is to use a stiff cardboard template. Cut a V-shaped notch with its point 5.5cm (2¼in) in from the end of the piece of card and then position it with its unnotched end flush with the table edge. Move it around the table, making light pencil marks at the apex of the notch. These can then be joined up to make a line following the edge of the table. Cut another piece of card and mark a line 8cm (3¼in) in from the edge to give a 2.5cm (1in) broad band.

6 Divide the band into 4cm (1½in) sections. With an artists' lining brush, paint them alternately faded green and blue. Run a line of reddish tan colour through the centre of the band then paint short lines across the middle of each blue section.

7 When dry, coat with sanding sealer and leave to dry before applying clear, matt varnish.

For further freehand projects see:
Colour-washed oak sideboard pp98–9; Freehand painted tables pp110–12; Kitchen accessories pp138–41.

Decorative painted chairs

Y OU WILL NEED an unfinished wood chair to start either of these projects. The gilded chair, combining luxury with informality, is a true work of art and will become a family treasure. Gilding gives a brilliant effect and the 'distressed' look is not too difficult to achieve if you follow the instructions carefully. The stamped chair is deceptively easy, too; the artichoke motif makes a fine, compact decorative shape and it also gives a hint of luxury. Stamps come in a great variety of shapes and sizes, so you can choose any motif that takes your fancy.

Gilded chair

❖ YOU WILL NEED ❖

Abrasive paper

Tack rag

Matisse pimento water-based paint

Household paintbrushes

Gold-leaf size medium (with an open-time of at least an hour) and brush

Cotton gloves

Silk scarf

Gold leaf sheets

Shellac

Oil-based varnish

1 Sand the chair and remove the dust with the tack rag. Apply two or three coats of base coat, allowing each to dry.

2 Apply the size medium to the chair and allow it to 'set'. The size is ready when your fingers will glide along it. Put on the gloves and have the scarf and gold leaf to hand. Never touch the sheets of gold leaf with your bare hands, as the oils from your fingers will discolour them.

3 Position a sheet of gold leaf above the surface and gently lower it onto the seat and lightly pat it down with your fingertips. The gold sheet will immediately bond when it comes into contact with the size.

4 Roll the scarf into a small, tight ball and rub it over the gold leaf to flatten the surface. Do not worry about gaps between the sheets; this creates an interesting effect, but touch up any bare areas.

5 Coat with shellac and then apply three or four coats of oil-based varnish, leaving each coat to dry.

For further gilding projects see:
Gilded mirror frame pp119–21.

Stamped artichoke chair

❖ YOU WILL NEED ❖

Fine grade abrasive paper

Tack rag

Household paintbrushes

Gouache paints in light olive and dark red oxide

Stamp with artichoke motif

Manila card, acetate or plan trace

Scalpel (or cutting blade) and cutting mat

Piece of chalk

Stencil brush

Kitchen paper

Black waterproof ink pad

Satin varnish

1 Sand down the chair with abrasive paper to achieve a smooth finish. Wipe it clean thoroughly with the tack rag to remove all dust particles.

2 Using a household paintbrush, apply two coats of red oxide gouache paint all over the chair. Allow each coat to dry thoroughly.

3 Stamp the manila card, acetate or plan trace with the artichoke stamp. Then cut around the outline with a scalpel to create a stencil.

4 Mark the position of the artichoke stamps on the chair with a piece of chalk.

5 Place the stencil on the marked positions. Dip the stencil brush into light olive gouache paint and dab it onto kitchen paper. Apply paint through the stencil, working in a circular motion to build up the depth of colour and create artichoke shapes.

6 Use a waterproof ink pad and stamp over the outlines to fill in the detail on the artichokes.

7 When the chair is dry apply two or three coats of satin varnish, leaving each to dry.

For further stamping projects see:
Sponge-stamped floor pp128–9; Sponged pots pp214–15.

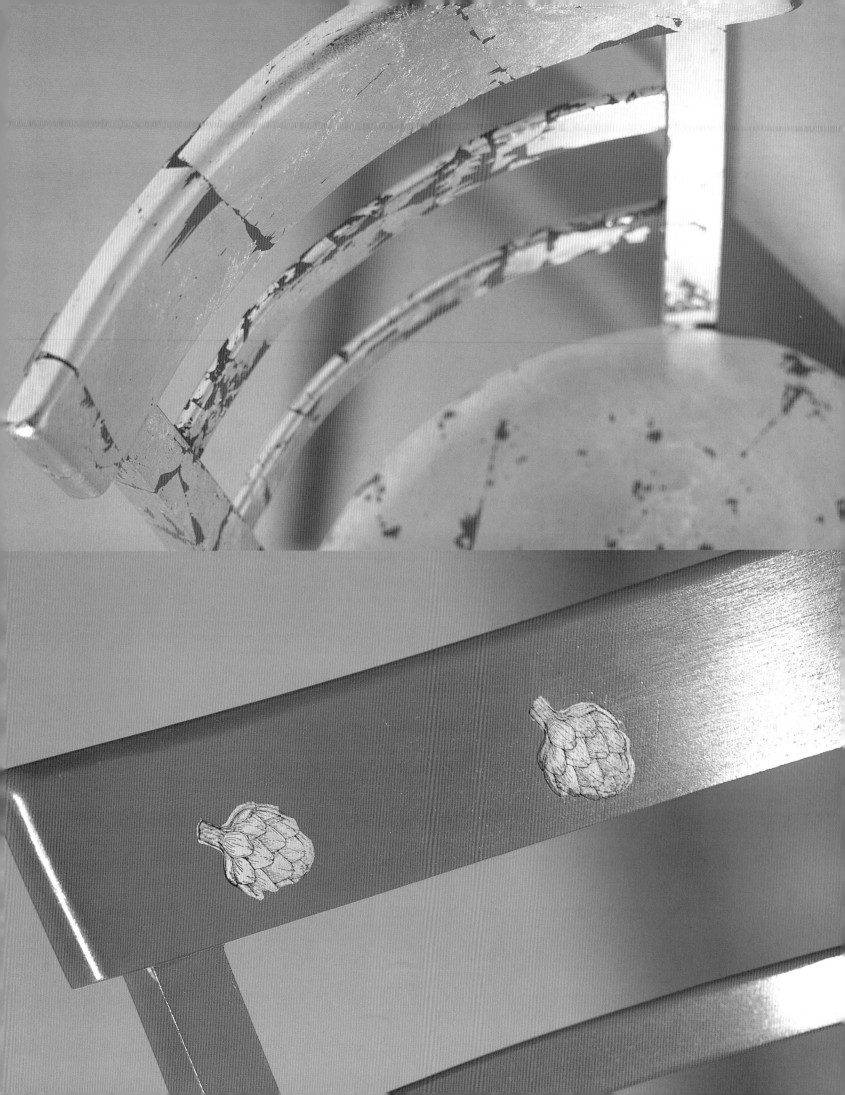

Antiqued table

THIS TABLE WAS SPLIT AND DAMAGED when it was rescued from a junk yard – even some corners were missing. However, it was given a new lease of life with a distressed finish in a vibrant turquoise. Even the damaged surface and missing corners took on a certain charm once the table was painted. This antiquing technique simply uses a few pots of acrylic paint and works best on bare or primed wood. Surfaces that have been varnished or sealed should be rubbed down well with abrasive paper to provide a good key before primer can be applied.

❖ YOU WILL NEED ❖

Wood filler

Medium grade abrasive paper

Tack rag

White acrylic primer

Household brush

Acrylic paint in brown and turquoise

Clean cloths

Methylated spirit (optional)

Dead flat matt acrylic varnish

1 Fill in any large splits or holes in the table with wood filler, then rub down with the abrasive paper and wipe with a tack rag. Apply a coat of primer to the table so that the acrylic paint will adhere well. When this is dry, apply a base coat of brown acrylic paint. Leave until this is thoroughly dry.

2 Apply a coat of turquoise acrylic paint over the dark brown base coat. Cover the surface completely, making sure that the paint reaches into every corner and inside edge of the table. Turn the table upside down as you work. Do not let this coat of paint dry out completely before the next step.

3 While the paint is still slightly wet, wipe off small patches from the edges and corners of the table with a cloth; these are the areas that would be first to wear naturally. Use a damp cloth or one dipped in methylated spirit on any areas that are drying too quickly. If the paint comes off too easily and smoothly, reapply it and start again.

4 Once the table is completely dry, seal it with two coats of dead flat matt acrylic varnish. This dries quickly and can easily be recoated the same day – usually after an hour, depending on the temperature.

HINTS & TIPS

• If you find it difficult to judge the drying time for rubbing off the acrylic paint, an alternative method is to apply wax to the edges of the table after the brown base coat is dry. Then paint over this with the turquoise paint and later chip it off to reveal patches of the brown underneath.

• To distress the finish further, you can apply a coat of crackle glaze between the base and top coats.

For further ageing projects see:
Antiqued iron bed frame pp178–9; Distressed chest pp198–9; Aged rustic chair pp212–13.

▲ Apply the top coat very thoroughly.

▲ Carefully wipe paint from the edges.

▲ Finish the table with two coats of varnish.

Porphyry picture frame

THIS FRAME IS not particularly old but needless to say it was bought secondhand and was extremely cheap. It was an enticing item offering a range of interesting possibilities in terms of decoration because it was so wide and had an inset and some carving to add to its attraction. The paint spattering technique gives the effect of porphyry – an attractive, classical finish in black, cream and gold. As a finishing touch a tartan ribbon was added to fit in with the decor in the rest of the room where the frame would eventually hang.

❖ YOU WILL NEED ❖

Damp cloth

White semi-gloss paint

2 x 4cm (1½in) household paintbrushes

Fine grade abrasive paper

Tack rag

Artists' oil paints in light red, yellow ochre and black

Mineral turpentine

Small natural sponge

Stencil brush

Piece of newspaper

Gold bronzing powder

Artists' acrylic varnish

Fine artists' paintbrush

Clear, satin polyurethane varnish

Tartan ribbon (same width as frame inset)

Tube of non-staining glue

1 Clean the frame thoroughly with a damp cloth. Apply a coat of white semi-gloss paint and leave for 24 hours to dry. Rub down with abrasive paper and wipe with the tack rag. Apply a second coat, leave to dry and rub down and tack the frame as before.

2 Mix a little white semi-gloss with some red oil paint and a little yellow ochre and black to make a terracotta colour. Add a tiny amount of turpentine and sponge all over the main part of the frame. Leave to dry for an hour or two until no longer shiny.

3 Mix a little yellow ochre and the white paint to make a cream colour and thin to a milky consistency with turpentine. Dip the end of the stencil brush in the mix and spatter some onto a piece of newspaper by drawing your thumb across the tips of the bristles. This will remove any drips or blobs that may spoil the frame.

4 Spatter cream paint over the frame. Leave to dry for a few minutes then spatter over a little dilute black oil paint.

5 Mix a little gold bronzing powder with some acrylic varnish and spatter this lightly over the frame. Then, using the fine artists' brush and the same gold mixture, carefully pick out the indented lines around the frame and paint the raised inner edge.

6 Leave the frame to dry overnight. Then apply a coat of clear, satin polyurethane varnish to protect it from wear and tear.

7 Cut the tartan ribbon into lengths to fit the frame inset. Mitre the corners by following the original mitring on the frame. Glue the ribbon onto the frame, smoothing it down carefully so it lies quite flat.

HINTS & TIPS

• If you have one, a glue gun is an easy way of sticking the ribbon to the frame.

For further picture frame projects see:
Limed picture frame pp230–1; Painted frames pp232–3; Golden pear picture frame pp234–5; Poppies picture frame pp236–7.

▲ Spatter the frame with green paint.

▲ Use a glue gun to attach the tartan inset.

USED FOR SOCIALIZING, REST AND
PLAY, THE LIVING ROOM IS ONE OF
THE MOST FLEXIBLE IN THE HOUSE
AND CAN BE TREATED AS
SOMETHING OF A BLANK CANVAS
FOR YOUR CREATIVE ENERGIES.
START WITH SOME MODEST
ACCESSORIES, OR GO WILD AND
DECORATE THE WHOLE ROOM IN
PAINT EFFECTS. THE RESULT WILL
BE A ROOM THAT IS COMFORTABLE,
STYLISH AND UMISTAKABLY STAMPED
WITH YOUR PERSONALITY.

Living Room Projects

Freehand painted tables

A REPETITIVE DESIGN on a nest of tables makes an unusually attractive item out of a very practical piece of furniture. Many people baulk at the idea of handpainting a set of tables, on the grounds that although painting one successfully might be possible, painting the others to match would be too much to attempt. Once you have made your design for the largest table, however, nothing could be easier than copying it onto the other two. The painting does not require great artistic skill – patience and concentration are more important.

❖ YOU WILL NEED ❖

Wood filler

Palette knife

Fine grade abrasive paper

Tack rag

2 x 4cm (1½in) household paintbrushes

Primer

Pale yellow semi-gloss paint

Artists' oil colours in yellow ochre and raw umber

Jam jar

Mineral turpentine

Old tablespoon

Natural sponge

Clear satin polyurethane varnish

Drawing paper and pencil

Tracing paper

Ruler

Masking tape

Soft pencil

Ballpoint pen

Artists' paintbrush

Acrylic craft paints

Sheet of glass (optional)

Candle

These battered old tables were covered in varnish and had to be stripped before work could begin.

1 The tables should be stripped of any varnish before you start – these have been stripped professionally. If there are any cracks or chips, apply wood filler using a palette knife with a thin, flexible blade.

2 When dry, rub down the tables, with abrasive paper, then dust them with the tack rag.

3 As the stripped tables are extremely porous, apply a coat of primer. Allow this to dry, then apply a coat of yellow semi-gloss. Leave to dry for 24 hours, then lightly rub the tables down and tack them again. Apply two more coats of paint, rubbing down and tacking after each one.

▲ Rub the tables down with abrasive paper.

4 Prepare a slightly darker yellow paint to sponge the tables by putting some yellow ochre oil paint into a jam jar and adding a small amount of raw umber. Mix to a creamy consistency with a little turpentine. Stir in some of the semi-gloss paint until the jar is about one-quarter full.

5 Smear a little of this mixture onto the dry table-top to see if the colour is dark enough – if not, carefully add a little more yellow ochre and raw umber until it is. When you are satisfied with the shade, top up the jam jar with an equal amount of turpentine. The jam jar should now be half-full of paint glaze.

6 Clean the experimental paint smear from the table with a cloth soaked in turpentine. Turn one of the tables upside down, apply glaze to the legs and then sponge it off with the natural sponge. Turn the table up the right way again and complete the top in the same way.

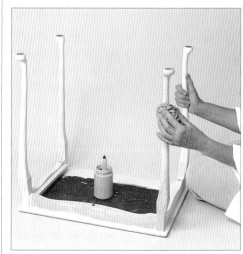

▲ Turn the table over to apply glaze to legs.

7 Sponge the other tables in the same way and leave them to dry for 24 hours. Apply a coat of varnish to each table.

8 The next stage is to map out the design on your table – in this case a border of very stylized ribbon and a bow taken from some Victorian tiles were used. Measure the top of the largest table and draw its proportions onto a large sheet of paper. Draw a border 6.5cm (2$\frac{1}{2}$in) in from the first line.

9 Copy the design freehand along the border line, twisting the ribbon symmetrically as it turns each of the four corners. Mark the position of the bow halfway across the border at the front of the table and draw it in line with the ribbon.

10 When you have completed the border design for the largest table, tape a piece of tracing paper over the top of your piece of paper and take a tracing. Working on this tracing, measure along the longest sides of the border and make a mark halfway along each side. Using a ruler, join these marks with a pencil line that stretches across the centre of the drawing. Repeat with the shorter sides so that the two pencil lines cross at right angles in the middle.

11 Take a soft pencil and repeat this on the table-top to give two lines crossing at right angles. Using the same soft pencil, scribble all along the border on the back of the tracing paper. Then, placing the paper scribbled-side down, tape the tracing to the top of the table so that the crossed lines on the drawing match up with those on the table-top, thus ensuring that the border is straight.

12 Carefully go over the drawing on the tracing paper with a ballpoint pen – the graphite on the back of the drawing will accurately transfer the design to the table. Still using the original as your guide, paint the ribbon and bow with acrylic paints.

▲ Apply a coat of varnish over the sponged glaze.

13 To prepare the design for the two smaller tables, reduce the size of the outer border (the distance between the table edge and the painted border), by 12mm ($\frac{1}{2}$in) on each table. Proceed in the same way for the middle size table: prepare your design on a sheet of drawing paper using your original tracing for the corners and the bow and filling in the slightly shorter sides freehand as before. Then trace the design, scribble on the back, transfer it to the table and paint it in the same way as the larger table.

14 For the smaller table, the ribbon will need to be slightly thinner to keep the design in scale, so once you have established the outside edge of the table and the position of the border on a sheet of drawing paper, you will need to copy the design freehand.

15 Once you have made the modified drawing for the smallest table, finish it in same way as for the other two, and then varnish all three tables.

16 Some tables have insets that take a sheet of glass on the top – if so, you can have a piece cut for each as an added protection. For tables that don't have this feature, an extra coat of varnish is advisable. Finally, before stacking the tables together again, rub a candle along the runners and the sides of the tables so they will run smoothly and reduce the risk of chipping the paint.

HINTS & TIPS

• Use a natural sea sponge for sponging; its absorbency and irregular structure will create the most attractive effect.

• When tracing the design onto the table, don't lean too hard on the ballpoint pen or you could mark the table top. The graphite will transfer the design without the need to apply pressure.

For further sponging projects see:
Sponge-stamped floor pp128–9; Hand-painted blanket box pp164–6; Sponged pots pp214–15.

Old oak woodgrained floor

YOU MAY BE WONDERING why you would want to paint wood to look like wood. Perhaps your floorboards are beyond rescue – they have been filled too much and are too damaged to renovate to a good wooden finish, leaving paint as the only option. Or perhaps they have been painted already and repainting them is easier than stripping them down completely. Or maybe you prefer the look of a beautiful old oak floor. Woodgraining can be a very specialized art practised by master craftsmen to the highest exactitude, but don't worry; this project uses an easy, yet effective, technique to simulate a simple oak grain. You should plan to carry out steps one and two, preparing the floor, the day before you apply the woodgrain effect.

❖ YOU WILL NEED ❖

Wood filler

Palette knife

Shellac

Abrasive paper

Sand-coloured acrylic semi-gloss for base coat

Scumble glaze and colourizer

Bucket

Burnt umber artists' acrylic paint

Household paintbrush

Metal decorators' comb

Thin paintbrush

Soft brush to soften

Piece of real oak for reference (optional)

Tough floor coating to seal

1 The day before you plan to apply the woodgrain effect, fill in any holes and knots in the floorboards using the wood filler and allow to dry. If the wood is bare, seal any knots with shellac and sand to a smooth surface.

2 Prepare the floor by applying a base coat of the sand-coloured acrylic semi-gloss paint. You may have to apply two coats if you are painting onto an absorbent primer. If the surface is already painted, sand it down to provide a key for the new paint to adhere to. Remember to paint in the direction of the woodgrain and allow to dry thoroughly.

3 Prepare a coloured scumble glaze to apply the wood grain. Pour some scumble into a bucket and slowly add acrylic colourizer. Here a ready-mixed colourizer, the colour of medium oak, has been used.

▲ Add colourizer to scumble to make a glaze.

4 Paint on the scumble glaze in the direction of the grain. Paint the length of two or three floorboards at a time.

5 Add a dab of burnt umber acrylic paint straight from the tube onto the tip of your brush.

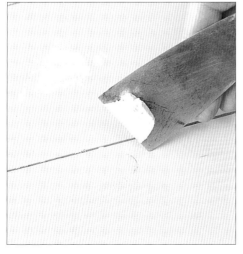
▲ Fill any holes or knots in the boards.

▲ Apply one or two base coats.

▲ Apply the glaze in the direction of the grain.

▲ Blend the burnt umber into the glaze.

6 Paint the burnt umber on the tip of your brush into the still-wet scumble glaze, blending it in. Pull a metal decorators' comb through the glaze in one direction to create a grain effect.

▲ Drag the comb across the scumble glaze.

7 Drag the decorators' comb over the glaze again, but this time hold it at an angle to produce a mottled effect. Work quickly before the scumble dries. Soften the comb lines with a brush if necessary. Leave to dry.

8 Paint on the quartered figuring by diluting some burnt umber acrylic paint and applying it with a small, thin brush.

▲ Drag the comb at an angle to the first lines.

▲ Apply the figuring with a small thin brush.

9 Look at a piece of real oak as reference for the flow and structure of natural figuring. Stand back periodically to have a look at the overall effect. Soften the figuring, working gently with a soft brush in an outward direction.

10 Add sharper, straighter marks across the grain to complete the figuring. When completely dry, varnish the floor with two coats of a tough floor coating.

▲ Use a large brush to soften the figuring.

▲ Complete the figuring with straight marks.

HINTS & TIPS

- Before embarking on this project, look at veneer samples of various grains and take photographs when you see interesting old oak gates, doors and floors. The more wood you look at, the easier it becomes to develop a feel for the flow and beautiful structure of natural grain and figuring.

For further floor projects see:
Geometric starburst floor pp90–1; Sponge-stamped floor pp128–9.

Craquelure lamp base and shade

PAINTED LAMP BASES, like this one, always look as though they are very expensive. Once you have mastered the craquelure technique, you will find it quick and simple to do and you can delight in the large amount of money saved. This cracked porcelain effect is achieved by brushing on two different varnishes, a slow-drying oil varnish followed by a quick-drying water-soluble one, then rubbing in oil colour to show up the cracks. The results are never quite predictable – the size of the cracks depends on how thickly you apply both layers of varnish. The thinner the layers, the smaller the cracks will be. The length of time left between applying the two coats also affects the size – the longer that you leave them, the finer the cracks will be.

❖ YOU WILL NEED ❖

White acrylic paint

Household paintbrushes

Flexible masking tape

Acrylic scumble

Water

Acrylic paint

Stencil brush

Water-based varnish

Varnish brush

Two-part crackle varnish

Soft synthetic brush

Raw umber artists' oil colour

Mineral turpentine

Kitchen paper

Satin oil-based varnish

1 Using a household paintbrush, paint the lamp base with two or three coats of white acrylic paint, allowing each coat to dry thoroughly before applying the next. A plain white acrylic paint was chosen because it makes the cracks highly visible. At the end of the treatment it will look cream rather than white.

2 Mask above and below the bands around the lamp where you want a contrasting colour. Use flexible masking tape to cover the curved surface of the lamp.

3 Mix a little acrylic scumble and water with some acrylic paint and stipple on the colour with a stencil brush. Leave to dry for approximately four hours and then seal the whole lamp base with a coat of water-based varnish. Allow it to dry thoroughly before you continue.

A plain lamp base was turned into a sophisticated piece using crackling techniques.

4 Brush the first part of the oil-based cracking varnish evenly over the lamp. Hold the lamp up to the light as you work to make sure that you have covered the entire surface. Leave this to dry (usually for between two and four hours) until it feels dry when you glide the back of your finger over the surface, but is still just tacky when you press your knuckle to it.

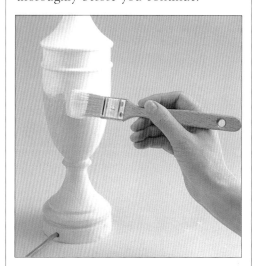

▲ Paint the lamp with acrylic paint.

▲ Stipple on the paint for the coloured bands.

▲ Brush on the oil-based cracking varnish.

5 Brush on the second part of the cracking varnish with a soft-haired synthetic brush. Work lightly and quickly so as not to leave any brush marks. Cover every part of the first coat. After about half an hour check to see if there are any areas you have missed and cover them with more of the second coat.

6 The cracks should appear as soon as the second varnish has dried, although they are hard to see at this stage. If they do not appear, leave the lamp base in a warm place or apply a gentle heat until they appear.

7 Dilute some raw umber artists' oil colour with a small amount of mineral turpentine until it reaches a creamy consistency and rub this into the surface with kitchen paper. Take a clean piece of paper and wipe it off, leaving traces of the raw umber paint in the cracks.

▲ Wipe off the raw umber paint.

8 Add a little additional mineral turpentine to the raw umber paint and dip a stencil brush into it. Run your index finger through the bristles to spray the surface of the lamp base with fine splatters. Soften the effect by dabbing it with a piece of kitchen paper. Leave the lamp to dry overnight or until it is completely dry and then seal it with a coat of satin oil-based varnish.

9 The lampshade was first sealed with a layer of water-based varnish and then given the same craquelure treatment as the lamp base. In order to retain the matt appearance of the lampshade, however, it was sealed with a final coat of dead flat varnish.

For further lamp base projects see:
Tortoiseshell lamp base and shade pp224–5.

• Remember that the second varnish is water soluble and care must be taken not to get it wet or touch it with damp hands.

• Avoid using this technique on a rainy or humid day as the cracks will need a considerable amount of encouragement to appear! A hair dryer can assist the process but use it on a gentle setting or you will finish up with a unnatural looking pattern. This may also happen if you leave your work in a hot sunny window. Leaving your decorated piece near a radiator or in an airing cupboard is usually effective.

• The effect can be successfully used to create an aged appearance over handpainted, découpaged and stencilled designs.

• Practise this crackling technique first on a piece of cardboard that has been sealed with water-based varnish.

• If you get into difficulty, you can remove the raw umber paint with mineral turpentine, wash off the water varnish and leave it to dry before starting again.

▲ Spatter the lamp base with turpentine.

Gilded mirror frame

THIS IS A NEW, very inexpensive, pine mirror that has taken on quite a different appearance by adding a few carved wooden mouldings bought cheaply at a fair. Mouldings can be used to give plain furniture a more decorative appearance. Many wonderful effects can be achieved using transfer metal leaf. Real gold and silver leaf are very expensive, but aluminium, copper, and bronze are also available. Traditionally, either oil size or a watery glue size is applied over several layers of gesso to receive the leaf but gilding has become simpler with the introduction of acrylic goldsize, which is ready to gild over in about 15 minutes and stays tacky indefinitely. Red ochre paint is used to imitate red bole or clay, which is traditionally used as a base for gold leaf.

❖ YOU WILL NEED ❖

Mouldings

Wood glue or PVA adhesive

Wood filler

Palette knife

Masking tape

Red ochre and white acrylic or traditional paint

Household paintbrushes

Acrylic gold-leaf size medium

Transfer metal leaf

Scissors

Bronzing powder

Brown shellac

Rottenstone

0000-grade steel wool

Methylated spirit

Clear or medium-brown wax

Soft cloth

1 Decide where you want to position the mouldings on your frame. Here they are concentrated on the upper part of the frame. Then, using wood glue or PVA adhesive, stick the mouldings in place. Fill any gaps in the frame with wood filler.

2 Stick masking tape all around the mirror edge to keep it clean, then paint the whole of the frame with two coats of red ochre paint, allowing the first coat to dry thoroughly before applying the next. Leave to dry.

3 Using a soft synthetic brush, apply acrylic gold–leaf size medium to the mouldings on the frame. The size will appear milky at this stage but it soon becomes transparent. After about 15 to 20 minutes, when the size is completely clear, it is ready to gild over.

Modern gilding techniques transformed this inexpensive pine mirror into a highly decorative piece.

▲ Glue the mouldings in place.

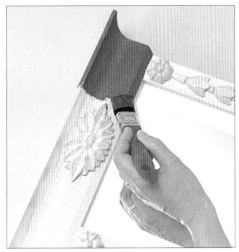

▲ Paint the frame in red ochre.

▲ Apply acrylic size to the mouldings.

▲ Use a brush to tamp the metal leaf down.

▲ Paint the frame with white acrylic paint.

• Bronzing powders come in a wide range of colours and, while they do not have the lustre of metal leaf, they are useful for filling in cracks in the leaf which are inevitable when gilding a carved surface.

• Both metal leaf and bronzing powders need to be sealed with a coat of shellac or vanish to prevent tarnishing.

4 Cut a sheet of transfer metal leaf in half with a pair of scissors and place this over the size. Tamp the leaf down with a firm-bristled brush so that it goes into the recessed areas as well as on the surface. Lift the backing paper off and continue in this way, using all remaining scraps on the sheets to fill in small gaps. When you have covered the moulding as much as you can, dust with bronzing powder to fill any remaining gaps.

5 Gently brush a coat of brown shellac over the gilded mouldings to seal and age the metal leaf. You can add a little rottenstone to the shellac if you want to give the frame a slightly more aged effect.

6 Paint the remainder of the frame with two coats of white paint over the red, allowing the first coat to dry before applying the second. When this is dry, rub down the painted

surface here and there with 0000-grade steel wool dipped in methylated spirit. If you have used a soft traditional paint, steel wool and water should create a sufficiently distressed appearance.

7 Mix some rottenstone with liquid clear wax and apply it to the frame, using a small brush to reach right up to the mouldings. If you prefer, you can substitute the clear wax with a medium-brown wax. Leave the wax to dry, then polish the frame using a soft cloth.

For further gilding projects see:
Gilded chair pp102–3.

▲ Brushing on a coat of brown shellac.

▲ Apply rottenstone and wax with a brush to achieve an aged effect.

Scumble-glazed table

SCANDINAVIAN PAINTED FURNITURE is noted for its elegant simple styling. The soft blue-grey used on this table is typical of colouring used on Swedish neo-classical furniture. The subtle dragged effect was achieved using a flat varnish brush and a transparent water-based scumble glaze mixed with acrylic paint. This replaces the oil-based glazes used traditionally and is quicker drying and non-yellowing. The scumble takes two to four hours to dry so avoid painting a surface adjoining one you have just worked on or you will spoil the finish.

❖ YOU WILL NEED ❖

Satin acrylic paint

Household paintbrushes

Artists' acrylic paint

Acrylic scumble

Flat varnish brush

Old teaspoon

PVA medium or glue and rottenstone, or acrylic paint in raw umber

Kitchen paper

Gilt cream

Soft cloth

Matt water-based varnish

▲ Apply two coats of acrylic paint.

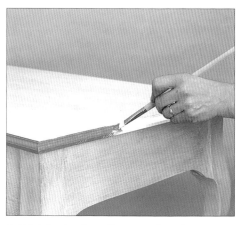

▲ Paint the border with an acrylic colour.

1 Paint the table with two coats of satin acrylic paint, allowing the first coat to dry before applying the second. Leave to dry.

2 Mix the acrylic paint and scumble to the colour required. Use a flat varnish brush to drag the glaze down the length of the top, a section at a time. Soften the effect with the brush. Next, drag the sides of the table. When completely dry to the touch, paint opposite surfaces on the legs, then the remaining ones. Leave to dry overnight.

3 Make an antiquing wash by mixing 1 teaspoon PVA medium or glue with 2 teaspoons rottenstone and 250ml (8fl oz) water. Alternatively, dilute some raw umber acrylic paint with water. Brush the wash on the surface of the table a section at a time, then wipe it off with kitchen paper to give a soft, aged effect.

4 Paint the border around the tabletop and the drawer using your choice of acrylic colour without added glaze. Here a mixture of ivory black, prussian blue, and titanium white satin acrylic, has been used.

5 Brush the gilt cream over the borders of the table. Leave it to dry completely and then buff it to a shine using a soft cloth. Varnish the whole table, except for the gold edges, with two coats of matt water-based varnish to protect it against everyday wear and tear. Allow the first coat of varnish to dry completely before you start to apply the second.

For further table projects see:
Tartan-band dining table pp100–1; Antiqued table pp104–5; Freehand painted tables pp110–12; Marbled dressing table pp162–3; Spray-painted table and chairs pp204–5; Painted tablecloth pp218–21.

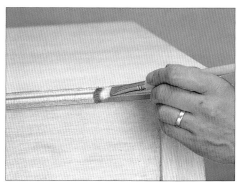

▲ Brush on the gilt cream.

The elegant lines of this delicate table lend themselves perfectly to this sophisticated painting technique.

Colourwashed wall

COLOURWASHING IS A TERM used so often to describe so many varied effects that it has almost become a generic term in the painting trade. It is actually a method for applying a thin glaze over the surface in such a way that the base colour shows through a mottled surface. In this project the glaze is brushed on and spread out while it is still wet.

A product known as scumble glaze is added to the paint to give it a slippery texture in order that the colour will move about more easily on the wall as you soften and spread with the brush. Colourwashing must be carried out on top of a base coat of vinyl silk or semi-gloss rather than matt paint. The slight sheen of the base coat is very important for the softening to be effective.

❖ YOU WILL NEED ❖

500ml (16 fl oz) oil-based paint

500ml (16 fl oz) scumble glaze

Approx. 1 teacup turpentine

Household paintbrush

Badger-hair softener

1 To make the colourwash glaze, mix the oil-based paint with transparent scumble glaze and stir well. Then add turpentine to thin the mixture until it is roughly the consistency of single cream.

2 Using a household paintbrush, apply the glaze over the wall, working quickly in large criss-cross strokes, in sections about 1m square (11ft square) at a time. Leave some of the white base coat showing through and overlap many of the brushstrokes.

▲ Apply the glaze in large criss-cross sections.

3 Spread the glaze with the same brush in crisscross directions as far as it will go. This requires some physical energy but is very easy to carry out. Work fast and keep the edges of each section wet, overlapping as you go.

4 Before the glaze dries, sweep a badger softener over the criss-cross marks in all directions. The soft bristles of the badger brush will obliterate most visible brushstrokes, but leave behind the variations of shade.

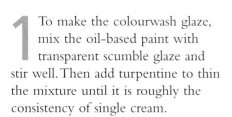

▲ Mix the colour wash glaze.

▲ Work fast to spread out the glaze.

▲ Soften the effect with a badger-hair brush.

HINTS & TIPS

• Occasionally, a thin glaze can become powdery, when dry. This can be caused by a bad batch of ready-made paint but is more usually the result of oil glaze that has not been stirred very thoroughly before use. To remedy a powdery finish, apply a single coat of acrylic glaze when the wall is fully dry. This is very thin and should be applied with a brush, not a roller, for best effect. It dries clear and serves as a washable and protective coat, a varnish and a cure for powdery glaze work. Acrylic glaze is very quick to apply and dries in about an hour.

• When softening the glaze, make sure you do not stop unless you are at a corner otherwise there will be a clear mark that will indicate the overlapping sections and spoil the effect.

For further wall projects see:
Chequered walls pp94–7; Painted panels pp133–5;
A kitchen frieze pp148–9; A bedroom frieze pp172–4;
Marble bathroom pp200–1.

Granite effect fireplace

PREVIOUSLY RIPPED OUT and discarded in favour of modern-day heating, fireplaces are now coming back as a popular feature of many homes. They provide a useful focus for any dining or living room, even if there is no working fire in place. The granite effect creates a good rustic feel and disguises pits and digs. However, seek professional advice before restoring a fireplace that you want to have properly installed. Specialist, heat-resistant paint must be used and fixings must be secure. Similarly, chimneys must be professionally checked before a fire is lit.

❖ YOU WILL NEED ❖

Warm, soapy water

Medium and fine grade abrasive paper

Tack rag

Spoon

Semi-gloss paint

Household paintbrushes

Paint kettle

Acrylic scumble glaze

Artists' acrylic paint in monestial green and viridian

Stirring stick

Dark green glitter

Fine silver glitter

Fine black glitter

Paper

1 Wash the fireplace outside with sugar soap solution. Then gently sand the surface using medium and then fine grade abrasive papers, before wiping with a tack rag.

2 Apply the semi-gloss colour (this should be paler than the chosen granite colour) and leave to dry. Gently sand with fine grade abrasive paper and wipe off the dust with the tack rag. Apply a second coat and allow to dry.

3 Put a spoon of the acrylic scumble glaze into the paint kettle and add two tube widths of the monestial green and viridian artists' colours. Mix until smooth and keep adding small amounts of colours in this ratio until you achieve the desired colour. Then add more acrylic scumble glaze until there is sufficient mixture (remember it is better to have too much than too little). Continue stirring until the consistency is like single cream.

4 Stirring all the time, gently tap in the small containers of silver, black and green glitters. Continue stirring until the glitters have been completely worked into the paint mixture.

5 Apply the glaze to the fireplace, taking care to cover all ridges, curves and corners. Leave the coat to dry and then apply a second coat. To increase the glittery effect, put some fine glitter onto a piece of paper and gently blow this over the surface while the glaze is still wet.

HINTS & TIPS

• Granite paint can be made in any number of colours. The fireplace here has been designed to have a two-tone look (using contrasting silver and green) but you can be as adventurous as you like.

For further stone effect projects see:
Porphyry picture frame pp106–7; Marbled pots pp214–15.

▲ Use a base coat paler than the granite finish.

▲ Apply the granite-coloured paint and glitter.

Sponge-stamped floor

THE CHARMING PATTERN on this varnished wooden floor was created with nothing more complicated than a stamp made from kitchen sponges. It took only one day to paint the floor, plus varnishing, and the result is bright and cheerful in an otherwise fairly sombre room. The sponge texture works well to break up the solid lines of colour. The turquoise-blue used to paint the design is the exact opposite colour to the terracotta on the walls. The inspiration for this design originally came from a fabric design – this is particularly easy because you can cut out the design and use it as a template to cut out the sponges. See pp84–5 for additional tips on how to source ideas from fabrics or alternatively design a pattern for yourself.

❖ YOU WILL NEED ❖

Woodstain

Floor varnish

Household paintbrushes

Sharp scissors

Design to copy

Scalpel (or cutting blade) and cutting mat

Flat cellulose sponges

Two wooden base blocks

PVA adhesive

Artists' acrylic paint in turquoise-blue

Piece of paper

1 Apply the stain to the floor and then give it a generous single coat of varnish. The varnish base prevents the paint from sinking into the wood grain and allows you to wipe away any mistakes quickly. It can be expensive to rectify any mistakes made on an unvarnished floor.

2 With sharp scissors, cut out the motifs from the fabric. Using these as templates, cut out the sponge shapes using the craft knife and cutting mat. Two stamps have been used here: one for the stripes and one for the flower. Glue the pieces to the base blocks using the PVA adhesive.

3 To test the stamp, apply an even coat of artists' acrylic paint with the brush and press the stamp firmly onto a spare piece of paper. Make any necessary changes to the shape using the craft knife.

4 Load the stamps with acrylic paint and stamp a border around the floor. Test the stamp each time you re-load it to ensure you have not put on too much paint. After re-loading, press lightly for the first print, then gradually harder for the next few.

5 When the design is dry (about one hour for acrylic paints) apply a further two coats of varnish to the whole floor.

HINTS & TIPS

• You can use any type of paint as long as it is sufficiently opaque to show up and thick enough not to run – it should be at least as thick as double cream.

For further stamping projects see:
Ivy-stamped chair pp150–1; Hand-painted chest pp206–7.

▲ Cut out a fabric motif as a template.

▲ Apply acrylic paint generously to the stamp.

▲ Finish the whole floor with a coat of varnish.

Stencilled balustrade

STENCILLING DOES NOT have to be done on a small scale; a large architectural stencil can give subtle impact to a room. This balustrade is a simple design that works to great effect in a room with little furniture. It is painted with exterior paints that contain some sand and are gently shaded to give a three-dimensional quality. The paint is very hard-wearing, so the finished work needs no special care – it is washable and simple to repair if it ever does become damaged. This design is an enlarged photocopy adapted to become a stencil by leaving gaps between the sections of the pillar. For the top and bottom of the design, which are straight runs along the wall, you will save time by using masking tape instead of cutting this section from the stencil.

❖ YOU WILL NEED ❖

Design for your stencil (see p246)

Craft knife and cutting mat

Manila card, acetate or plan trace

Low-tack masking tape

Metal ruler

Ruler

Spirit level

Pencil

Plumb line

Non-permanent adhesive spray

Cellulose sponges or small paint roller

Fine-textured exterior paint (containing sand) in two colours, light and slightly darker

Artist's crayons, oil or wax oil in white and yellow ochre or raw sienna

1 Enlarge your chosen design to the required size on a photocopier, bearing in mind that if your room already has a dado rail your design will have to fit snugly between this and the skirting board.

2 Position the enlarged design on a cutting mat underneath a piece of stencil plastic that is at least twice as big as the design and secure both in place with masking tape.

3 Carefully cut out the design in the plastic, using a craft knife and a metal ruler for the straight edges. (Cut two stencils if you are working with a partner.) Remember to cut out the balustrade in separate sections, leaving a gap of about 0.5cm (¼in) between each one, which will remain unpainted.

4 Now mark the position of your stencils on the wall; do this by marking the top and bottom of each pillar with a straight line or piece

▲ Tape the stencil paper over the design.

of masking tape (use a spirit level). Measure an equal distance between each pillar, so that they will be regularly spaced. Using a pencil, lightly mark a vertical line, which will run through the centre of each pillar, using a plumb line and ruler to guide you.

5 Spray the back of the stencil with non-permanent adhesive spray and position it carefully on the wall, following the guidelines that mark the centre. Secure the stencil further with small pieces of masking tape.

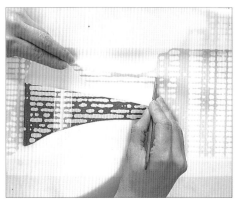

▲ Carefully cut out the stencil.

▲ Position the stencil over the pencilled guides.

▲ Fill the whole area with the lighter colour.

▲ Apply shading along the straight section.

▲ Add three-dimensional shading with crayons.

6 Using a chunk of cellulose sponge or a small paint roller, fill in the whole stencil with the lighter of your chosen colours of textured paint. Leave the stencil in place for the next step.

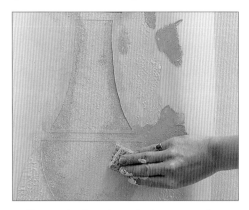

▲ Repeat shading along the bottom section.

7 Dip a small piece of sponge into your darker colour and dab off any excess paint onto paper or the edge of the stencil. Dab the darker colour through the stencil to shade it. Shade around the edges and at the bottom of each section of the pillar. Dab the two shades of wet paint together to blend the darker shade gently into the lighter shade. Peel away the stencil. Continue stencilling the pillars all around the room.

8 Mask off a straight section, along the top of your pillars, leaving no gap, as shown above middle. Using a cellulose sponge, fill it first with cream paint, and then apply the shading colour along the edges.

9 Repeat step 8 for the bottom section, painting the skirting board as well if your stencil continues down to the floor.

10 When the paint is dry, carefully shade the pillars with crayons to create a three-dimensional effect. Run a thin line of yellow ochre or raw sienna around the edges where the shadows will fall, down the right-hand side and along the bottom of each section. Using a white crayon, add highlights where the light will catch your balustrade to complete the three-dimensional effect. You will see in the photograph below that a line of white has been run down the left-hand side of each section, following the curve of the outline, a few centimetres in from the edge. A line of white has also been run along the top of each section.

HINTS & TIPS

• You can adjust the colour of your balustrade by mixing artists' acrylic paints into the textured paint.

• Enlarged photocopies are not always perfectly symmetrical. For perfect symmetry in your design, cut the stencil in two halves. First cut one half from the design and then turn it over and use it to cut out an identical shape in reverse for the second side.

For further stencilling projects see:
Frottaged and stencilled screen pp167–9; A bedroom frieze pp172–4; Children's balloon stencils pp184–5; Mexican-style bathroom pp190–2; Repeating border and dragged stripes pp208–11; Poppies picture frame pp236–7; Stencilled mirror frame pp242–3.

▲ A line of white down the left-hand side and along the top of each section completes the effect.

Painted panels

THREE DIFFERENT paint effects – dragging, ragging and bagging – work in harmony with each other here to give an elegant and welcoming hallway. The panels are created by attaching wooden beading to the wall. They are easy to assemble; if you have ever used a saw before then you will be able to panel your room following the instructions given here.

Before you start, decide how many panels you would like and how much beading you will need; you can buy this in lengths from a hardware store. In this hallway the colours are all shades of the same colour, selected from the paint-mixing strips of colours displayed in hardware stores. By choosing all your shades from the same strip you can be sure that your colours will go well together.

❖ YOU WILL NEED ❖

Wood primer paint

Household paintbrush

Sufficient lengths of beading to make panels, plus one length extra to allow for cutting loss

Tenon saw and mitre block

2.5 litres (80fl oz) of low-sheen acrylic paint in your 2 chosen base colours

Border and panel adhesive

Masking tape

1 litre (32fl oz) of transparent oil glaze

0.5 litre (16fl oz) of semi-gloss paint in your 3 chosen glaze colours

3 large plastic plant saucers

Mineral turpentine

Stippling brush (optional)

Cotton rags

Dragging brush

3 or 4 plastic carrier bags

1 Apply a coat of primer paint to the wooden beading if it is bare when you buy it. Leave the beading to dry thoroughly.

2 Cut the beading into accurate lengths using the tenon saw and mitre block as shown below left. Take care that your pieces will all be the correct way round and reverse the angle of the cut for the second of two corner cuts. You will soon get the hang of how the angles should be cut.

3 Paint above and below the dado rail with two coats of low-sheen acrylic paint in the colours you have chosen for your base coats. Here a very pale blue-green has been used for the top section and a deeper blue-green for the bottom section – both were chosen from the same paint-mixing colour strip. Remember that you will be adding an even darker glaze over the paint bases.

4 Using a pencil, mark the inside line of each panel on the wall for guidance. Stick the wooden beading into position on the wall to create the panels, using blobs of adhesive on the backs of the pieces or putting blobs onto the wall. Keep a close eye on the panels you have glued, as they sometimes slip. Secure them with masking tape if they do start to move. Fill any gaps where the corners join with more panel adhesive.

5 Now mix three trays of glaze in your chosen colours, using the plastic plant saucers as containers. Your colours should be about two or three shades apart on a paint mixing card, and darker than your base paint. Use one part transparent oil glaze, one part paint and one part turpentine. Keep the lightest and darkest glazes quite thick, but thin the medium glaze with a drop more turpentine so that it has the consistency of milk.

▲ Cut the beading into angled lengths.

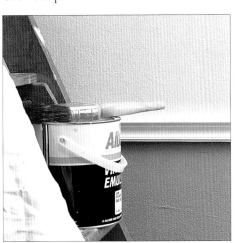
▲ Paint above and below the dado rail.

▲ Attach beading to the wall with adhesive.

133

▲ Brush the glaze over the inside of the panel.

6 Brush your lightest-coloured glaze evenly all over the inside of one panel and then immediately stipple away the brush strokes with light jabbing motions using a stippling (or household) brush. This stippling is optional but it prevents any of your brushstrokes from showing up on the finished work, so gives a more pleasing result.

▲ Draw the dragging brush evenly down the glaze, applying firm and even pressure.

▲ Dab a crumpled rag over the glaze.

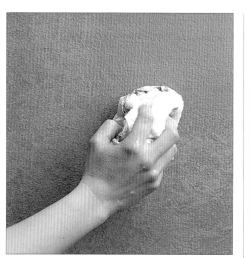

▲ Use a crumpled bag for a 'leathery' look.

▲ Paint the beading in a contrasting colour.

7 Immediately, dab quickly and evenly all over the glazed area with a piece of rag, crumpled into a ball. This is known as ragging.

8 Apply the thinner, medium colour glaze around the outsides of the panels. Lay the dragging brush onto the wet glaze, starting at the top or side of each section, and pull it down through the glaze, pressing firmly as you go to create a delicate striped effect. Use it vertically between the panels and horizontally along the top and bottom.

9 Apply the darkest glaze, which can be quite thick, to the painted area below the dado rail. Turn a plastic carrier bag inside out (to prevent any printing ink coming off on your work) and crumple it up in your hand. Dab this firmly all over the glaze.

10 Finally, give the dado rail and beading two coats of paint in a complementary colour. Using a deep shade from the same colour-mixing strip as your other colours creates a dramatic effect.

HINTS & TIPS

• Work quickly with glazing techniques or the glaze will start to dry and there will be a mark where you apply the next section.

• If the stripes fade out towards the end of the stroke when you are dragging, try applying more glaze. If this doesn't work, thin the glaze a little with some turpentine.

For further wall projects see:
Chequered walls pp94–7; Colour-washed wall pp124–5; A kitchen frieze pp148–9; A bedroom frieze pp172–4; Marble bathroom pp200–1.

THE KITCHEN TENDS TO BE ONE OF
THE BUSIEST AND MOST SOCIABLE
ROOMS IN THE HOME, WHETHER IT
IS A NEIGHBOUR DROPPING IN FOR A
QUICK COFFEE OR GUESTS HELPING
WITH THE PREPARATIONS FOR AN
INFORMAL DINNER. FURNITURE
AND ACCESSORIES NEED TO EARN
THEIR PLACE HERE, BUT THERE IS
NO REASON WHY THEY SHOULD
NOT BE EYE-CATCHING AS WELL.
THIS CHAPTER PROVIDES PLENTY
OF IDEAS FOR PAINTED PIECES THAT
WILL ADD WARMTH AND BEAUTY TO
THE HEART OF YOUR HOME.

Kitchen Projects

Kitchen accessories

HEN WANDERING AROUND markets, pine objects such as these seem to be everywhere, and even though you may have discarded something similar yourself only a couple of weeks before, the urge to buy can be overwhelming. It must be the lure of pine, which always looks attractive, but particularly when you evoke its Scandinavian connections. This is exactly what has been done with these pine pieces, which are decorated with a soft, dusty turquoise, a colour which turns up time and time again on old Swedish furniture.

Pine shelf

❖ YOU WILL NEED ❖

Wood filler

Palette knife

Medium and fine grade abrasive paper

Tack rag

Gouache paints in ultramarine, lemon yellow and raw umber

Jam jar

Old tablespoon

White acrylic paint

2 x 4cm (2½in) household paintbrushes

Clear matt polyurethane varnish

Paper

Pencil

Artists' paintbrush

Gouache or acrylic paints in various shades for applying the design

1 The amount of preparation you need to do will depend on the state of your shelf. This shelf has obviously once been painted white and only just survived a half-hearted attempt to strip it. It has also been knocked about and there are several little cracks and holes. Fill these in with a quick-drying wood filler using the flexible blade of the palette knife, making it as smooth as you can. If your shelf is in better condition than this, it may need no more than a wipe down to remove any dust and dirt.

2 Once the filler has completely dried, rub it down first with medium grade abrasive paper and then with a fine one. Then wipe the entire surface with a tack rag to leave it smooth and dust-free.

3 To mix this subtle shade of turquoise, squeeze about 2.5cm (1in) of ultramarine gouache paint into the bottom of a jam jar, then add just a little dot of lemon yellow. Mix the two together – at this stage you will have a very bluey green. Add just a touch of raw umber and a little water, then gradually spoon in white acrylic paint, mixing it in until the shade begins to look right.

4 Once you are happy with the colour, add more water until the paint is about the consistency of single cream – this will give the shelf a faded look when the paint dries.

5 Apply a coat of the turquoise paint mix over the whole shelf. If your shelf is in fairly good condition, one coat will be enough, and the colour will look effective with some of the wood grain showing through. If your shelf is quite rough, however, or if you have had to fill it extensively, you will need to give it a second coat after the first one has dried to cover up its worst features.

6 Book shelves can be difficult to decorate, since most of the surfaces are normally covered in books and the ends are often obscured by being positioned up against a wall. With this shelf, however, you can decorate both ends so that the design is visible even if one end is hung against a wall. Trim the front edges in a complementary shade to add some colour to the overall design, wherever the shelf is placed.

▲ Fill any cracks and rub down before painting.

▲ Paint a contrasting border along the edges.

7 If you are not very confident about painting your design freehand directly on to the paint, give your shelf a coat of clear, matt varnish at this point. Later, if you do happen to make a mistake, you can easily wash the paint off, using a little washing-up liquid and some steel wool, without disturbing the base coat underneath. However, if you are skilled and confident enough to take freehand painting in your stride, you can paint directly on to the paint using gouache or acrylic paints.

8 Practise your design on paper first until you feel reasonably confident about putting the design on the shelf freehand. Pine objects look great when decorated with simple Folk Art designs, so aim for a spontaneous, unsophisticated look. If you are taking your design from a plate or other object, you will need to make some scale drawings on paper in order to work out exactly how it will fit into the space at the end of the shelf.

9 Once you have found an arrangement that you like, lightly sketch a few basic guidelines on to the shelf and then copy the design from the plate freehand using simple brushstrokes. If you have varnished your shelf first, you will need to use acrylic paints for this stage; gouache paint does not take well on top of varnish and is easily removed by subsequent washing.

10 Once you have decorated both ends of the shelf to your satisfaction (remember, they do not have to be identical in every particular, as they cannot be viewed together), choose one of the dominant colours from the design and use it to paint a contrasting border along the front edges of the shelf.

11 Leave until the paint has dried thoroughly. Finally, give the shelf a coat of clear matt polyurethane varnish all over to protect your design from wear and tear.

For further freehand projects see:
Colour-washed oak sideboard pp98–9; Tartan-band dining table pp100–101; Cups and saucers chair pp146–7; Painted china pp152–4; Hand-painted blanket box pp164–6; Painted frames pp232–3.

HINTS & TIPS

• When sketching guidelines on to the shelf, keep them to a minimum or you will lose the fluidity of your design.

• Make sure you mix enough of the acrylic paint to do the whole shelf twice if necessary; you may find it difficult to match the shade if you have to mix extra.

Pine spice rack

❖ YOU WILL NEED ❖

Materials as for pine shelf on p138

1 This spice rack was in good condition and only needed a light rub down with fine grade abrasive paper. Paint it with the acrylic mixture as before, but leave the drawers and pots unpainted apart from their knobs and a little trim around the tops. Varnish before applying the design.

2 Take the design from the same source as the pine shelf, practise it on paper as before. It will need adapting for the long narrow space available. Once you are satisfied, pencil some guidelines on the rack and paint the design. Once dry, give the whole thing a final coat of matt polyurethane varnish.

Hand painting this plain pine spice rack gives your kitchen a touch of individuality..

▲ Adapt the design to fit the space available.

For further freehand projects see:
Colour-washed oak sideboard & pp98–9; Tartan-band dining table pp100–1; Cups and saucers chairs pp146–7; Painted china pp152–4; Hand-painted blanket box pp164–6; Painted frames pp232–3.

Pine spoon holder

Fine grade steel wool

Hot, soapy water

Cotton buds

Bleach

Lint-free rag

Wood filler

Palette knife

Medium and fine grade abrasive paper

Tack rag

Gouache paint in ultramarine, lemon yellow and raw umber

Jam jar and old tablespoon

White acrylic paint

2 x 4cm (1½in) household paintbrushes

Paper and pencil

Clear matt polyurethane varnish

Artists' paintbrush

Artists' acrylic paints in various colours for applying the design

1 This spoon holder needed a lot more preparation than the shelf or the spice rack because it was stained and greasy. To remove the grease, scrub it well with fine grade steel wool using hot soapy water. However, if you have to give a wooden item a thorough clean up in this way, try not to make the wood too wet as this will lift the grain and leave you with a great deal of rubbing down to do.

2 To remove the ink, use a cotton bud dipped in bleach – this will take time and patience. Once the spoon holder is sufficiently clean, wipe the whole thing down with a lint-free rag wrung out in cold water and leave it aside until dry.

3 Fill any holes with wood filler and a palette. Then rub the spoon holder down with some fine or medium grade abrasive paper and remove the dust with a tack rag.

4 Apply two coats of the acrylic mixture as for the shelf and spice rack on pp138–9. Leave some of the pine showing so it matches the spice rack. Map out the design and varnish the spoon holder before applying the design, Finally, paint it to match the other two items and apply a coat of clear matt varnish.

For further freehand projects see:
Colour-washed oak sideboard pp98–9.

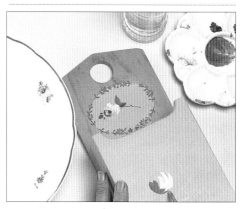

▲ Use single brushstrokes to apply the design.

Key holder

Fine grade steel wool

Methylated spirit

Fine grade abrasive paper

Tack rag

2 x 2.5cm (1in) household paintbrushes

Brunswick green enamel paint

Piece of chalk

Size 3 artists' brush (sable or synthetic mixture)

Small pots of enamel paint in crimson, bright red, yellow, white, lime green and tan

Gloss polyurethane varnish

3 screw-in brass hooks

1 Remove the mirror and hooks from the key holder and wipe the base with fine grade steel wool and methylated spirits to clean it. If the varnish on the base is shiny and undamaged, rub it down lightly with some fine grade abrasive paper to give it a slight 'key' for the paint.

2 Go over the key holder with a tack rag. Apply two coats of Brunswick green enamel paint, leaving six hours between each coat.

3 Work out your design on a piece of paper. Chalk circles on to the dried enamel as a guide to where the flowers will go. Use the artists' paintbrush and bright enamel colours to paint in the roses, then carefully paint in the leaves and the daisy centres. Add petals to the roses and leave the pot to dry overnight.

4 Varnish the key holder, leave it to dry for 24 hours and apply a final coat. Finally, clean and replace the mirror and treat the revamped key holder to three shiny, new brass hooks.

For further freehand projects see:
Colour-washed oak sideboard pp98–9; Tartan-banded dining table pp100–1; Cups and saucers chair pp146–7; Painted china pp152–4; Painted frames pp232–3.

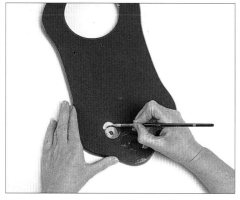

▲ Paint each petal with a single brushstroke.

Lined clock cupboard

THIS ATTRACTIVE WALL CUPBOARD has been made from old pine floorboards. The cardboard clock face is transformed using a craquelure technique. A simple découpaged pear motif has been used for the door and three tones of yellow chosen to complement this. The middle tone is a creamy yellow – white has been added to the central panel and raw umber pigment to the darker panel surround. A lining technique has been used on the cupboard. A sword liner is ideal for this because it holds a good amount of paint for a continuous flow and it can produce a variety of line sizes, depending on the pressure used when applying paint. Sword liners are available from paint specialist decorating suppliers, or you can use a 6mm ($^1/_4$in) long-haired flat artist's brush instead.

❖ YOU WILL NEED ❖

Medium grade abrasive paper

Wood filler

Filling knife

Acrylic or traditional paint in three shades

Household paintbrushes

Masking tape (optional)

Pencil

Ruler

Sword liner or 6mm ($^1/_4$in) artists' brush

Fruit print

Manicure scissors

Paper glue

Glue brush

Sponge

Satin water-based acrylic varnish

Varnish brush

Two-part crackle varnish

Kitchen paper

Raw umber pigment

Matt oil-based varnish

Brown wax

Soft cloth

The clock's simple lines call for unfussy decoration.

1 Rub down the cupboard with medium grade abrasive paper, then fill all cracks with wood filler. Apply a coat of the middle tone of paint to the whole cupboard except the door panel, then paint the central panel with the lightest tone. When dry, paint the panel surround with the darkest colour.

2 Using a pencil and ruler, lightly mark the clock where you want to position the narrow lines. Load a sword liner brush with the dark paint colour and drag the brush along the pencilled line, applying an even pressure the whole time.

▲ Apply the darkest tone to the panel surround.

3 Cut out the print with manicure scissors. Glue it to the panel and wipe off excess glue with a sponge. When dry, go over any white edges on the cut-out with the pencil.

4 Apply two coats of acrylic varnish to the entire cupboard, then a further eight to ten coats over the découpaged panel, leaving each coat to dry before applying the next. Use one coat on the clock face, then apply the two crackling varnishes.

5 When the second coat is dry, use kitchen paper to rub in the raw umber pigment. Seal the surface with a matt oil-based varnish the next day. Then apply a brown wax, again using kitchen paper, over the entire cupboard, including the clock face. Leave to dry, then polish with a soft cloth.

For further cupboard projects see:
Colour-washed oak sideboard pp98–9.

▲ Disguise any white edges with a pencil.

Painted chairs

TRANSFORMING A CHAIR can make a quick, refreshing change to a kitchen. Simplicity is the key to success for both of these techniques – do not cover the chair in fussy detail. In the first project, little pigs in a pale shade are painted on a strongly coloured background, making an ideal rustic stencil design for a chair in a country-style kitchen. Choice of colour is important when planning the second project, a crackling effect. This eye-catching design in French blue and pale cream gives an elegant result suitable for a sophisticated setting.

Stencilled pigs chair

❖ YOU WILL NEED ❖

Abrasive paper

Tack rag

Gouache paints in teal and oyster pearl

2.5cm (1in) household paintbrush

Manila card, acetate or plan trace

Fine-point permanent marker pen

Craft knife and cutting mat

Masking tape

Stencil brush

Kitchen paper

Satin varnish and brush

1 Sand the chair to remove any old paint or varnish and create a smooth surface. Wipe over with the tack rag to remove all dust.

2 Using the base-coat brush, apply two coats of teal paint and allow it to dry.

3 Tape the acetate over the patterns on pages 246 and carefully trace the designs with the marker pen. Using the craft knife and cutting mat, cut out the design.

4 Position the pig stencil in the centre of the chair back and use masking tape to hold it in position. Dip your stencil brush into the oyster pearl paint. Dab the brush onto the kitchen paper to eliminate excess paint. Apply paint over the stencil, working in a circular motion to build up as much colour as required.

5 Repeat step 4 on the front of the seat and add hearts to the rungs of the back and the front legs.

6 Leave to dry for 24 hours. Apply two or three coats of varnish and allow to dry.

For further stencilling projects see:
Stencilled cane chair pp160–1; Frottaged and stencilled screen pp167–9; Stencilled newspaper rack pp238–9.

Crackled effect chair

❖ YOU WILL NEED ❖

Abrasive paper

Tack rag

2.5cm (1in) household paintbrush

Gouache paints in oyster pearl and French blue

One-part crackle medium

Satin varnish and brush

1 Sand the chair to create a smooth surface. Wipe it over with the tack rag to remove all dust particles.

2 Using the household paintbrush, apply two coats of oyster pearl paint and allow it to dry.

3 Then, use a clean household paintbrush to apply a smooth, even coat of the one-part crackle medium over the dry oyster pearl base coat and leave it to dry until it is smooth and no longer tacky to the touch (this will take approximately 20 minutes to 1 hour).

4 Use French blue paint to apply an even coat of paint over the dry crackle medium. The crackle medium will begin to take effect right away. Do not re-work the final coat of paint because this will ruin the effect.

5 Leave the paint to dry for at least 24 hours. Then apply two or three coats of satin varnish, leaving each coat to dry before applying the next. For a smooth finish lightly sand after each of the first two coats.

For further crackle projects see:
Aged rustic chair pp212–13.

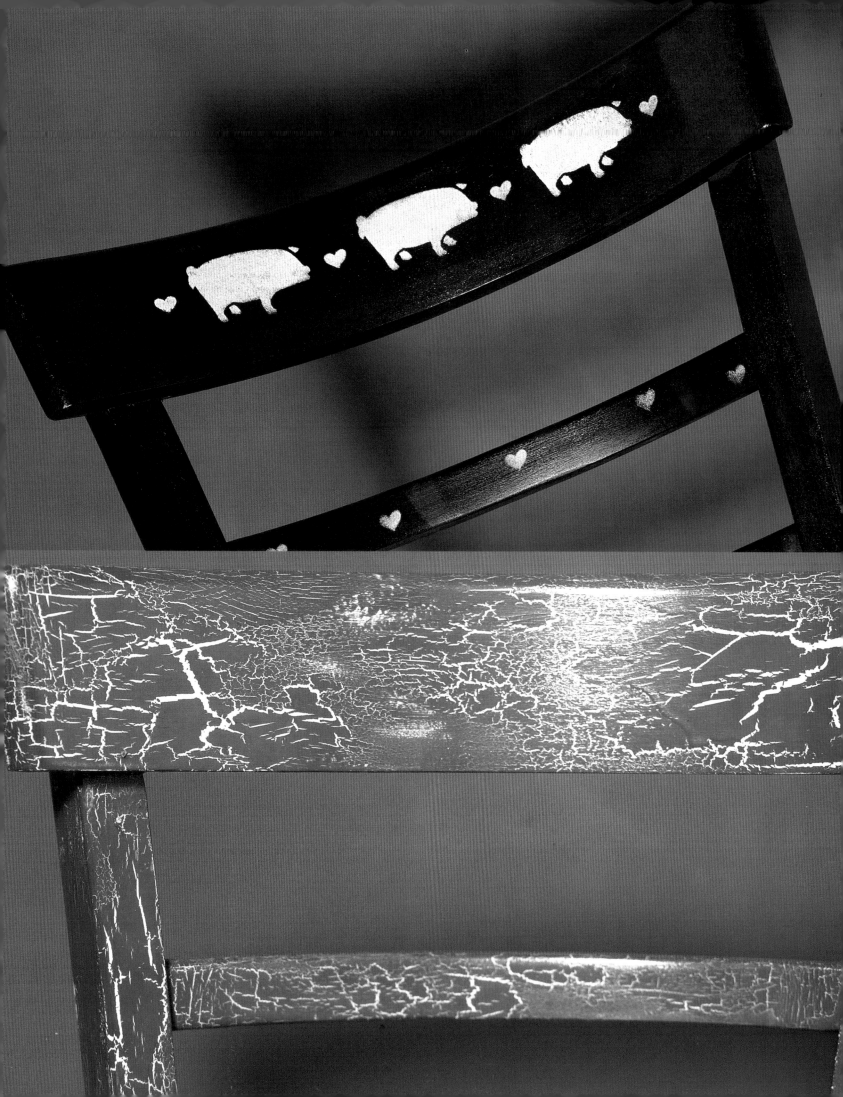

Cups and saucers chair

THIS IS THE PERFECT KITCHEN chair with its cup and saucer design. All you need to re-create this work of art is a sturdy chair that has been stripped back to the raw wood, some paints and the patterns in this book (see p246). If desired, the chair can be varnished or waxed to give a sturdier, more hard-wearing finish. This cup and saucer design was inspired by 18th-century Minton pattern books, which depicted designs for tea-bowls and saucers. After about 1800, the tea-bowls were replaced by the new fashion of the time – cups with handles.

❖ YOU WILL NEED ❖

Abrasive paper

Tack rag

Household paintbrushes

Acrylic paints in smoked pearl, warm white, carbon black, yellow oxide and ultra deep blue

Cloth

Tracing paper

Design for your stencil (see p246)

Pencil

Carbon paper

Stylus or ballpoint pen

Crackle glaze

Sword liner

Satin varnish (optional)

1 Sand the chair with abrasive paper to create a smooth surface and then wipe it over with the tack rag. Paint the chair with watery, warm white paint. Apply one section at a time and wipe with a cloth to give an uneven effect.

2 Trace the outline of one of the cups and saucers (see pp246) on to tracing paper. Then, using carbon paper and the stylus or ballpoint pen, transfer it to the back of the chair. Paint the cup and saucer shape in smoked pearl. Then apply the crackle glaze to the cup and saucer shapes and leave it to dry. Paint warm white paint (with a little water added) over the crackle glaze in order to activate it.

3 Place the traced design back on to the chair, slip the carbon paper under it and again trace the cup and saucer shape. Mix smoked pearl with a touch of yellow oxide and carbon black, and add shading to the cup and saucer. Add the lines and decoration in ultra deep blue using a liner brush.

4 Using ultra deep blue, draw freehand lines around the back struts and around the edge of the top of the seat. The chair can be varnished with a clear varnish or waxed with beeswax or furniture wax.

For further chair projects see:
Decorative chairs pp102–3; Spray-painted table and chairs pp204–5; Aged rustic chair pp212–13.

A. Paint the shape in smoked pearl.

B. Apply the crackle and let it dry.

C. Activate the crackle with warm white paint.

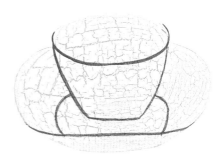

D. Trace the shape with carbon paper.

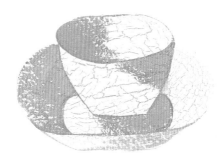

E. Add the shading to the relevant areas.

F. Add the decoration in ultra deep blue.

A kitchen frieze

SINCE IT IS RARELY advisable to hang wallpaper in an area where steam and heat are produced, the hardwearing finish of stencilling is ideal for adding some life and interest to this room. However, restrict stencils to surfaces that are receptive to paint if you want the designs to survive. Paint on modern laminates will not look good for long, and painting on ceramic tiles should only be attempted with specialist tile paint, which is unsuitable for stencilling. Timber-fronted units will, however, take stencilled designs that will endure most things if properly varnished. The stencilled kitchen shown here uses an appropriately culinary stencil with a bold outline and simple shapes. The technique and design appear both around the walls and on objects in the room.

❖ YOU WILL NEED ❖

Design to copy

Artists' acrylic paints in assorted colours

Household paintbrushes

Tracing paper

Pencil

Manila card, acetate or plan trace

Scalpel (or cutting blade) and cutting mat

Non-permanent adhesive spray or masking tape

Bathroom sponge

Heat-resistant varnish

1 When you have chosen your stencil design, photocopy or draw it to the size required. Paint the design in colours that you wish your final stencils to be. Follow this 'master' design when applying the stencils.

2 Trace the master onto a piece of card, acetate or plan trace and use a scalpel and cutting mat to cut out the outline shape of the design.

3 Hold the stencil firmly in the position with non-permanent adhesive spray or masking tape. Then, using a dryish bathroom sponge, apply a rough-textured coat of pale ochre acrylic paint.

4 When the base coat is dry, add the detail freehand with a paintbrush. Following your master, colour the various different elements in the design using watered-down acrylic paints over the ochre base. Do not worry about being too precise when painting in the detail – the rustic look of this design is actually improved and enhanced by some irregularity and roughness.

5 Stencils on a kitchen wall should always be varnished. Here, the stencilled baskets received several coats of varnish, and the stencil design on the tray was treated with several coats of a heat-resistant varnish to protect it from hot mugs or plates.

For further stencilling projects see:
Stencilled balustrade pp130–2; Painted chairs pp144–7; Stencilled cane chair pp160–1; Frottaged and stencilled screen pp167–9; A bedroom frieze pp172–4; Cherub wardrobe pp180–3; Children's balloon stencils pp184–5; Mexican-style bathroom pp190–2; Fish stencil shower glass pp193–5; Repeating border and dragged stripes pp208–11; Poppies picture frame pp236–7; Stencilled newspaper rack pp238–9; Stencilled mirror frame pp242–5; Monogrammed box pp244–5.

▲ Sponge on the ochre base coat.

▲ Follow the master design.

▲ Apply heat-resistant varnish to a tray.

Ivy-stamped chair

THIS RUSTIC CHAIR was given an ageing paint finish before the stamps were applied. The design was taken directly from nature – a sprig of ivy was picked from the garden and the stamp was made out of a potato. The chair was purchased flat-packed and assembled prior to painting. When an item like this is painted after it has been assembled, the paint helps to fill some of the gaps between the pieces of wood. Do not prime the chair because you do not want the white or pink colour of the primer to show through when you rub away the paint. Oil-based paint will not dry well without a primer base, so add few drops of paint drier to the paint.

YOU WILL NEED

Chair

Spirit-based wood stain

Green-grey semi-gloss paint

Fine grade sandpaper or sanding block

Household paintbrushes

Wet stain

Ivy leaf

Craft knife

Potato

Small artists' paintbrush

Brown paint

Oil-based varnish

1 The assembled chair was stained all over with a spirit-based wood stain. This is purely a stain and not a coloured varnish. The stained chair was left to dry overnight and then painted with two coats of green-grey semi-gloss paint. As the paint is applied, it begins to take on an aged appearance as some of the stain mixes with the paint. This mixing of the stain cannot be controlled other than by applying additional coats of paint. Use a paler shade than required on the finished item.

2 When the paint is completely dry, continue the ageing process by rubbing back the paint to the stained bare wood with medium and then fine sandpaper or a sanding block. Concentrate on areas where the chair would have worn if it were old, such as on the edges of the legs and seat. Don't worry at this stage if you rub right through the stain to the new wood.

3 The final ageing is achieved by brushing more wood stain onto the chair and then stroking over the wet stain with a clean, dry brush, working in the direction of the grain.

4 To make the ivy stamp, cut around the outline of an ivy leaf with a craft knife onto half a potato. Then cut away the background so that the design to be printed stands proud. Vegetables give off water so blot the potato with tissue. This chair was printed with three different-sized leaves and the stems were hand painted using a small artists' brush and brown paint.

5 Finally, varnish the chair with a couple of coats of oil-based varnish to protect the wood and to maintain the distressed look.

For further stamping projects see:
Hand-painted chest pp206–7; Ethnic stamped CD box pp240–1.

▲ Stain the chair with woodstain.

▲ Sand the chair to make it look old.

▲ Apply wet stain with a clean, dry brush.

Painted china

THINK TWICE BEFORE abandoning your old, dull crockery in favour of something bright and new, because you can completely rejuvenate your ceramics using special paints. As with painted glasses (see pp155–7), simple designs usually look most effective. For example, bold spots and stripes work well, as do simple flowers and leaves. You could even choose a design that echoes those found around the kitchen or dining room already – on patterned curtains, tiles or ceramics. These designs are applied to white china, but painting on any plain pastel-coloured crockery would also give attractive results. However, ensure that the colour scheme you choose matches the base colour of the china. You can check this by experimenting with a test piece.

❖ YOU WILL NEED ❖

Warm, soapy water

Methylated spirit

Soft cloth

Paper or test piece of china

Pencil

Old plate

Ceramic paints

Paintbrush

Damp cloth

▲ Use a pencil to draw light marks that will serve as a guide.

1 Wash and wipe dry the china that is to be painted. Then wipe it with a cloth soaked in a little methylated spirits in order to remove any traces of grease.

2 On a piece of paper or with a test piece of china, work out your design before you begin to paint. Then, mark the design on to the china very faintly with a pencil to act as a guide as you work. The pencil marks will be covered over when you apply the painted design.

3 In order to achieve the desired colours, use a paintbrush to mix the paint on an old plate, the same colour as the china that is to be decorated. You can also use the plate to practise painting your design before you begin. This experimenting will allow you to judge the success of your design and make any adjustments. It will help you to decide how much paint you need to apply in order to achieve the effect you would like.

▲ Choose ceramic paints in various colours.

▲ Mix the paints on an old plate.

▲ Do not overfill your brush when applying paint circles to your ceramics.

• Ceramic paints that are baked in the oven will be more durable than those that are simply left to dry.

• Painting is a great way to personalize a piece of china, such as a child's breakfast bowl, or mum's special mug and items such as these make very special gifts.

• You could use different paint colours to indicate different contents in kitchenware – for example, blue for salt, red for pepper and yellow for vinegar in a cruet set.

For further freehand projects see:
Tartan-band dining room table pp100–1; Freehand painted tables pp110–12; Kitchen accessories pp138–41; Hand-painted chest pp206–7.

4 Apply the paint sparingly if you are painting circles, or in long even strokes if you choose to paint stripes. Do not apply additional paint to an area you have already painted because this may cause the paint to smudge or smear. Instead, wait for it to dry completely and then apply another coat.

5 If you make a mistake or you are not happy with the result of your design, simply wipe the paint away using a damp cloth, then try again.

6 Once the design is complete, leave the piece to dry, or bake it in the oven according to the paint manufacturer's instructions.

▲ Wipe away any unwanted areas of paint.

Brilliant painted glass

MANY KITCHENS house various shelves and ledges that, unless you are incredibly self-disciplined, can end up covered in all sorts of cooking equipment and general household clutter. The best way to avoid this problem is to keep the kitchen surfaces hard-working as areas of storage. So, make a determined effort to clear away all those bits and pieces from your kitchen shelves and replace them with this useful and attractive glassware, which will brighten up the room and keep the clutter at bay. The simplest patterns are often the most effective and will add decorative splashes of colour to a dull shelf or the supper table. Choose colours and a pattern or design that co-ordinate well with your kitchen decor or your table setting.

❖ YOU WILL NEED ❖

Warm, soapy water

Methylated spirit

Soft cloth

Coloured pens

White paper

Spare piece of glassware (optional)

Old plate

Translucent glass paints

Fine artists' paintbrush

Cotton buds

▲ Work out the design on a piece of paper.

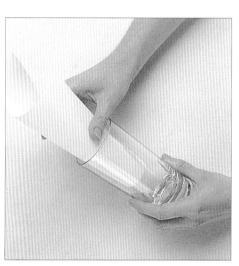
▲ Insert a piece of white paper into the glass.

1 Wash and dry the glasses thoroughly, then wipe them gently with a soft cloth and a little methylated spirit to remove any stubborn traces of grease.

2 Work out your chosen design and colourways with coloured pens on a sheet of white paper. You do not need to be a great artist to do this because you will find that even simple, random designs will produce quite stunning effects. If possible, it is also a good idea to practise on a spare piece of glassware before you begin.

3 Before you start to paint, insert a piece of white paper or a crumpled white tissue inside the glass – this will allow you to see your design more easily as you work. You may also find it helpful to work on a plain white surface, such as white paper or cardboard.

4 Using an old white plate as a palette, mix up small amounts of the glass paints in order to achieve the colours that you require for your designs. However, do not mix too much paint at once because it will dry quite quickly while you work and will be wasted.

▲ Mix the desired paint colours.

155

5 Apply the paint carefully using a fine paintbrush. Take care not to apply too much paint as this will cause it to dry unevenly or to drip (dab the paintbrush on a spare piece of paper first to remove any excess). However, too little paint will cause brush marks to show.

6 Do not worry if you make a mistake. You can simply neaten any edges with a dampened cotton bud. If all else fails and you need to start again, you can wipe off the wet paint with a damp cloth.

▲ Apply the paint with a fine paintbrush.

HINTS & TIPS

• If you want to make use of your glassware for drinks, it is best not to apply paint too near the rim because frequent usage will eventually wear away the painted design. Start your design 2.5cm (1in) below the rim. Treat your glasses with respect by hand-washing them carefully in warm soapy water. Avoid using the dishwasher as this will shorten the life of your decoration.

• It is so simple to paint your glassware that you will probably be tempted to try out your ideas on lots of different glass objects. Choose colours that co-ordinate with other items in your kitchen or your table setting.

▲ Remove unwanted paint.

For further glass painting projects see:
Painted decanter and glasses pp92–3;
Fish stencil shower glass pp193–5.

THE BEDROOM SHOULD BE
A SANCTUARY — CALM, QUIET
AND RELAXING. IT IS ALSO A PLACE
WHERE YOU SHOULD FEEL FREE
TO REFLECT YOUR PERSONAL STYLE
AND TURN YOUR DREAMS INTO
REALITY. ADD SOME TOUCHES OF
COMFORT AND LUXURY WITH A FEW
EXQUISITE ACCESSORIES, OR TAKE A
FLIGHT OF FANTASY AND
TRANSFORM AN UNINSPIRING PIECE
OF FURNITURE INTO A THING OF
BEAUTY AND ELEGANCE.

Bedroom Projects

Stencilled cane chair

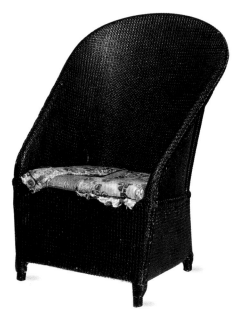

THIS LITTLE CHAIR is covered in the kind of weave often mistakenly labelled as Lloyd Loom. Whatever its real name, its smooth surface is far more amenable to stencilling than the genuine article. Unfortunately, this specimen had been smothered in black paint, which was painted on rather than sprayed, so the weave was completely clogged up. If you find something in this weave that is still in its original state, it will look a lot better if you spray it or brush on several diluted coats of paint rather than brushing on two or three layers straight from the tin.

❖ YOU WILL NEED ❖

Oil-based spray paint

Tape measure

Drawing paper

Pencil

Design from fabric or source of your choice

Masking tape

Tracing paper

Technical drawing pen or fine felt pen

Manila card, acetate or plan trace

Scalpel (or cutting blade) and cutting mat

Acrylic craft paints

Saucer

Stencil brush

Spare piece of paper

Warm, soapy water

1 Measure the area that you want the design to occupy on the chair. On a piece of paper, draw a shape slightly larger than you want the finished stencil to be and begin to draw the design within the shape, copying from your source and simplifying the shapes.

2 Tape a piece of tracing paper over your drawing and, using a technical drawing pen, trace over the design, refining and simplifying it as you go. Tape the tracing onto a work surface, then tape the plastic film over it, matt side up. Using the same pen, trace the design onto the film.

3 Lay the plastic shiny-side up on the cutting mat. Using a sharp scalpel and cutting as accurately as possible, cut out the stencil. When you finish, check to make sure that there are no jagged edges. Try the stencil out on a spare piece of paper to see if it needs any final adjustments.

4 Measure the back of the chair and lightly mark the centre. You will need to use the stencil twice on the chair back (the right way round on one side of the mid-line and flipped over on the other). Fix the stencil in position with masking tape.

5 Pour a little of the acrylic craft paint into a saucer and take some of it up on the end of the stencil brush. Dab the brush onto a spare piece of paper until you have worked most of the paint off – the less paint you have on the brush, the better.

6 Dab the brush onto your stencil, using your free hand to hold the adjacent edges of the stencil down. You can graduate the colour on the roses and leaves by using different shades of green and pink.

7 Remove the stencil and wash off the paint with warm soapy water. Dry it and tape it opposite the first design, in reverse. Complete the second side to match the first. You can also use part of the stencil to make a motif at the base of the chair.

For further chair projects see:
Decorative chairs pp102–3; Painted chairs pp144–7; Ivy-stamped chair pp150–1.

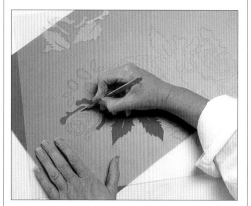

The chair had been thickly painted in black, and needed several coats of cream paint to cover it up.

▲ Use a very sharp knife to cut out the stencil.

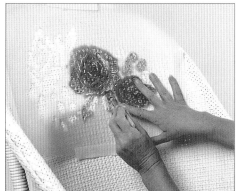

▲ Hold the stencil firmly in place as you paint.

Marbled dressing table

THIS CLASSIC KIDNEY-SHAPED dressing table came from a junk market. It was covered in layers of thick white paint, which needed to be stripped off professionally. When the dressing table returned from the strippers, the mirror frames had been reduced to a bundle of sticks which then had to be repinned by a picture framer. The main body was painted in white semi-gloss, then a range of soft pinks were used to create the faux marbling effect on the top. Frills and curtains in a floral print were added to complete the feminine effect.

❖ YOU WILL NEED ❖

Fine and super-fine grade abrasive paper

Tack rag

White primer

White semi-gloss paint

Mineral turpentine

2 x 4cm (1½in) household paintbrushes

Artists' oil colours in rose madder, cadmium yellow and raw umber

3 small non-plastic containers

Transparent oil glaze

Piece of white paper

Lint-free rag

Artists' paintbrush (sable or synthetic mixture)

Badger-hair softener

Clear satin polyurethane varnish

Clean rag

1 Rub down the table with fine grade abrasive paper to as smooth a finish as possible. Remove any dust with a tack rag then apply a coat of white primer and leave to dry.

2 Lightly rub down the primer with the fine grade abrasive paper and tack the surface again. Slightly thin some semi-gloss paint with turpentine. Apply three or four coats of semi-gloss, leaving each coat to dry, rubbing down with super-fine grade abrasive paper and removing dust with a tack rag between coats.

3 Using artists' oil paints and white semi-gloss paint, mix up three colour shades (pink in this case) to match the fabric. The darkest shade will be used for the marble veins.

4 Mix the first two colours in separate containers and dissolve them with enough turpentine to give them a creamy consistency. Gradually add the transparent oil glaze and stir it into the mixture. Finally, stir in the rest of the turpentine to produce a mix that is fluid and looks transparent when brushed onto white paper, but that is not so thin that it does not hold its pattern and shape when ragged onto a surface.

5 Paint irregular patches of one colour glaze on the top of the table. Partially fill the open areas with similar patches of the second glaze. Leave some of the white base coat showing through. While the glaze is still wet, take a crumpled piece of lint-free rag and press it firmly and quickly all over the glazed area.

6 Using an artists' paintbrush, loosely add the darkest colour to make the veining. For a more realistic effect, ensure that the veins

▲ Paint on the 'marble' veins.

travel diagonally and either begin or finish on the edge of the piece or where they connect with each other. Use a badger-hair softener to dust the veins lightly and soften the effect. Leave to dry for 24 hours, then apply a coat of clear, satin polyurethane varnish.

7 Paint the mirror frames with irregular patches of the first two glazes. Dab firmly with a clean rag to leave the glaze mainly in moulding. Varnish when dry.

For further marbling projects see:
Marble bathroom pp200–1; Marbled pots pp214–15.

▲ Rag the table top to create a random effect.

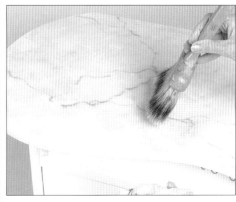

▲ Soften the effect with a badger-hair softener.

Hand-printed blanket box

Painted betrothal chests were traditional in Europe for centuries and they would often include the bride's initials and the date of marriage. Although the design of this project is not traditional, the use of a painted panel, the oak-leaf motif and the printing technique are. Today, the blanket box would make an original personalized wedding gift or could be adapted to make a lovely birth or christening present, by varying the colouring and decorating the chest with the child's initials and date of birth. Draw around paint tins to get the curves for the template and make the oak-leaf print by drawing the shape onto a sponge and cutting it out with a scalpel knife. You can make the gold paint yourself – use a deep gold bronzing powder and an artist's acrylic medium to get the shade and degree of lustre that you want.

❖ YOU WILL NEED ❖

Rubber gloves

Soft cloths

Dark brown french enamel varnish or water-based woodstain and clear shellac

Kitchen paper

Liquid wax

Brush for applying wax

Acrylic or traditional paint in 2 colours

Household paintbrushes

Water-soluble pencil

Cardboard

Ruler

Scalpel knife

Flexible masking tape

00-grade steel wool

Medium grade abrasive paper

Baby's bath sponge

Plate

Gold paint

Alphabet tracing paper

Transfer paper

Brown wax

This stencilling project will enable you to personalize furniture such as this chest.

1 The first thing that you need to do is stain and seal the chest. Make sure that the chest is clean and dry before you begin. Wearing rubber gloves to protect your hands

▲ Rub French enamel varnish over the chest.

and using a soft cloth, stain the chest by rubbing french enamel varnish over the surface. This is shellac based and therefore seals the wood at the same time as staining it. On the other hand, a water-based woodstain and a coat of clear shellac would make an equally successful alternative. If you do choose to use a woodstain, make sure that you go over it thoroughly with clear shellac.

2 The next step is to apply liquid wax with a paintbrush over the areas that would naturally wear. This will ensure that the wood has a perfect finish. Then, when the chest is completely dry, paint it in your main choice of colour.

▲ Draw around the template to create the panel.

▲ Paint inside the panel in a different colour.

▲ Dip the sponge in the paint and press on chest.

3 Draw your panel shape onto a piece of cardboard using a ruler to check your measurements. Cut the template out using a scalpel knife, put in the centre of the chest and draw around it with a pencil.

4 Mask the panel, using flexible masking tape where necessary, and paint inside it with the second colour of paint. Remove the tape and rub back the whole of the chest with steel wool and sandpaper.

5 Cut out an oak-leaf shape from the sponge. Brush some of the darker coloured paint onto a plate, dip the sponge into this and press it down flat onto the edge of the blanket box. Continue in this way until you have formed a border all the way around the edges. Print in gold over the existing oak leaves using the same process.

6 Transfer the initials and dates onto the central panel using transfer paper. Using a fine brush, paint a gold line over the darker colour around the edge of the panel. Then carefully fill in the lettering and the date.

7 Apply a coat of brown wax to the blanket box with a cloth; leave it for approximately half an hour before you start to buff it. If you have used chalky paints, this will completely transform the appearance of the blanket box and bring out all the richness of the paint colours.

▲ Carefully fill in the initials, date and panel outline with gold paint.

HINTS AND TIPS

• If you prefer, you can make a stencil of three or four oak leaves and cut them out to form a border. You will then need to mark horizontal and vertical lines onto the blanket box with a pencil, where you want to position the border. Begin stencilling by placing the centre of the stencil in the middle of a pencilled line and working outwards from there.

For further freehand projects see:
Colour-washed oak sideboard pp98–9, Tartan-band dining table pp100–1; Kitchen accessories pp138–41; Hand-painted chest pp206–7; Painted tablecloth pp218–21; Painted frames pp232–3.

Frottaged and stencilled screen

THE IDEA OF DECORATING a three-panelled screen can be quite daunting. Such screens are often decorated with fabric and the combination of paint effects used here will give the impression that it has been covered in trompe-l'oeil antique damask and surrounded by a ribbon border. Although there are numerous layers, each one is quick and simple. However, for the effect to be a success, it is absolutely essential that you mark out the vertical lines accurately and make sure that the horizontal ones line up on each of the panels. The pattern here is adapted from an embossed wallpaper design and will fit screens of various different sizes.

❖ YOU WILL NEED ❖

Yellow acrylic or traditional paint

Paint roller and tray

Water-based gold paint

Paint brushes

Acrylic or traditional paint in a colour of your choice

Tissue paper

Stencil film

Scalpel (or cutting blade) and cutting mat

Flexible and straight masking tape

Ruler

Pencil

Long ruler or straightedge

Set square

Stencil brush or natural sponge

Kitchen paper

Medium grade finishing paper

Matt water-based varnish

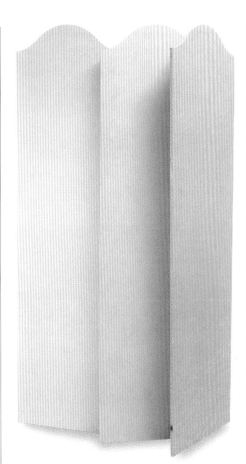

You can build your own screen out of MDF.

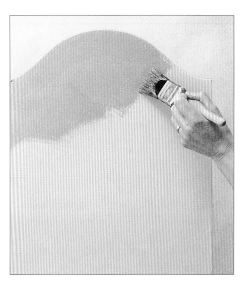

▲ Apply two layers of gold paint to the screen.

1 The first thing you need to do is create texture for the screen by applying two coats of yellow paint over the surface with a paint roller. Allow the first coat of paint to dry thoroughly before you start to apply the second. Yellow is a good colour to use because it helps to disguise any thin area in the final gold layer but you can use another colour if you prefer. Using a paintbrush, apply two coats of gold paint over the yellow, allowing the first coat to dry thoroughly before applying the second.

2 When the gold paint has dried thoroughly, paint the colour that you have chosen over approximately one-third of one of the screen panels. You will find it easiest to use a large, wide paintbrush for this.

▲ Use a wide paintbrush to apply the colour.

167

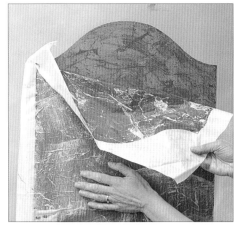

▲ Use tissue paper to create this textured effect.

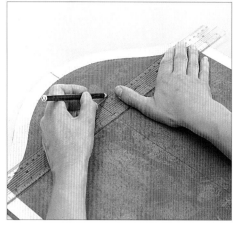

▲ Ensure that the lines match up perfectly.

▲ Paint a border of gold paint around the edge.

3 Immediately press a sheet of tissue paper against the wet surface of the screen, pressing it flat with your hand, then peel it off. This creates a textured effect, which will cover all the paintbrush marks. This paint effect is known as frottage. Complete the rest of this panel and the other two panels in the same way.

4 Trace the pattern on page 247 onto stencil film with a pencil and mark the line down the middle of the stencil. Cut out the design, including the registration marks (the little diamond on each corner) with a scalpel knife, using a cutting mat or thick cardboard to protect your work surface. Stick masking tape around each panel, using flexible tape for the curved area at the top.

Draw a line down the centre of each panel exactly in the middle. To do this, make a series of dots at regular intervals down the length of each panel, checking that the distance between the dot and the edge of the panel on one side is equal to the distance on the other side. A centring ruler is very useful here. Join up all the dots with a light pencil line using a long ruler or straight edge. You will find it easier if you lay each panel on a flat surface for measuring and marking.

5 Draw a line across one of the panels near the top. Make sure that it is horizontal by checking its position in relation to the line down the centre, using a set square. Place another panel level next to it and continue the line in exactly the same

position on this, then finally on the third panel.

6 Place the stencil in the position for starting, lining the centre of the stencil with the line down the middle of the screen. Secure with some masking tape and then draw a horizontal line on the stencil film to match that on the panel. This will ensure that the starting point is the same for each panel.

Dip the stencil brush into the gold paint and wipe off the excess onto a piece of kitchen paper. Dab the paint through the stencil, varying the amount that you use in order to give the design a faded appearance. Make sure that you dab a little paint through the diamond registration mark. You will need this in order to line up the next stencil. Do not worry that these registration marks will spoil your design because they will be lost in the overall effect of the paint. Move the stencil down the screen, lining up

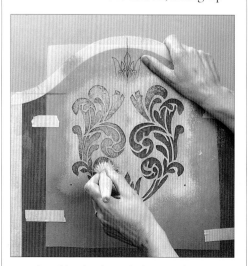

▲ Dab gold paint through the stencil.

the diamonds at the top with the gold ones at the bottom of the previous stencil. Continue all the way down the panel and on the sides, matching up the registration marks. Stencil the pattern on all the panels in the same way.

7 Place a second row of masking tape just inside the existing tape before removing it. Brush gold paint around the edge of the screen. Use the paint sparingly with the brush fairly dry, so that the red paint shows through.

8 Rub back the surface of the screen gently with a medium-grade finishing paper, then seal the screen with a coat of matt water-based varnish.

HINTS AND TIPS

• The stencilled area is quite big and you will find it much quicker to work with a large stencil brush. Try to find one that is not too close-textured for greater flexibility and ease of use. Alternatively, you can use a natural sponge or a brush. It is important to have plenty of kitchen paper handy for removing the excess paint.

• The colour used here is red ochre, which looks very good with the gold, but deep shades of green or blue would also look extremely striking.

For further stencilling projects see:
Stencilled balustrade pp130–2; A kitchen frieze pp148–9; Stencilled cane chair pp160–1; Stencilled headboard pp170–1; A bedroom frieze pp172–4; Stencilled animal prints pp175–7; Children's balloon stencils pp184–5; Poppies picture frame pp236–7; Stencilled newspaper rack pp238–9.

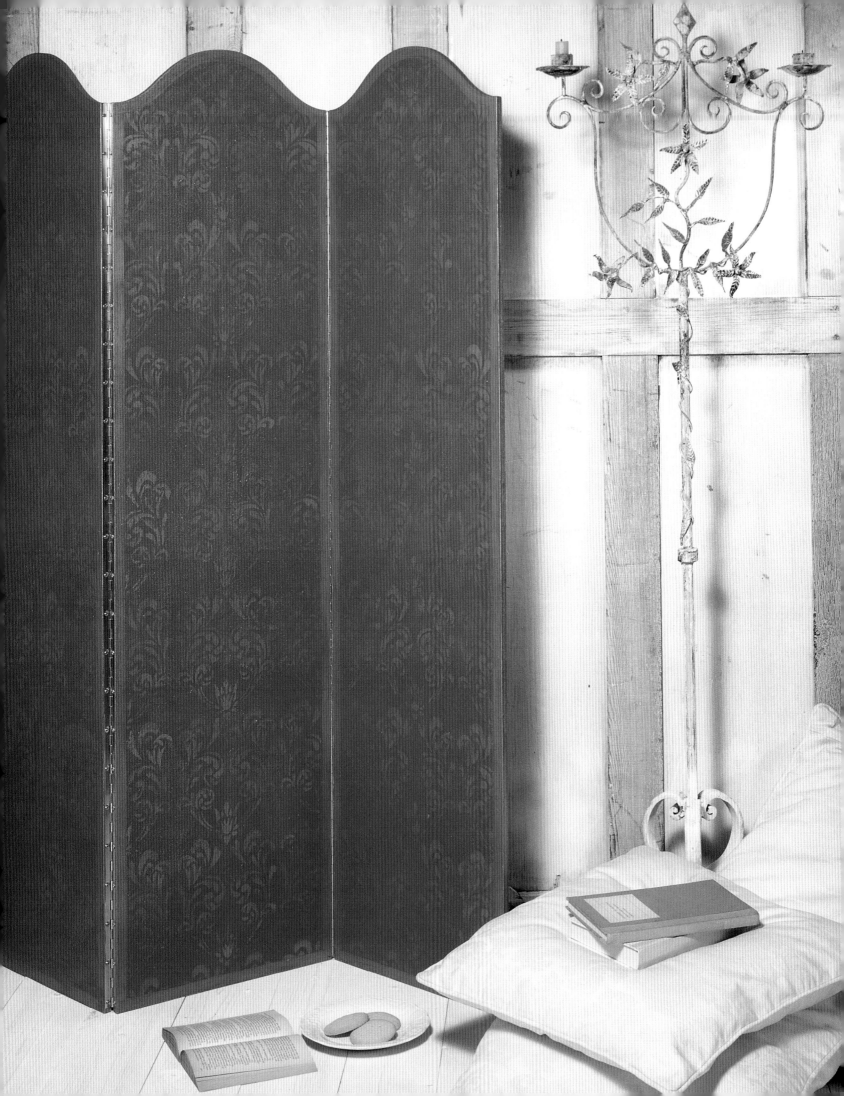

Stencilled headboard

THE DESIGN USED FOR THIS old-fashioned headboard is a pretty, modern version of the French 18th-century pattern known as 'Toile du Jouy'. It is an intricate and delicate pattern, but the strong lines and emphatic shapes, together with the variety of separate motifs, have a great deal of scope. To add more interest to the design, a 'drop shadow' effect was created by a light sponge application of a pale, warm grey. When this had completely dried, the design was stencilled in terracotta acrylic paint to match the fabric. The large design here offered plenty of opportunity for a range of techniques. Different densities of paint add interest and life to a pattern. Notice how effective using the same stencil twice can be in adding depth to the design.

❖ YOU WILL NEED ❖

A piece of MDF

Tape measure

Plumb line

Pencil

Stencil

Non-permanent adhesive spray

Warm grey acrylic paint

Bathroom sponge

Terracotta acrylic paint

Fine paintbrush

Clear polyurethane varnish with yellow ochre

1 This bedhead was made by cutting a piece of MDF into a shape that complemented the motif. The bedhead was screwed into the plaster and painted to match the wall.

2 Measure the central point of the bedhead and suspend a plumb line from the top at this point and lightly mark in the vertical line running down the centre.

3 Note the height of the pillows and position the design around them. Losing the end of a design behind pillows looks informal, but if too much is obscured, it may just look messy.

4 Align the stencil with the centre mark and then move it down and to the left by a few millimeters. Apply warm grey acrylic, using a bathroom sponge and leave the paint to dry completely.

5 Align the central line of stencil to the central mark of the bedhead and apply terracotta acrylic paint with a bathroom sponge.

6 Sharpen up the shapes with a fine paintbrush to give a highly polished finish.

7 Add a little yellow ochre to the varnish to give a mellow antique effect. Apply two coats of varnish to protect the headboard from knocks and scrapes. If you are feeling adventurous, you can repeat the jug motif on the walls.

For further stencilling projects see:
Stencilled balustrade pp130–2; A kitchen frieze pp148–9; Stencilled cane chair pp160–1; Frottaged and stencilled screen pp167–9; A bedroom frieze pp172–4; Stencilled animal prints pp175–7; Children's balloon stencils pp184–5; Poppies picture frame pp236–7; Stencilled mirror frame pp242–3; Monogrammed box pp244–5.

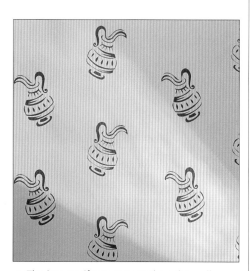

▲ The jug motif was repeated on the walls.

▲ Checking the alignment of the stencil.

▲ Position the design so it is not obscured.

A bedroom frieze

CONTINUING THE PATTERN of the curtains on to the plain walls by painting a stencilled border beneath the cornice is a good way of integrating the space in your bedroom. The colours of this stencil were taken from the curtains: dark biscuit, dark pink, light pink and greenish-grey. The design for the stencil was an amalgamation of several of the elements of the curtain pattern. The upper half of the fruit bowl made a good starting point for the border. The grapes were left out because their pattern was too dense, which left a gap in the bottom corner. This was then filled by repeating a few of the flowers from the top of the design. The elegant curved bow was then added and the whole design simplified.

❖ YOU WILL NEED ❖

Tracing paper

Design for your stencil from fabric or source of your choice

Pencil

Acrylic paint in dark biscuit, dark pink, dusky pink and green-grey

Paint kettle or saucer (for mixing paints)

Spare piece of paper or card

Manila card, acetate or plan trace

Scalpel (or cutting blade) and cutting mat

Spirit level

Non-permanent adhesive spray

Bathroom sponge

1 Trace the elements in the curtain design that you want to incorporate into your stencil. Adapt and simplify as necessary.

2 Mix up the paints into the three colours of your choice. Start by putting the base colour (the biscuit colour in the curtains in this case) into three pots. To the first, gradually add a dusky pink and mix thoroughly until you achieve the shade you require; to the second, add green-grey; and to the third, add a tiny amount of a dirty wine-coloured paint.

3 Plan the colours of the design by painting onto a full size photocopy of the stencil design. As well as marking out where the colours will go clearly mark the areas where the wall colour is to be used as an element of the design. Some of the pattern elements here, such as the rim of the grapefruit and the highlights on the apple and the leaves, were created by leaving the light base colour blank. Bear in mind that light stencilling allows much of the base wall colour to show through, which allows for quite subtle variations of shade. Mark these areas on the design plan. For example, light shades of green and pink were created by applying them lightly over the base colour. Other colours can also be created by applying one colour on top of another.

▲ Plan the colours of the design on paper.

▲ Source your design from the curtain pattern.

▲ Trace and adapt the design.

▲ Mix the tints and try them out.

▲ Trace the outline of each colour.

▲ Check the effect on a piece of card.

HINTS & TIPS

• When mixing the wall paints, use the small colour registration circles, found inside the seams of your curtain fabric, as a guide so that you can match the tones perfectly.

• If you work cleanly and methodically, there is no real limit to the amount of colour you can use through one stencil.

For further stencilling projects see:
Stencilled balustrade pp130–2; A kitchen frieze pp148–9; Stencilled cane chair pp160–1; Frottaged and stencilled screen pp167–9; Children's balloon stencils pp184–5; Poppies picture frame pp236–7; Monogrammed box pp244–5.

4 Break the final design into three colour stencils by tracing the outline of each area of colour on to a separate sheet of tracing paper. Make sure that the centre lines are accurately marked on each of the colour traces.

5 Transfer each colour stencil and its centre lines from the tracing paper on to a piece of manila card, acetate or plan trace. Then, using a scalpel on a cutting mat, cut out the stencil pattern from each piece of card. Start by removing the smallest areas first to keep the stencil firm and always cut away from your body.

6 Cut a V-shaped groove at either side of each piece of card along the horizontal centre line. These grooves will enable you to line up the stencils accurately.

7 Check that the finished effect works before applying it to the wall – try each stencil out on a piece of card and practise lining them up on top of each other.

8 Plan the position of the stencils on the wall. Draw a light pencil line to follow using a spirit level and mark the position of each stencil.

9 Apply the first colour with a bathroom sponge and mark the centre of the stencil in pencil on the wall. This will enable you to position the other stencils accurately.

10 Leave the paint to dry completely before applying the next stencil colour. When the stencils are completly dry, rub off the pencil lines.

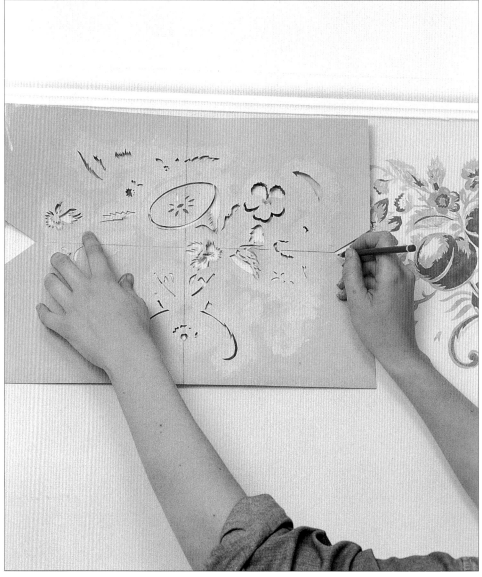

▲ Make pencil marks on the wall to help you line up the stencils correctly.

Stencilled animal prints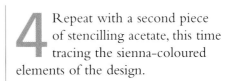

ANIMAL PRINTS are very popular in today's fashion and are found more and more in the interiors of people's homes. They can be used on curtains, pillow cases, cushion covers or throws to bring a sophisticated look, or an element of kitsch to your bedroom. Combine them with themed accessories such as pictures of a sunset over the savannah or elephant ornaments to evoke an exciting African or Indian atmosphere. You can find leopard, zebra, giraffe and tiger prints on many fabrics. Look around to find the texture and colour of material that you like best. Suedette, mock satin and even velvet are all suitable fabrics on which you can stencil animal prints. To fill a large area, simply work in sections, washing the acetate stencils carefully between uses.

❖ YOU WILL NEED ❖

Fabric of your choice

Iron

Design for your stencil (see page 247) or design from source of your choice

Paper

Fabric paint in sienna natural and black

Non-permanent adhesive spray

Stencilling acetate

Permanent pen

Cutting mat

Scalpel (or cutting blade) and cutting mat

Blotting paper

Two size 2 stencil brushes

Palette

1 Wash your chosen fabric in order to remove any residues which might react with the paint, then dry and iron the fabric so that it is free from creases.

2 To stencil the leopard print design, use a photocopier to enlarge the two templates on page 247 to the required size. Alternatively, copy a print from another source such as a piece of material or a picture in a book.

3 Draw a template of the shapes on white paper and colour as you want the final design to look using black and sienna. Spray a thin coat of non-permanent adhesive on to the back of a piece of acetate, manila card or plan trace and place it over the leopard design. Trace the outlines of the black shapes on the acetate with a permanent pen.

4 Repeat with a second piece of stencilling acetate, this time tracing the sienna-coloured elements of the design.

5 Peel each piece of acetate off the paper, place it on a cutting mat and cut out the stencil design following the pen outlines with a scalpel. Cut away from your body as you work. Push out the cut pieces carefully (acetate tears easily).

6 Place the fabric down flat on a piece of blotting paper and secure the first stencil on top using non-permanent adhesive spray.

7 Dip the stencil brush into a small amount of sienna natural fabric paint in your palette and dab off any excess. Apply the paint evenly through the stencil, working gently in a circular motion.

▲ Copy the design from a piece of fabric.

▲ Cut out the stencil carefully.

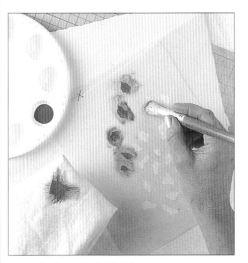

▲ Apply the paint in the first stencil.

▲ Apply the second colour through the stencil.

8 Leave the paint to dry for a couple of hours then carefully peel off the first stencil.

9 Place the second stencil on the painted fabric, aligning it carefully. Use black fabric paint and a clean stencil brush, to apply the paint in the same way.

10 When you have finished leave the paint to dry for a couple of hours and then peel the acetate away carefully.

11 Position the first stencil below or at the side of the completed section, leaving space for the black of the first stencil to show around the edges.

12 Paint the fabric in sections until it is completely covered with the pattern. To fill in small gaps, use just the dots from the first stencil. Allow the paint to dry – refer to the manufacturer's recommended drying times.

13 Most fabric paints have to be fixed by heat before they can be washed or dry cleaned (check the label). Simply place a clean cloth over the completed stencil and heat-seal with a hot iron.

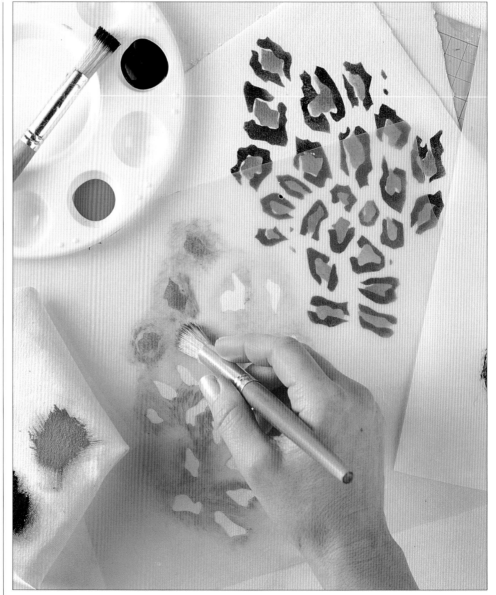

▲ Repeat the stencil until you achieve the desired pattern.

HINTS & TIPS

• If you find the idea of using two stencils daunting; use a deeper shade of fabric, such as the mock suede in the bedspread, and only use the second stencil.

• Think about incorporating pearlized or metallic fabric paints into the design. They will complement textured fabrics perfectly.

• Clean the stencils gently with warm water after use.

For further stencilling projects see:
Stencilled balustrade pp130–2; A kitchen frieze pp148–9; Stencilled cane chair pp160–1; Frottaged and stencilled screen pp167–9; Children's balloon stencils pp184–5; Poppies picture frame pp236–7; Monogrammed box pp244–5.

Antiqued iron bed frame

YOU MIGHT THINK that it is all very well being tempted to buy an old jug from a junk shop, because you know that prior to it taking up pride of place on your dresser it will meet with a thorough wash or a keen dusting down. However, if the piece you intend to purchase is likely to be the weight of a small cart horse and rusty with it, the idea of cleaning such a large object might not be so appealing. This project shows that with a little determination and some elbow grease, it is quite possible to rescue and revamp a large cast iron bed frame, thus combining the elegance of an age gone by with the comfort and convenience of today's lifestyle.

❖ YOU WILL NEED ❖

Warm, soapy water and cloth or stiff brush

Rubber gloves

Cloth or scrubbing brush

Coarse and medium grade abrasive paper

Household paintbrush

All-purpose acrylic primer or anti-rust primer

Acrylic paints in white, pink and pistachio

Fine artists' brush

Soft cloth

Raw umber paint pigment

Acrylic varnish

Dragging brush

Silver metallic paint

1 Remove the surface dust and dirt with a large bowl of warm soapy water and a cloth or a stiff brush. Sand off any rust and old paintwork with coarse grade abrasive paper. Using a household paintbrush, apply a coat of all-purpose acrylic primer. If the frame is rusty, use anti-rust primer. Allow to dry.

2 Paint a coat of white acrylic over the bed frame, watching out for any runs or drips. Leave to dry, and apply a second coat if needed.

3 Using a fine artists' brush, pick out any details or ornamental features of the bed frame's design in pale pink acrylic. Then, using a soft cloth, rub away some of the pink paint on the details to create the look of wear and tear.

4 Paint fine lines of pistachio-coloured acrylic over the ornamental details to highlight the intricate metalwork. Allow to dry.

5 Using medium grade abrasive paper, rub down the paintwork on the bed frame to reveal patches of previous paint layers and bare metal. This will add to the aged and worn feel that an old bed would have.

6 Make some ageing glaze by mixing a tablespoon of raw umber paint pigment in a pot

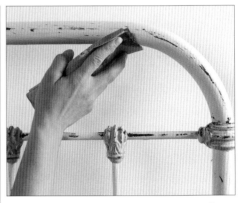
▲ Rub down the paintwork for an aged effect.

of acrylic varnish. Brush a coat of ageing glaze over the frame using a long-haired soft dragging brush. Allow the glaze to pool in some areas, but do not allow any runs to occur.

7 Using a fine artists' brush, carefully apply silver metallic paint in order to pick out and highlight any intricate mouldings. Allow to dry thoroughly.

For other ageing projects see:
Antiqued table pp104–5; Distressed chest pp198–9; Aged rustic chair pp212–13.

▲ Sand off any old paintwork and rust.

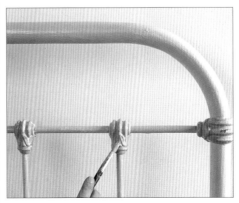
▲ Apply pink acrylic paint on the details.

▲ Varnish with a coat of glaze.

Cherub wardrobe

Tᴴɪꜱ ᴡᴀʀᴅʀᴏʙᴇ, which has been rag-rolled and stencilled with a light, bright, whimsical cherub theme, was originally a gentleman's wardrobe. It is made from good, solid wood, with shelving up one side and a hanging rail, and would be ideal for a child's bedroom or a small guest room. The flat doors lend themselves well to the paint techniques of stencilling and rag rolling. If the door handles are unsuitable for painting, or do not blend in, replace them with silver or glass knobs. Two inexpensive silver tassels add a stylish finishing touch.

❖ YOU WILL NEED ❖

Screwdriver

Wood filler

Palette knife

Medium and fine grade abrasive papers

Tack rag

Primer

Household paintbrushes

Semi-gloss base coat

Paint tray

Small roller with sleeve for oil-based paint

Transparent oil glaze or acrylic or ready-made acrylic mix

Paint kettle

Black artists' oil paint

Mineral turpentine

Pink flesh-tone semi-gloss paint

Stippling brush

Clean lint-free cotton rags

Manila card, acetate or plan trace

Design for your stencil (see page 248)

Permanent pen

Scalpel (or cutting blade) and cutting mat

Non-permanent adhesive spray

Acrylic paintbrush

Acrylic satin glaze

Black and white stencil sticks

Medium-sized stencil brush

Two glass knobs

Two silver tassels

1 Remove the handles to make sanding and painting easier. Fill any holes with wood filler. Allow to dry and then rub down with medium grade abrasive paper, following the grain of the wood. Wipe off any dust with a tack rag, then apply a coat of primer and allow to dry completely.

2 Pour the semi-gloss base coat into the paint tray. Using a small roller, fitted with a sleeve for oil-based paint, apply paint to the wardrobe. Finish edges with a small paintbrush and leave to dry. Rub down any uneven areas with fine grade abrasive paper, tack,and apply second coat.

3 Place a tablespoon of transparent glaze into the paint kettle, then squeeze in a tube width of black artists' oil paint and stir until smooth. Add more transparent glaze plus mineral turpentine in the ratio of two to one, finally adding one spoon of pink flesh-tone semi-gloss, until you have enough to cover the wardrobe.

A dark solid piece of wooden furniture can easily be brightened up.

The consistency of the mix should be similar to that of single cream.

4 With a well-loaded stippling brush, apply the glaze over one section of the wardrobe.

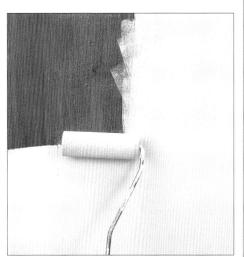

▲ Roll on the first coat of semi-gloss base coat.

▲ Use a stippling brush over the glaze.

Work quickly and do not overbrush. While the glaze is still wet, apply the stippling brush with a moderate up-and-down stabbing motion in order to remove the brushstrokes and create a fine speckled-effect finish. Move on to the next step immediately.

5 Cut up the cotton material into large rag pieces. Screw up a piece of rag, twisting it into a sausage shape. Place the rag at a top corner and roll it down to the bottom of the wardrobe, using your fingertips and applying even pressure. Return to the top of the wardrobe door and position the rag next to the side of the last section. Repeat the movement, making sure that you overlap the last 'run' slightly to avoid hard edges. Then repeat steps 4 and 5 on the next panel, and gradually work around the wardrobe.

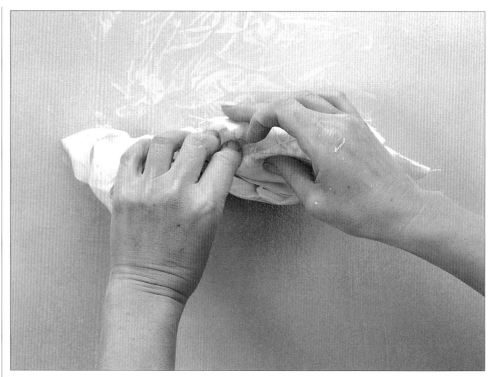

▲ Roll a rag into the glaze and work down the wardrobe gradually.

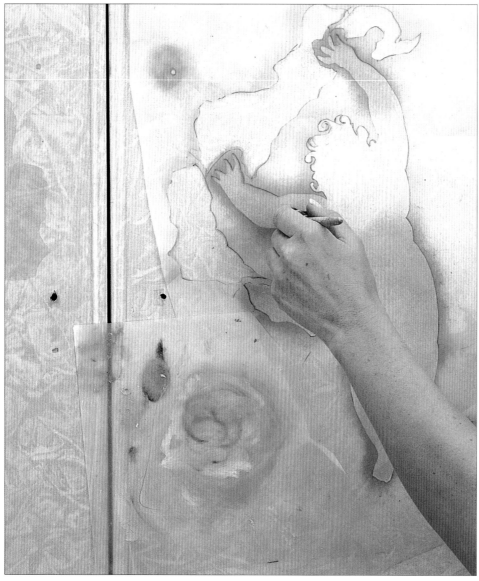

▲ Stencil part one of the design in pale grey.

6 To make the cherub stencil, position the film over the template for part one of the cherub stencil on page 248, and trace the outline with a fine-tip permanent pen. Allow extra stencil film around the edges to mix colours, and for the positioning marks. Cut along the lines with a scalpel and cut out the circular line-up dots, which will enable you to position the second stencil correctly. On a separate piece of film repeat the same for part two of the stencil.

7 Apply adhesive spray to the reverse side of the part one stencil and stick it into place on the wardrobe door. Check the position and adjust if necessary before applying the colour. Break the seals of the stencil sticks (manufacturers' instructions are given on the packaging) and work black and white on to the spare area of the film. Mix the colours together until you produce a pale grey shade. Working the stencil brush into this mix, cover all of the cut-out areas of part one, using a circular and stippling motion. Add positioning marks to the surface to help you when you come to lining up the next stencil, before carefully peeling part one away.

▲ Stencil part two of the design in dark grey.

▲ Detail of the darker parts of the stencil.

HINTS & TIPS

• Do not be tempted to overload colour on to the brush, because heavy paint will cause smudging and the stencil design will lack the required soft texture.

• If a stippling brush is not available, place a clean sleeve for oil-based paint on the small roller and very gently roll over the glaze to smooth out the brushstokes.

• During the stencilling process, it is normal, at first, to feel that not enough paint has been applied but when the stencil is removed the design will be much heavier than you imagined.

• Keep a small dish or saucer of water and lots of cleaning fluids to hand, to remove any smudges or dribbles immediately.

For further dragging projects see:
Painted panels pp133–5; Repeating border and dragged stripes pp208–11.

8 Apply adhesive spray to the reverse side of part two of the stencil, then position it correctly over part one of the stencil by aligning with the position marks.

9 Mix the stencil sticks as before but make a darker grey colour, and keep some neat black beside this to use for highlighting small areas. Colour all the cut-out areas of part two with dark grey, accentuating some intricate parts and features by stippling with a small amount of black.

10 Peel the stencil off and wipe away the line-up marks. Then clean the stencil with a clean rag moistened in mineral turpentine, and allow to dry. Repeat the stencilling process on the other door by reversing the stencil. Wipe off the marker lines and leave both doors for at least 24 hours to dry thoroughly.

11 Using the acrylic brush, finish the wardrobe by applying two coats of acrylic satin glaze. This glaze will initially give the appearance of a milky finish but it will dry clear, so do not be tempted to overwork the medium. Allow the manufacturer's recommended drying time between coats.

▲ Detail of a finished cherub.

Children's balloon stencils

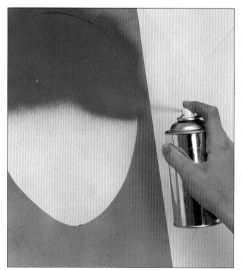 F ALL THE ROOMS in the house, the stencilled nursery has become an enduring favourite. This is probably due to the fact that nursery stencils at their best are simple and bright. Although complicated stencils of figures or locomotives accurately reproduced down to the last piston are undeniably lovely, it's a matter of debate whether such sophistication is appreciated by the room's inhabitants. While the children are still young, go for bright, saturated, all-over colours, which tiny new-formed eyes do seem to notice and enjoy. This type of random project is ideal for tackling a little at a time. More than one nursery has remained incomplete at the arrival of its new occupant. The beauty of this scheme is that there is no definitive finishing line.

❖ YOU WILL NEED ❖

Manila card, acetate or plan trace

Scalpel (or cutting blade) and cutting mat

Non-permanent adhesive spray

Scrap paper for masking

Craft spray or acrylic paints in assorted colours

Face mask

Black permanent marker pen

Pen

Masking tape

Pin or needle

1 For the balloon shape, draw a straight line of a suitable length and connect the top and bottom ends with a curve. Trace the shape onto manila card, acetate or plan trace and then flip it over from the central line and trace a mirror image to give a symmetrical balloon shape. Cut out the balloon shape with a scalpel.

2 Mask the area around the stencil. Lightly spray the base colour through the stencil. When the base colour is dry, tape a pin or needle to side of a can of contrasting coloured paint so that it interrupts the spray of paint producing larger spots of colour.

3 Add a highlight to each balloon stencil with a short burst from the white spray. Draw in the curling balloon string using a black permanent marker pen.

For further stencilling projects see:
Stencilled balustrade pp130–2; A kitchen frieze pp148–9; Stencilled cane chair pp160–1; Stencilled headboard pp170–1; Stencilled animal prints pp175–7.

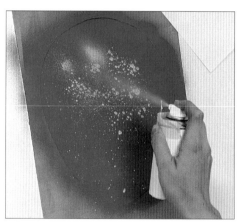

▲ Spray on the contrasting colour.

▲ Spray on the base coat.

▲ Detail of the finished overlapping balloons.

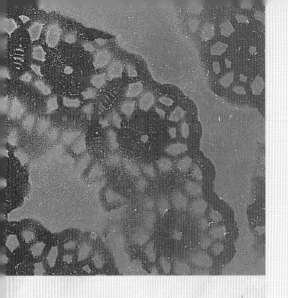

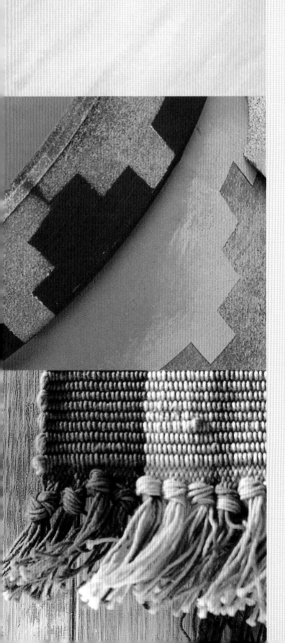

OFTEN CROWDED WITH UNATTRACTIVE BUT NECESSARY ITEMS SUCH AS LAUNDRY BASKETS AND TOWEL RACKS, THE BATHROOM CAN BE QUITE A DECORATIVE CHALLENGE. HOWEVER, A LITTLE PLANNING WILL DEAL WITH THE CLUTTER, AND THE FOLLOWING IDEAS FOR BRIGHT PAINTED PROJECTS WILL INSPIRE YOU TO TRANSFORM THOSE UNINSPIRING BITS AND PIECES. WHEN YOU HAVE FINISHED, RUN A DEEP BATH, LIE BACK FOR A LONG SOAK AND ADMIRE YOUR HANDIWORK.

Bathroom Projects

Verdigris mirror and door handles

THESE DAYS, WE SEEM to have an obsession for making things look worn and neglected. We can't wait to make objects look rusty, crazed, fly-blown, distressed or just plain dusty. Of all the antiquing techniques, however, verdigris, which is the effect you get when certain metals, such as copper and brass, are left to their own devices and become discoloured and corroded with age, is one of the most striking. The metal of this mirror and door handles was definitely not worth cleaning up but it was very decorative and lent itself well to a verdigris finish.

❖ YOU WILL NEED ❖

Hot, soapy water and cloth

Masking tape

Jam jars

Acrylic paints in dark blue-green, peppermint green, pale blue, pale turquoise

4cm (1½in) household paintbrush

Old tablespoon

Methylated spirit

Sieve

Whiting

Several hog's-hair artists' paintbrushes

Cloth

PVA adhesive

1 Wash the metal in hot, soapy water to get rid of any dust and grease and then dry everything thoroughly. Mask off the mirror to protect it while painting.

2 Make up half a jam jar of diluted dark green acrylic paint (1 part acrylic paint to 3 parts water). Apply a coat of the diluted acrylic paint to the mirror frame and stand, and to the door plates and knobs. Leave them to dry thoroughly.

3 To make up the verdigris pastes, place a tablespoon of the pale blue and pale green acrylic paints into separate jam jars and stir two tablespoons of methylated spirits into each colour. Add enough sieved whiting to each of the jars to make a firm mixture.

4 Start with the mirror only and, using a hog's-hair brush, go over the whole frame and stand in all three paint colours. Try to make the distribution of colour and texture as random as possible. When the verdigris paste is completely dry, which should not take very long, go over the mirror again, lightly dabbing it all over with water on a clean brush.

5 While the frame is still damp, sprinkle on some additional sieved whiting – dab and push this gently into the moulding of the frame with your fingers. Take a little of the diluted base green colour and trickle a very small amount here and there, but be careful not to overdo this because it could end up spoiling the final effect.

6 As the frame begins to dry out go over it with a dry cloth, rubbing some of it back to the green base coat and some small raised areas back to the metal. Leave most of it untouched.

7 While the frame is drying, give the finger plates and door knobs the same treatment.

8 When they are fully dry, seal with a coat of diluted PVA adhesive (2 parts water to 1 part PVA).

HINTS & TIPS

• If you have trouble getting hold of dark green acrylic in a small size you will probably find that the little trial pots of acrylic, which most paint manufacturers produce, will give you plenty of paint.

For further ageing projects see:
Antiqued table pp104–5; Antiqued iron bed frame pp178–9; Distressed chest pp198–9; Aged rustic chair pp212–13.

▲ Mix up the verdigris paste.

▲ Dab on the whiting with your fingers.

Mexican-style bathroom

BATHROOMS ARE BEST APPROACHED with a degree of whimsy and fun. Many can have a very cold feel, due to the large expanses of shiny white ceramic and direct overhead lighting. A strong, perhaps daring, approach to colour offers instant improvement, and an ideal opportunity to explore a particular theme. In this bathroom, the bright warm colours and primitive patterns of Mexico have been used as a starting point. The theme is continued throughout, from the mellow terracotta walls and the traditional Mexican patterns on the hanging shelf and walls and windows to the small details on the eye-catching, brightly coloured plant pots.

❖ YOU WILL NEED ❖

Tracing paper, newspaper or scrap paper

Pencil or felt pen

Manila card, acetate or plan trace

Scalpel (or cutting blade) and cutting mat

Warm terracotta matt acrylic paint

Non-permanent adhesive spray

Acrylic paints in assorted colours

Bathroom sponge

Coarse grade abrasive paper

Clear polyurethane varnish

Upholstery nails

Matt spray varnish

Protective face mask

Matt car spray

1 Make the Mexican-style stencils by designing or tracing a Zigarat pattern and star shapes. Transfer them onto stencil material and cut them out using a scalpel and mat.

2 Colour wash the walls with terracotta matt acrylic paint and then attach the Zigarat stencil to the wall using non-permanent adhesive spray. Apply the paint in the colour of your choice using a bathroom sponge. Allow to dry and then apply the paint through the star stencil. Distress the surface with coarse grade abrasive paper. When they are dry apply a layer of varnish.

3 The shelf was suspended from the ceiling to clear the sloping wall in this attic bathroom. Design and cut a simple symmetrical stencil design and apply to the shelf using bright colours. The edge of the shelf was then stencilled with a bright pattern. First, apply a layer of thinned-down warm terracotta acrylic straight into the grain of the untreated timber of the shelf and overstencil using bright primitive colours. Provide additional detail with upholstery nails. Keep the stencilled motif as rough and splodgy as possible

to give a rustic feel. The colours were chosen to match the Mexican pottery on the shelves.

4 The colourful collection of terracotta flower pots was stencilled with brightly hued acrylic paints. The colours were chosen with the traditional pottery of Mexico in mind. The pots could just as easily have been handpainted because acrylics are opaque enough to allow you to cover up any mistakes. First, give the pots a base coat of acrylic paint.

5 It is far easier when stencilling a curved and tapering object to make a stencil that fits it like a glove so that the paint is less likely to smudge or seep. To make the stencil, roll a large cone shape from a sheet of tracing paper, newspaper or scrap paper. Follow the top and bottom edges of the flower pot with a pencil or felt pen. Make light marks in pencil to show the position of the stencil then carefully

▲ Use abrasive paper to distress the wall.

▲ Make the stencil to fit the flower pots.

▲ Apply the paint using a sponge.

unwrap the paper, and you will have an exact template of the flower pot from which you can derive your stencil. Using the pencil marks as a guide, draw the stencil pattern onto some manila card, acetate or plan trace. Then use the scalpel and mat to remove the sections where you want the paint to come through onto the pot. Place the flower pot inside the stencil and apply the paint, using a bathroom sponge in a dabbing motion. When the paint is dry, add a little freehand detailing and leave to dry. To protect your ceramics, finish with a couple of coats of gloss varnish.

▲ Spray the window with matt varnish.

6 Obscure, or textured, glass is rarely attractive, and sandblasted glass is very expensive. On the other hand, matt car spray, when sprayed directly on to glass, gives a very plausible and attractive sandblasted effect. It is also durable and practical enough for most windows. Various effects similar to sandblasted glass can be achieved to give a good-looking alternative to textured or opaque glass bathroom windows. The stencilled window also solves a common problem in bathrooms – it is a very good idea to have glass that lets in light, while still being opaque enough to prevent you from being seen. One of the joys of this technique of stencilling on window glass is that when direct sunlight streams through the stencilled glass, the unsprayed areas creating the motif are projected perfectly onto the opposite wall. Re-use the stencils that you made for the wall. Mask the window frame and stick the motifs to the glass with non-permanent spray adhesive. Wearing a protective face mask gently spray the window with matt car spray.

HINTS & TIPS

• Many interesting effects can be achieved by using a variety of household items as a mask for your spray stencil pattern. Use paper doilies for lace-like effects, leaves for a forest-glade – even large paper clips can create interesting effects.

• This technique can be used for a variety of applications. If you prefer a Victorian-inspired bathroom, ordinary paper doilies will give a lace-like finish while leaves attached to the glass with a PVA adhesive will give you a ready-made forest glade. Panes of glass and mirrors can be bordered with the simple use of masking tape and a straight line. For example, a particularly elegant window above a front door can be stencilled with the number of the house. To do this, simply trace the existing brass number from the front door and make a mask from manila card. Then use a masking tape border to create a clear frame around the pane.

For further stencilling projects see:
Stencilled balustrade pp130–2; A kitchen frieze pp148–9; Stencilled cane chair pp160–1; Frottaged and stencilled screen pp167–9; Children's balloon stencils pp184–5; Poppies picture frame pp236–7; Monogrammed box pp244–5.

▲ Doilies can be used as stencils to create interesting effects.

Fish stencil shower glass

THE FISH STENCIL was not intended to bring a marine theme into this bathroom, rather it was selected because of its simplicity and its unusual appearance. Inspired by a slightly more complicated Art Deco design, it has been greatly simplified and is used modestly in order to break up one or two of the straight lines in the bathroom and soften the effect. There are two methods for frosting glass yourself, both very effective, much more cost effective than buying etched glass and readily available from craft shops. One method is to use sheets of sticky backed plastic in a frosted finish and to cut pieces carefully with a knife and apply them to clean glass. The second method, shown here, is a touch more professional and definitely longer lasting.

❖ YOU WILL NEED ❖

Design to copy

Manila card, acetate or plan trace

Marker pen or crayon

Scalpel (or cutting blade) and cutting mat

Repositionable spray mount

Scrap paper for masking

Frosting spray

1 Either make your own design or select one design from a book or piece of wrapping paper, making sure that it can be simplified into sections and enlarged on a photocopier if necessary. This fish design is already in sections and is extremely easy to work with.

2 Trace the image onto the plastic stencil material, simplifying the design, if necessary, as you go. You will see here that the eye and face area have been reduced into one part each.

3 Cut the stencil using a scalpel and cutting mat. Cut the smaller pieces out first then the larger ones so that the stencil remains firm. Take care not to split the stencil as this will cause leaks when the frosting spray is applied.

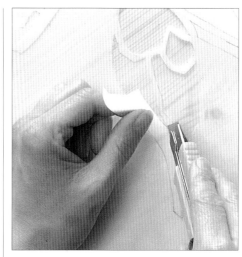

▲ Cut out the stencil with a scalpel.

4 Apply the stencil to the glass and hold it firmly in place using a repositionable spray mount. Make sure that it is correctly positioned on the glass and press it flat against the surface, smoothing out any wrinkles or bubbles which could spoil the effect.

▲ Select a design that can be easily simplified.

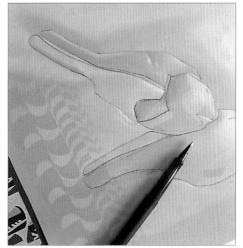

▲ Trace the image onto the stencil material.

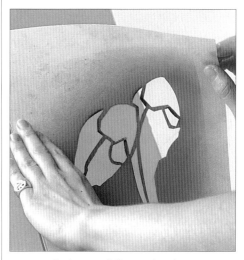

▲ Smooth the stencil flat on the glass.

193

▲ It is important to mask all around the stencil.

• The spray goes on almost clear and dries to a frosted finish. Let it dry for a few minutes before removing the stencil fully.

• You could also use the fish stencil to decorate your bathroom walls. Spray paints are perfect for a soft and misty stencil. Practise working them on a spare piece of paper or board first because every spray can acts differently in terms of how much paint is released when you press the button. Car paints are superb for painting directly onto tiles because the cellulose ingredients are long-lasting and water-resistant.

For further stencilling projects see:
Stencilled balustrade pp130–2; A kitchen frieze pp148–9; Stencilled cane chair pp160–1; Frottaged and stencilled screen pp167–9; Children's balloon stencils pp184–5; Poppies picture frame pp236–7; Monogrammed box pp244–5.

5 To protect the surrounding area from stray spray, mask it off with scrap paper. Spray the frosting solution through the stencil in short sharp bursts as lightly as possible. Leave it to dry for a few minutes then repeat.

6 Peel back a small corner of the stencil after a couple of minutes to check the depth of frosting you have produced. You may need to apply another coat so don't remove the stencil fully until you have achieved the effect that you want. Any errors can be removed by carefully scraping them away with a flat blade, but take care not to scratch the glass.

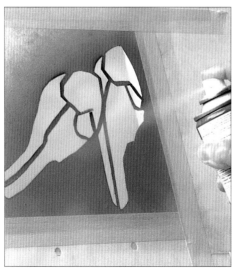

▲ Spray the paint in short bursts.

▲ Peel back the stencil and check the depth of the frosting.

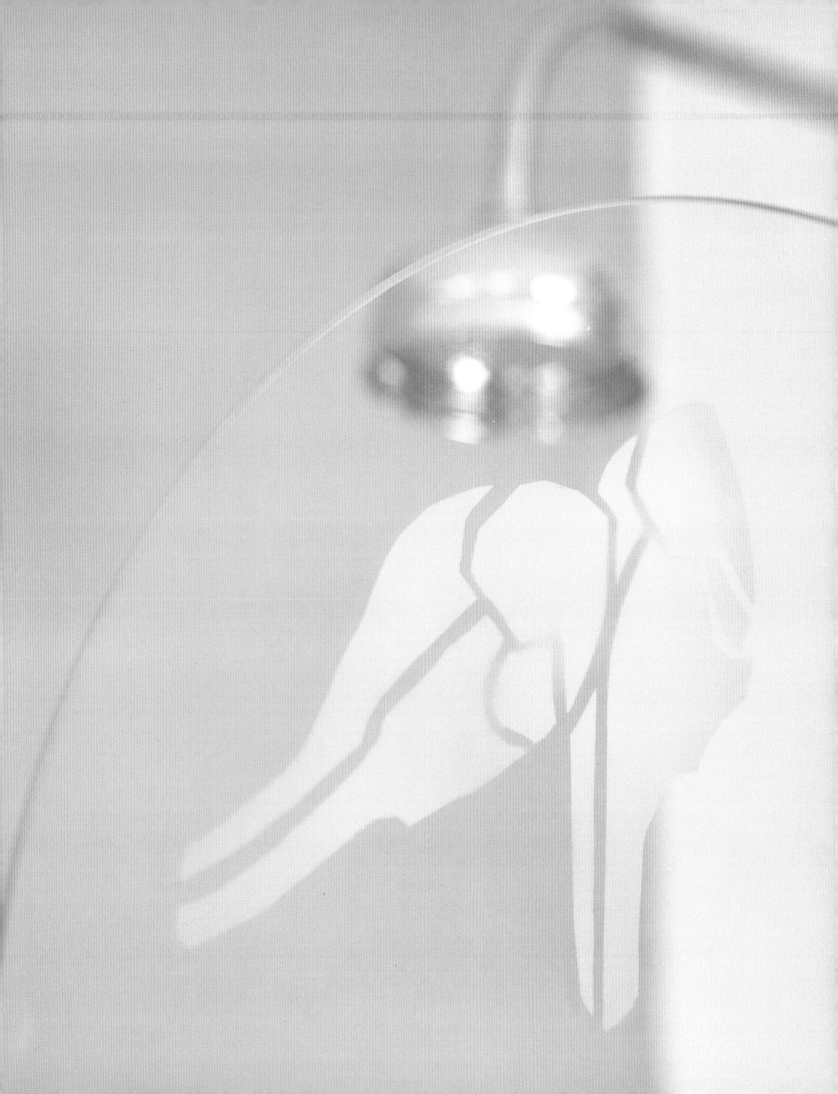

Limewashed bath panels

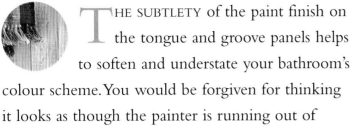

THE SUBTLETY of the paint finish on the tongue and groove panels helps to soften and understate your bathroom's colour scheme. You would be forgiven for thinking it looks as though the painter is running out of paint because that is exactly how this technique is carried out – using a half-loaded paintbrush. The pale colour used here is the same colour as the walls of the bathroom. Once the base coat of paint is complete, this effect takes very little time and is dry in minutes. It is therefore convenient for those forced to put the new-look bathroom back into service quickly. Of course, dry-brushing is not reserved exclusively for wood panels and can be transported onto any surface. It works just as well on panelled doors.

❖ YOU WILL NEED ❖

5cm (2in) household paintbrush

2 litres (½ gallon) of primer

2 litres (½ gallon) of base colour paint

3cm (1¼in) wide paintbrush

0.5 litre (⅒ gallon)
of paint for the streaks

Spare piece of wood

1 It is very important to prime the wood with a good quality waterproof primer before you start to paint it. Carefully prime right up to the edges, because raw paint will absorb moisture and eventually rot.

2 When the primer is dry, apply a good coat of paint in the chosen base colour. One coat will be sufficient if it is well-applied. Water-based low-sheen paint will work well if you are confident of the quality of the priming. Otherwise use an oil-based semi-gloss paint.

3 For the soft-brushed effect; dip the tip of a small paintbrush (about 3cm/1¼in wide) into a shallow tray of the lighter colour paint. The lid of the can is good for this. Wipe off any excess drips on the side of the can.

4 Tickle the brush up or down one of the planks of wood, following the direction of the grain. The brush will leave thin streaks. Turn it over and exhaust the paint on the other side as well before stroking it up and down gently to spread the paint

▲ Use the can lid as a paint tray.

streaks that you have just applied. You may like to test this step on a spare piece of wood before going on to the actual panels so that you can perfect your technique.

For further liming projects see:
Limed picture frame pp230–1.

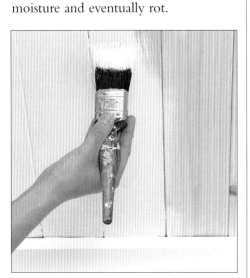

▲ Prime right up to the edges of the wood.

▲ Apply the base coat colour.

▲ Lightly streak the panels with your brush.

Decorative bathroom chests

EITHER OF THESE CHESTS would grace any bathroom and provide practical storage space for towels or toiletries. Their beauty lies in the subtlety of the paint effects that are used. In the first project, checks in cream and two tones of pink were painted on and left to dry before they were rubbed down with abrasive paper to produce the distressed finish. In the second project, a meandering ivy stencilled pattern in soft green adds an elegant touch to the small chest of drawers. The craft materials used are available from most craft shops.

Distressed chest

❖ YOU WILL NEED ❖

Abrasive paper

Tack rag

2.5cm (1in) base coat brush

Gouache paints in oyster pearl and blush

Ruler

Chalk

Masking tape

2.5cm (1in) and 1cm (½in) paintbrushes

Light and dark pink acrylic paint

Extender medium

Palette or old plate

Varnish

1 Rub down the chest and remove any dust with the tack rag. Remove the drawer knobs. Using the base coat brush, apply two or three coats of oyster pearl. Allow to dry.

2 Mark out the design with a ruler and chalk. Mask off the areas that are to be painted dark pink. With the 2.5cm (1in) brush, paint the dark pink checks with blush. Allow the paint to dry and then remove the tape.

3 Mask the areas that are to be painted light pink. Mix light pink acrylic paint with oyster pearl and blush and apply with a 2.5cm (1in) brush. Allow to dry and remove the tape.

4 Place some extender and blush paint on a palette. Load extender on to the 1cm (½in) brush, wipe the brush over the paint then blend the extender and blush paint on the palette. Paint this transparent pink on to the routed edges of the drawers, top of the chest and knobs.

5 Distress the chest by rubbing it down with wet abrasive paper. Allow to dry. Remove any dust with a tack rag then replace the knobs. Apply two or three coats of varnish.

For further ageing projects see:
Antiqued table pp104–5; Old oaAined floor pp113–15; Aged rustic chair pp212–13.

Stencilled chest

❖ YOU WILL NEED ❖

Abrasive paper

Tack rag

2.5cm (1in) base coat brush

Gouache paints in oyster pearl and colonial green

Manila card, acetate or plan trace

Fine point permanent marker

Scalpel (or cutting blade) and cutting mat

Masking tape

Stencil brush

Extender medium

Palette or old plate

Varnish

1 Sand the chest well, removing dust with a tack rag. Remove knobs. Using the base coat brush, apply two or three coats of oyster pearl, and allow the chest to dry between coats.

2 Tape the acetate over the stencilled mirror frame pattern on page 248 and trace the design with a marker pen. Using the scalpel, cut out the design.

3 Work out the position of the stencil, and tape it in position with masking tape. Start at the top drawer, and try to create an effect that looks natural.

4 Load a stencil brush with colonial green and dab off any excess. Apply paint in a circular motion.

5 To highlight the routed edge, drawers and top of the chest with a transparent green, place some extender and colonial green on the palette. Dab a flat brush into the extender then wipe it over the green.

6 Allow to dry for 24 hours. Replace the drawer knobs. Apply two or three coats of varnish.

For further stencilling projects see:
Stencilled headboard pp170–1.

Marble bathroom

SIT BACK IN YOUR BATHTUB and enjoy the flowing and relaxing movements of this simple paint effect that seems to swish and cascade down the walls. Low cost, low preparation and speedy, this is a super treatment for walls that are already painted or have paper on them that is still in good condition. This is not a lesson in how to imitate marble – good marbling takes more than a weekend to master. It is a decoration inspired by the look of natural marbles, but uses no glazes or specialist brushes. It is not even a very messy job.

❖ YOU WILL NEED ❖

3 x 1 litre (32fl oz) cans of semi-gloss finish paint in your chosen colours

3 flat paint trays

Bristle 'dusting brush' or a wide, bristle decorating brush

Spare piece of paper

Masking tape

1 Prepare the room for painting, by making sure that the walls are clean. Mask off any fixtures such as taps, light switches and the point at which the walls meet the ceiling. Prepare three flat trays of paint with only 1cm (½in) of paint in each. Semi-gloss paint is used here because it is water resistant when dry (and is excellent for bathrooms) and it dries more slowly than acrylic paint, offering more time for blending.

2 Starting with the darkest paint colour, dip the tip of the dusting brush into the tray. Do not overload the brush – if any paint drips from the brush, dab it off on a some paper before you start stippling.

3 Working in patches about 60cm (2ft) across, hold your brush with the long side following the direction of the intended 'flow'. Stipple the paint onto the wall with a sharp but light jabbing motion. Follow a general, wiggly diagonal flow. Go easy on the darkest shade. Avoid making any large or noticeable 'X' shapes. If you make any of these by mistake, quickly blend them out with the other shades.

4 When you have run out of paint on your brush, immediately dip the tip into the medium shade and apply some diagonally flowing lines to the wall, next to the dark lines. Blend the two colours together where they meet by dabbing the brush into the dark lines, which will still be wet, then back into the lighter shade.

5 Repeat the process with the lightest shade of paint (here it is white), filling in all the spaces and blending into both colours.

▲ Stipple on the lightest shade, blending it in.

6 Finally, stand back from the wall and check that your colours are well blended. Add extra lines in any shade where you think it necessary. Look out for any obvious marks left by the jabbing motion of your brush and gently stipple them away. Repeat steps 4 and 5, regularly stepping back to check your work and blending until all the walls are covered. Wash out the brush and remove the masking tape.

For further marbling projects see:
Marbled dressing table pp162–3; Marbled pot pp214–15.

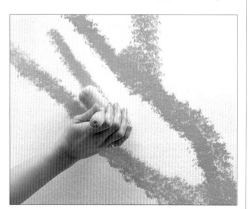
▲ Stipple the darkest colour onto the wall first.

▲ Move onto the medium shade immediately.

▲ Adjust the finish as necessary.

Renovating a neglected piece of furniture is a creative and economical way of adding character to your garden, whatever style of garden you have, be it a rambling natural wilderness or a tiny pot-filled patio, the projects in this section will fuel your imagination. Conservatories provide the perfect oppportunity to run wild with projects that might be too dramatic for the house or too fragile to withstand the elements all year round.

Garden & Conservatory Projects

Spray-painted table and chairs

Garden furniture has to withstand the elements and if it is not maintained well it can get into quite a state. However, renovation can save and rejuvenate an old tattered garden table and chair set. These white chairs were also rather uncomfortable, so a set of pretty cushions were added to help with the visual effect but also to make the chairs a more practical feature of the patio. The garden table was partly metal and partly wood, but luckily the anti-corrosive paint could handle both. A jaunty new tablecloth completed the smart final effect.

This table and chairs will be out in the elements so they will have to be treated with protective paint.

1 Give the metal a good wash in hot, soapy water then rub off any loose paintwork with steel wool.

2 When the metal is completely dry, treat the rust spots with rust remover and steel wool until the bare metal is gleaming.

3 Strip the table-top and then rub it down, first with some medium grade and then with some fine grade abrasive paper. Go over the surface with a tack rag to remove any dust. Prime the wood, painting as smoothly as possible and working in the same direction as the woodgrain.

4 When the primer is dry, rub it down lightly and tack once more. Then give it four or five applications of anti-corrosive paint. It is best to use spray paint because of the curly nature of wrought ironwork.

5 If the metal chairs are dirty or in bad condition, treat them in exactly the same way as the metal table legs. Once the rust has been treated, apply the same spray paint. First, turn the chairs upside down and spray all the surfaces you can see from that angle then turn them the right way up and repeat the process.

HINTS & TIPS

• A word of caution regarding spray paints, especially if you have had little or no experience of them: do follow the instructions carefully and don't attempt to put too much paint on at any one time or you will get runs or drips. Even so, with this type of paint the layers do have to be built up in fairly quick succession so that they can meld together before the paint begins to 'cure'.

• If possible, work outside on a wind-free day to paint and protect the area around where you are working.

For further table and chair projects see:
Tartan-band dining table pp100–1; Decorative chairs pp102–3; Antiqued table pp104–5; Freehand painted tables pp110–12; Scumble-glazed table pp122–3; Ivy-stamped chair pp150–1; Stencilled cane chair pp160–1; Aged rustic chair pp212–13.

▲ Rub down the wooden table-top.

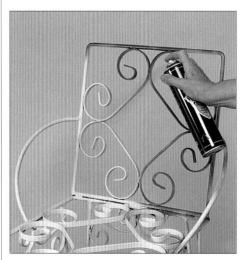

▲ Spray the wrought-iron chair thoroughly.

Hand-painted chest

THIS CHEST will probably be familiar to many of you as it comes from a well-known furnishing store and is very inexpensive. The draw arrangement on the chest is unusual and attempting individual decoration of each drawer could look uneven. One solution is to treat the piece as a whole and this design, with the help of a photocopier, fits neatly between the top and bottom of each drawer. It was adapted from a traditional Indian embroidery design and the red and white colouring gives it an appealing freshness. The design was transferred to the chest using a transfer paper, which comes in various colours. The red paper used here was close in colour to the paint and completely invisible once the chest had been lightly sanded. Ths project can be time-consuming but is not difficult – all you need is a steady hand.

❖ YOU WILL NEED ❖

Acrylic paint in deep red and white

Household paintbrushes

Fine grade abrasive paper

Masking tape

Pencil

Tracing paper

Transfer paper

Fine-pointed artists' paintbrush

Deep red artists' acrylic paint

Matt water-based varnish

Steel wool

Clear wax

Soft cloth

This chest came from a high-street furnishing store.

1 Paint the entire chest with two coats of red acrylic paint, allowing the first coat to dry thoroughly before applying the second. Then, when this is dry, paint two coats of white acrylic paint over the top of the chest.

▲ Sand the chest until the red shows through.

2 Rub the white paint lightly with sandpaper so that some red shows through, particularly around the edges of the chest. Link the two middle drawers with masking tape, avoiding the surface to be decorated. Repeat for the three top drawers. You will then be able to treat them as one surface.

3 Trace the design from the template (see page 248) and place the tracing paper in position on the chest. Slide a piece of transfer paper underneath and secure the design in place with masking tape. Transfer the design by drawing over it with a pencil. Do not remove the tracing paper until you have transferred the whole design, as it is difficult to reposition accurately. Continue for the remaining areas of the chest.

4 Using a fine-pointed artist's brush, carefully fill in the design with deep red acrylic paint.

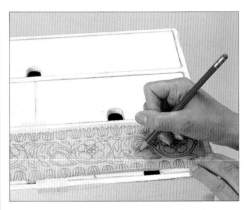
▲ Carefully trace your design onto the chest.

▲ Use a dark red paint to fill the design.

5 When the paint has dried thoroughly, rub it down lightly with steel wool to distress it. Finish the chest by brushing it with a coat of matt water-based varnish and applying a clear wax over this. Buff to a shine with a soft cloth.

For further freehand projects see:
Colour-washed oak sideboard pp98–9; Kitchen accessories pp138–41; Cups and saucers chair pp146–7; Painted frames pp232–3

Repeating border and dragged stripes

Unusual wall finishes below a dado can be extremely effective. A decorative border can be used to look like a dado. The design chosen to define this dado was a simplified 'egg and dart' motif, once common in wallpaper designs. Its close repeat means that awkward corners, such as those around a chimney breast, can be easily accommodated, without showing up any missed or botched repeats. Broad vertical stripes look attractive and can also be used as an effective device for increasing the height of a room but can sometimes be a little too bold if used over an entire wall. Restricted to the area below a dado rail, however, they add a note of old-world elegance and increase the feeling of space without overpowering the rest of the scheme.

❖ YOU WILL NEED ❖

Design to copy

Tracing paper

Manila card, acetate or plan trace

Scalpel (or cutting blade) and cutting mat

Spirit level

Pencil

Rubber

Tape measure

Warm grey artists' acrylic paint

Household paintbrushes

White flake artists' acrylic paint

Clear polyurethane varnish

Calculator

Stiff mounting card

Set square

Plumb line

Low-tack masking tape or manila card

Non-permanent adhesive spray

Oil-based glaze

Refined linseed oil

Raw umber oil pigment

Mineral turpentine

1 The first thing you need to do is to trace your dado design. The one used here was taken from a book of classical architectural mouldings. Photocopy it to a size that works well within the space available – in this case, it was 5cm (2in) high. The straight lines along the upper and lower edges prevent the border from looking messy or isolated on the wall.

2 Transfer the tracing onto manila card, acetate or plan trace, shade in and then cut out the 'negative' areas with a scalpel. Then cut a second stencil the same shape as the egg, but about 5mm (¼in) smaller all round.

3 Select the position on the wall where you want the dado to run. The traditional height of a dado, is exactly one-third of the height of

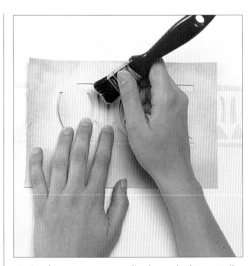

▲ Apply warm grey acrylic through the stencil.

the room. Adjust this to suit your particular room. Low ceilings will seem higher with a lower dado and a high ceiling can seem lower with a tall dado. Ensure that the dado clears any radiators and does not pass over the mantle shelf, or directly over the windows. Mark a line around the whole room in pencil using a spirit level to draw perfectly straight lines.

4 Because of the close repeat of the design, you can start applying the stencil at any point on the wall. Mix some warm grey acrylic with some of the background colour of the wall and apply with a stiff, dry brush leaving a light finish. After about 5 minutes go back to the beginning of each stencil and apply additional paint to the top to give a flat, darker area between the mouldings, which will look like shadow.

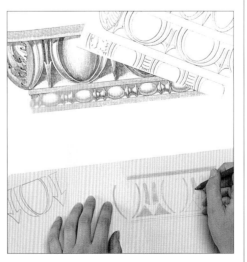

▲ Trace your stencil design.

▲ Highlight the bottom right area of each egg.

5 Mix some white flake with the wall colour acrylic to make the light-coloured paint that will form the highlights in the stencil pattern. Using a dry paintbrush, apply it through the second stencil, working from the bottom right to the top left, leaving less and less paint on the wall as you go. Finally, apply a coat of matt varnish.

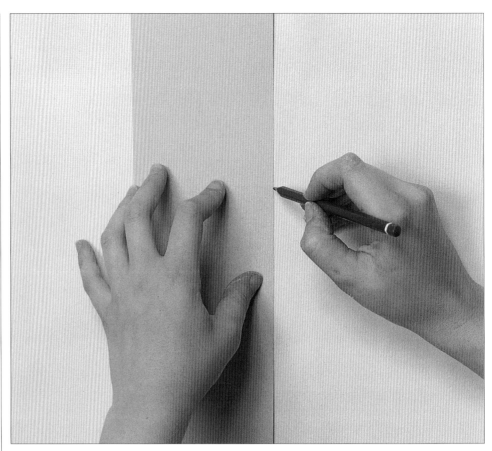

▲ Using the card template as a guide, lightly mark in the position of the stripes on the wall.

6 Calculate what size of stripe will fit best on to each wall. If the stripes are a subtle shade, they can accommodate being split on corners, though bolder colours where the stripes are very defined might require greater consideration.

7 Cut a piece of stiff mounting card to the width and height of the stripes. Use a set square to ensure that all the corners are right angles. Then use this as a template to mark out the stripes in pencil around the room, starting from the middle of the wall that will be most visible. Use a spirit level and plumb line as you work.

8 Mask off the edges of a few stripes using either low-tack masking tape (trimmed in half so as not to obscure neighbouring stripes) or manila card and non-permanent adhesive spray.

9 Mix an oil-based glaze, combining half a small tin of matt varnish with a dash of refined linseed oil, and some raw umber dissolved in turpentine.

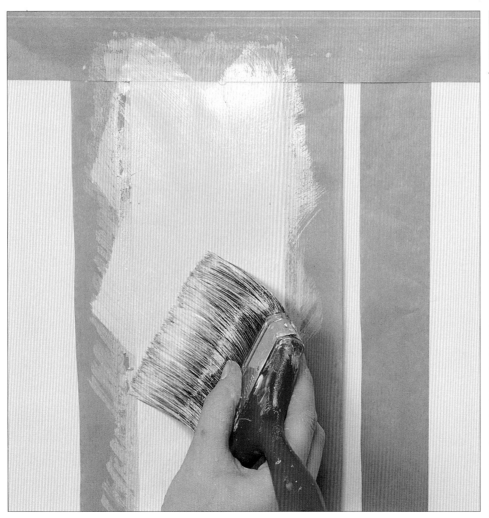

▲ Mask off the area around the stripes and apply the paint with a large paintbrush.

▲ Drag a coarse dry brush down through the glaze to give a worn texture.

the brush at a right angle to the wall. This dragging technique will produce lovely mellow stripes which have an attractive delicately 'worn' texture. If acrylic paint is used, seal with varnish.

HINTS & TIPS

• The easiest stripes are those that are equidistant or that have the same width for both the stripe and the space between.

• Ordinary masking tape, whatever the manufacturers may claim, can be very good at pulling off existing paintwork. Low-tack masking tape is not difficult to find from a good paint merchant, and is not only re-usable, but also very easy to apply in a straight line.

• Acrylic paint could obviously be used but, if you want to disguise a radiator in the paint scheme, you will need to use an oil paint or spray. No amount of coaxing will keep acrylic paint on a radiator for long.

• You could use other techniques with rags, sponges or plastic bags to create texture in the paint.

• If when you remove the tape or manila mask you find the glaze has seeped underneath and smudged, quickly remove the unwanted paint with a cotton bud soaked in mineral turpentine.

• It is always a good idea to start painting in an area that you know will be hidden by a piece of furniture. This will give you an opportunity to gain confidence before tackling the more visible areas such as alcoves on either side of the chimney breast.

• Because a varnish-based glaze was used on this project, an additional coat of varnish was not needed. But bear in mind that acrylic stripes are easily scuffed unless they are sealed with a tough matt or satin varnish.

10 Apply the glaze in short diagonal strokes working from the middle of the stripe outwards so that the brush is drier as it hits the tape.

11 While the glaze is still wet, go over the stripes again with a coarse dry brush, this time literally dragging the paint downward over the surface. While you work hold

For further wall projects see:
Chequered walls pp94–7; Colour-washed wall pp124–5; Painted panels pp133–5; A kitchen frieze pp148–9; A bedroom frieze pp172–4; Marble bathroom pp200–1.

Aged rustic chair

IT IS EASY TO IMAGINE this rustic Greek chair, with the worn paint cracked by the heat, being sat upon year after year by customers enjoying a glass or two of retsina outside a whitewashed taverna. Lovely Mediterranean blues were used for the chair – the colours were created by mixing cerulean blue and ultramarine powdered pigments with white acrylic paint. The chair would make a cheerful addition to a garden room or conservatory. Good results are achieved with both ordinary acrylic and traditional paint, but there can be a variation in the extent of cracking between different brands of paint and even different colours from the same manufacturer. Whichever paint you choose ensure it is not too thick and has a good flow.

❖ YOU WILL NEED ❖

Acrylic or traditional paint in 2 contrasting shades or white acrylic paint and 2 shades of powder pigment

Household paintbrushes

Crackle glaze medium

Medium grade abrasive paper

Sanding block

Matt water-based varnish

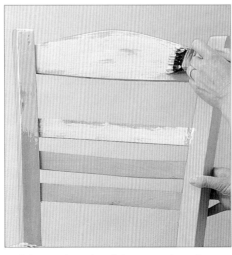
Bright colours gave this chair a Mediterranean look.

1 Paint the paler of the two colours on the chair rather patchily so that both bare wood and paint will be revealed beneath the cracks and add to the illusion of age. Leave to dry.

2 Brush on the crackle glaze. The thicker you apply it, the larger the cracks will be. Leave the chair to dry before applying the next coat of paint. The medium becomes more stable and easier to handle if you leave it for at least four hours or overnight.

3 Brush on the second darker paint colour, again in a random fashion, but covering most of the first colour. Try to work quickly and confidently and do not go over an area you have just painted more than once or you will reactivate the glaze and the paint will start to skid and slide. Wait for the paint to dry thoroughly then fill in any bits you have missed with more paint. Allow to dry.

4 Using medium grade abrasive paper wrapped around a sanding block, rub back the paint to reveal more of the base coat and soften out any hard edges. Seal with one or two coats of water-based varnish, working quickly so as not to activate the crackle medium. Allow the varnish to dry between coats. If you do not seal the surface and the chair gets wet, the paint surface will be disturbed.

▲ Brush on the crackle glaze.

For other ageing projects see:
Antiqued table pp104–5; Antiqued iron bed frame pp178–9; Distressed chest pp198–9.

▲ Paint on the paler of the two colours first.

▲ Rub back the paint to produce a worn look.

Decorated pots

TERRACOTTA POTS CAN be customized and given a more personal touch. The first project below shows you how to create a marbled effect and, unlike some marbling techniques, is extremely easy to achieve. The second project, a simple sponged finish will enhance a terracotta pot without drawing the eye away from the plant that it holds. Pots that are used outdoors should always be finished with an oil-based or weatherproof varnish or else all your hard work will be ruined by the rain. Remember, oil-based products can be used over water-based products, but you must never use a water-based product over an oil-based one.

Marbled pots

❖ YOU WILL NEED ❖

All-purpose water-based sealer

Household paintbrushes

Acrylic gouache paints in oyster pearl, warm beige, pearl white and carbon black

Glaze

Stencil brush

Cling wrap

Water-based satin varnish

1 Seal the pot both inside and out with the all-purpose sealer and allow it to dry completely.

2 Using a paintbrush, apply one or two coats of oyster pearl paint to the inside and outside of the pot, and allow to dry.

3 Next, you need to apply one generous coat of glaze to the outside of the pot.

4 On your palette, place warm beige, pearl white and carbon black. Be generous with your portions of paint, as this helps to maintain the same colour throughout.

5 Using the stencil brush, dab each colour at random over the outside of pot while the glaze is still wet.

6 To create the 'marbled' effect, wrap the pot in cling wrap. Press it to the pot and then remove it. Use the same cling wrap to rewrap the pot and press it again. Repeat until the desired effect has been achieved.

7 Allow the paint to dry for twenty-four hours and then apply two or three coats of satin varnish to protect the pot.

For further marbling projects see:
Marbled dressing table pp162–3.

Sponged pots

❖ YOU WILL NEED ❖

All-purpose water-based sealer

Household paintbrushes

Acrylic gouache paints in ocean blue, ultramarine light and pearl white

Sponge

Kitchen paper

Water-based satin varnish

1 Seal the pot both inside and out with the all-purpose sealer and allow it to dry completely.

2 Using a paintbrush, apply one or two coats of ocean blue to the inside and outside of the pot. Allow it to dry.

3 On your palette place some ocean blue, ultramarine light and pearl white paint. Be generous with your portions of paint, as this helps to maintain the same colour mix for the whole project.

4 Dab your sponge into the three colours, starting with the darkest colour. Blot the sponge once before applying it to the pot.

5 Dab the pot with the sponge. When reloading your sponge, blot it before applying it to the pot.

6 Leave the pot to dry for twenty-four hours and then apply two or three coats of satin varnish.

For further marbling projects see:
Marbled dressing table pp162–3.

Brightly coloured pots

A S TERRACOTTA is an absorbent porous surface, acrylic paint can be painted straight on to it. Bold colours have been used to jazz up these terracotta pots. The crackle glazed effect is an easy and fun way to use strong colours together – the red under the pink and the blue under the bright yellow, for example. It also creates an impression of age. Because acrylic paint dries quickly, it can always be repainted in a different colour if you are not happy with the final look. Once the pots have been varnished, they will be wipeable and hardwearing.

❖ YOU WILL NEED ❖

Acrylic paint in blue and yellow

Household paintbrush

Crackle glaze medium

Artists' paintbrush

Dead flat varnish

1 Apply a base coat of acrylic paint in your chosen base colour. Allow to dry and apply a second coat. The cracks will appear in the direction you apply the paint. Here the paint has been applied in brushstrokes around the pot.

2 Once the base coat is dry, apply the crackle glaze in the same direction as the base coat. For strong cracks, as shown here, allow the first coat of glaze to dry out completely, then apply a second coat.

3 Once the crackle glaze has completely dried, apply the top coat of acrylic paint in a contrasting colour in the same direction as before. Apply the paint in one sweeping motion and do not go back over an area that has just been painted – this will pull the glaze off and ruin the effect. If this does happen, let it dry, then start again. Use enough paint just to cover the area and allow to dry. Large cracks will start to appear.

▲ Apply the crackle glaze.

4 Line the rim of the pot once it is dry. Apply a new base coat. Leave it to dry then apply a coat of crackle glaze, followed by the top coat. Use a small artists' brush to create an even finish. Leave the pot to dry, then apply two coats of dead flat varnish, allowing each coat to dry.

For further crackle projects see:
Aged rustic chair pp212–13.

▲ Paint the first base coat.

▲ Paint on a contrasting colour.

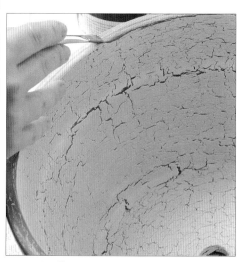

▲ Finish off with an artists' paintbrush.

Painted tablecloth

A RED AND WHITE check tablecloth brings a cheerful touch to dining alfresco. Made from medium weight canvas, this tablecloth is marked out with a grid pattern and then painted with fabric paint. This is a no-sew cloth – the edges are turned under with double-sided bonding film, or, for an even simpler method, you could fray the edges. Eyelets are hammered in on the corners so that you can hang weights to ensure the cloth will stay put in a strong wind. Stones with natural holes worn in them will keep the cloth still. A string of shells is purely decorative, but gives the right feel. Or, you could buy some heavy beads and use them instead. Keep the cloth in the car for when you come across one of those opportune picnic spots.

❖ YOU WILL NEED ❖

350g (12oz) cotton duck canvas

Scissors

Tape measure

Pencil

Straightedge

Fabric paint

Glass jar

Household paintbrush

Iron

Spare piece of material

Double-sided bonding film

Black felt pen

Eyelets

Eyelet cutting tool

Hammer

Stones

String

1 Cut the cotton duck canvas into a square. The easiest way to do this is by folding the cloth diagonally, to make a triangle, then cutting along the raw edge.

2 Mark the cloth along the edge every 10cm (4in). Then use a straightedge to draw lines across the cloth, joining the marks lightly with a pencil. This will produce the check pattern and will give you a guide when painting.

3 Use the fabric paint container as a measure to water down the fabric paint in a glass jar, in the proportion 1 part paint to 6 parts water. Diluting the paint in this way will make it easier to use and it will also go further. Using a thinned down paint mix also means that you can create interesting shades where two blocks of colour overlap.

▲ Mark outlines with a pencil.

4 Use a wide paintbrush and follow the pencil guidelines to apply the paint in rough stripes, working first in one direction across the fabric. The paint will sit on the surface of the canvas to begin with, so you may need to work it in to the fabric a bit with the brush.

▲ Cut the cloth to the right size and shape.

▲ Paint one set of stripes across the cloth.

▲ Paint the second set of stripes on.

5 When you have finished one lot of vertical stripes, allow them to dry completely then paint the rest of the stripes at right angles to create a checked effect.

6 Seal the paint with a hot iron when it is dry following the paint manufacturer's instructions. Place a clean cloth over the tablecloth so as not to scorch it. Make sure that you iron over the whole tablecloth.

▲ Iron over the whole cloth through another piece of material to seal the paint.

▲ Iron a hem in place using double-sided bonding film.

7 Turn under a 3cm (1in) hem all the way round onto the wrong side of the tablecloth and press in place with double-sided bonding film to give a neat edge that will not fray. Then turn the tablecloth the right side up and use a felt pen or fabric pen, to outline the squares where the two lines of paint cross; this outline does not have to be precise. A rough look will fit in with the intended final effect of rustic simplicity.

▲ Outline the squares where the stripes meet.

▲ Insert an eyelet in each corner of the cloth.

8 Draw a freehand leaf in the centre of each marked square. Alternatively, if you are not confident when drawing freehand, use a stencil or stamp, or appliqué a fabric design on to the cloth. Insert an eyelet in each corner of the tablecloth. Mark the position with a pencil and use the tool supplied with the eyelets to cut the hole. Thread string or raffia through the eyelet and hang stones collected from the beach that have natural holes, large beads, or any small heavy objects that will anchor the tablecloth down in the wind.

▲ Thread stones through the eyelets to act as anchors.

HINTS & TIPS

• On some fabrics, watering down fabric paint will give an attractive watery edge to the paint, similar to that of watercolour paint on paper.

• If the fabric is too thick to hammer the eyelet through, snip it away with a pair of scissors until the hole is big enough to take the eyelet.

For further fabric painting projects see:
Stencilled animal prints pp175–7.

GARDEN & CONSERVATORY PROJECTS

Details matter and each of the small items featured in this chapter will add a finishing touch to your home that has more impact than anything you could buy ready-made. Most of the projects can be completed in a relatively short time, and the basic objects can be picked up in markets and junk shops at little cost. Why not make one as a unique and personal gift to let a friend know how special they are? Your thoughtfulness will be long remembered.

Gift & Accessory Projects

Tortoiseshell lamp

THERE ARE MANY wonderful ways of using varnishes to make tortoiseshell effects that are almost indistinguishable from the real thing. This method is blatantly faux, but it is great fun to do and gives a smart new finish to the elderly base and the brand new lampshade. The lamp base was beautifully turned and had a fascinating, red bakelite switch, but it was also covered in layers and layers of green paint that had to be stripped off. If you don't like the rich effect of gold on tortoiseshell, you could try a dark brown or even a white trim.

❖ YOU WILL NEED ❖

Fine grade abrasive paper

Tack rag

Primer

2 x 4cm (1½in) household paintbrushes

Warm, light yellow semi-gloss paint

Artists' oil paints in raw umber, burnt sienna, light red and black

Transparent oil glaze

Palette or old plate

Artists' paintbrushes

Mineral turpentine

Palette knife

Badger-hair softener brush

Gold bronzing powder

Acrylic varnish

Mid-sheen, clear, satin polyurethane varnish

The lamp base had to be stripped of old paint before it could be given the tortoiseshell treatment.

1 Strip the lamp base and, when it is dry, rub down with fine grade abrasive paper and dust with a tack rag. Paint the base and lampshade with primer and allow to dry. Apply three coats of semi-gloss paint, leaving 24 hours between coats and rubbing down and tacking after each application.

2 Lay out each of the oil paints and a tablespoonful of transparent oil glaze on the palette. Using an artists' brush, mix a little of the raw umber oil paint with some turpentine and then add some transparent oil glaze with a palette knife. When this mixture is well integrated, add a few drops more of turpentine until the glaze is about the consistency of milk. Paint this glaze on to the lampshade in random squiggly lines, which move in a diagonal direction, leaving patches of the base colour showing through.

3 Make up the other glazes in the same way. Apply burnt sienna glaze along the same diagonals as the raw umber, but in separate, broad, curly strokes. Dab on a light red glaze sparingly in little groups of two or three brushstrokes. Then, using the black glaze sparingly, paint on small groups of curly, comma-shaped brushstrokes. Use the softener brush to soften the overall effect and blend the colours into each other, brushing the glaze gently up and down the diagonals, only just allowing the bristles to touch the glaze. Imagine another set of diagonals in the other direction, and lightly brush up and down these until the colours begin to merge.

4 Leave to dry for 24 hours and then mix some of the gold bronzing powder into a little acrylic varnish. Paint this mixture around the binding of the lampshade and pick out some of the moulding on the base. When the gold is dry give the whole piece a coat of satin varnish.

For other lamp projects see:
Craquelure lamp base pp116–18.

▲ Apply small black comma-shaped marks.

▲ Soften the effect with a badger-hair brush.

Malachite painted box

S MALL WOODEN BOXES are quite easy to find at a reasonable cost. Often gifts such as wine and cigars are packed in wooden boxes that can be totally transformed. Boxes can be finished in many ways, such as by applying stencilling, hand-painted designs, découpage, paint techniques and distressing, to personalize them as gifts. This project shows you how to produce a wonderful sheen finish simulating the polished-stone effect of malachite. The technique requires some work but the end result is well worth the effort.

❖ YOU WILL NEED ❖

Screwdriver

Fine grade abrasive paper

Tack rag

Rabbit skin glaze

Pot that fits into the saucepan

Saucepan

Sieve

Gilders' whiting

Small paintbrush

Soft brush or mop for applying gesso

Sealer or primer

Varnish

Raw linseed oil

Mineral turpentine

Pale sea green oil-based semi-gloss paint

Pencil

Straightedge

Transparent oil glaze

Artists' oil pigment in viridian and burnt sienna

Liquid driers

Piece of stiff card

A roughly finished wooden box is ideal for transforming from its raw state into a beautiful gift.

1 If possible, take the lid and the hinges off the box before you start so that it is easier to work on. If it has a lock, you may be able to remove this too. Thoroughly rub down the surfaces with abrasive paper and wipe over with a tack rag to remove any dust.

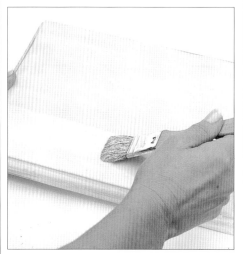

▲ Apply the gesso in quick, straight strokes.

2 Gesso is the key ingredient for this technique. The recipe for gesso is 1 part rabbit skin size to 16 parts water (by volume). Whiting is added later. Place the size in a suitable container with 6 parts of water. Let this stand for two hours. Add the remaining water, then place the pot in a saucepan of hot water on a low heat until melted. Take off the heat, put aside a small amount of size and then sieve gilders' whiting into the remaining warm size. Keep adding whiting until it is about 6mm (¼in) below the surface of the size, and gently stir (the consistency should be that of single cream). Leave in the fridge overnight.

3 Using a brush, apply the size (the original mixture that you have put aside before adding whiting) to all the surfaces of the box. Allow to dry overnight. Warm the gesso in a saucepan of hot water on a low heat to blood heat. Using a soft brush, apply a

▲ Rub down the gesso surface.

coat of gesso in quick, straight, brush strokes. Look along the surface and, as soon as the sheen has disappeared, apply the next coat by stippling on with the soft brush, still maintaining the gesso at blood heat. Apply more coats of gesso as the sheen disappears, stippling every other coat until you have applied at least five coats. Allow to dry for 24 hours.

▲ Apply at least two coats of pale green base coat.

4 Carefully rub down the surfaces with fine abrasive paper to a smooth finish – this makes a mess, so do it somewhere that is easy to clean and away from where you are going to do any painting.

5 Apply a coat of sealer or primer with a mixture of varnish (part by volume), mineral turpentine (part by volume) and raw linseed oil (one half-part by volume). Leave to dry completely overnight.

6 'Denib' all surfaces (lightly rub down with fine abrasive paper). Apply at least two coats of oil-based pale sea-green semi-gloss paint, allowing to dry overnight between each. You need to rub down the surface lightly with fine abrasive paper and remove any dust between coats.

7 Using a pencil and a small straightedge, mark out irregular sections covering each surface of the box.

▲ Draw uneven sections with a pencil.

▲ Use a piece of card to emulate malachite.

▲ Define the edges of the shapes by wiping with a clean rag.

10 Wipe the box with a clean, dry cloth. Apply a coat of gloss varnish; allow to dry overnight and then gently rub the surface with a fine finishing glasspaper. Repeat until you have a high gloss shine (this may take several coats). Do not rub down the final coat.

HINTS & TIPS

- The inside of the box can be finished with a contrasting colour such as deep red or a complementary colour such as black, or lined with a fabric of your choice.

- It may be a good idea to have a piece of genuine malachite, or a photograph of the stone next to you as you work, to help you create a realistic effect.

For further stone effect projects see:
Marbled dressing table pp162–3; Verdigris mirror and door handles pp188–9; Marble bathroom pp200–1; Tortoiseshell lamp base and shade pp224–5.

8 Mix a rich green colour, using transparent oil glaze and viridian pigment, with just a touch of burnt sienna to sage the green slightly and stop it being too blue. Make the gilp with 1 part oil, 2 parts mineral turpentine and 5 drops of driers. Then thin the glaze slightly with the gilp.

9 Using a paintbrush, apply glaze to alternate sections that have no adjoining edges. Take a piece of stiff card and, using a straightedge, tear off a piece slightly larger than the section marked. Drag this piece of card through the glaze with a shaky movement to emulate the lines and swirls that are so characteristic of malachite. Vary the direction of each separate section when dragging through the glaze to create a realistic effect of malachite stone. Use a straightedge and clean rag to wipe the excess glaze back to the drawn shape. Let the glaze dry thoroughly overnight. The following day continue to fill in the remaining shapes, wiping back the excess glaze as before. Allow to dry overnight. Continue until all the sections have been filled in.

▲ Varnish the painted box until you have a high gloss shine.

Limed picture frame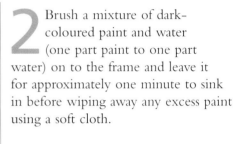

THE TECHNIQUE OF LIMING has been used on furniture for centuries, originally to protect it from fungus and insects, then later as a decorative effect. The caustic properties of lime make it very unkind to skin, so nowadays we use a white pigment added to wax. It is possible to buy a water-based liming paste and, if you can get hold of this, follow the same instructions as below but apply the clear wax after you have removed the excess paste. Liming is a traditional way to treat oak, which is often very dark and has a marked and open grain. However, the technique can be used very effectively on pine if it is first brushed with a wire brush and then colourwashed with paint or stained with wood dye. Choose a dark colour to contrast with the white liming wax.

❖ YOU WILL NEED ❖

Wire brush

Dark-coloured acrylic or traditional paint

Household paintbrush

Two soft cloths

Liming wax

0000-grade steel wool

Clear wax

Liming will give this pine picture frame an attractive decorative finish and a more aged appearance.

1 Open up the grain on the wood by brushing the surface of the picture frame vigorously with a wire brush, always brushing in the direction of the grain. This could take about 15 minutes.

2 Brush a mixture of dark-coloured paint and water (one part paint to one part water) on to the frame and leave it for approximately one minute to sink in before wiping away any excess paint using a soft cloth.

3 When the paint has completely dried, apply the liming wax to the surface using steel wool. This will tone down the colour of the paint. Leave it for at least half an hour or until it is dry.

4 Using steel wool, rub the surface of the frame with clear wax to remove the excess liming wax. Leave the wax to dry for about half an hour and then buff the frame to a shine with a soft cloth.

For further liming projects see:
Limewashed bath panels pp196–7.

▲ Rub down the wood with a wire brush.

▲ Remove the excess paint with a cloth.

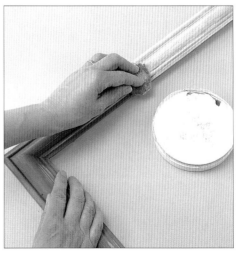

▲ Apply the liming wax over the paint.

Painted frames

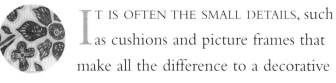

It is often the small details, such as cushions and picture frames that make all the difference to a decorative scheme. Picking out a pattern or theme throughout a room can create a feeling of continuity and harmony. If you have a couple of hours to spare and a fabric design that you would like to reflect in other areas of your home, then decorating simple

picture frames may be the answer. Plain, flat picture frames are easiest to work with and they are readily available. Choose small frames that are not too daunting in size because they will not take too long to complete. Before you start work, spend some time studying the fabric and picking out the detail of the design. If you want to use it at a different size, use a photocopier to reduce or enlarge it.

Chequered frame

❖ YOU WILL NEED ❖

Fine grade abrasive paper

Tack rag

Acrylic paint in the colours of your choice to match the fabric

Small household paintbrush

Fabric to copy design

Masking tape

Ruler

Artists' paintbrush

Blue marker pen

Clear varnish

1 Strip and rub down the frame with fine grade abrasive paper, then remove any dust with a tack rag. Paint the frame using a background colour that matches the background on the fabric. Use the masking tape to create the straight lines. The fabric will provide a template so that you can position the tape at intervals of the correct width.

2 Leave to dry, then draw in the dark blue lines with a marker pen and a ruler. Apply a protective coat of clear varnish.

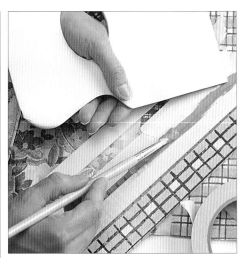

▲ Copy the fabric pattern on to the frame.

Periwinkle frame and box

❖ YOU WILL NEED ❖

Acrylic paint in colour of fabric background

Fabric to copy design

Scissors

Carbon paper

Small and very fine artists' paintbrushes

Artists' paint in the colour of your choice

1 Paint the frame and box to match the background of the fabric and leave to dry completely. Then cut out sections of the fabric and trace the design directly onto the frame with carbon paper.

2 First, the pale blue outlines of the flowers were painted on using a small soft artists' brush. The centre of each flower was filled with a deep-blue acrylic colour and, finally, the detail was copied onto each flower and leaf using a tiny brush, referring to the fabric all the time.

▲ Trace the pattern directly onto the frame.

Golden pear picture frame

THE TRADITIONAL TECHNIQUES of folk art painting (see Hints and Tips below) can be used to great effect to create beautiful painted picture frames. Some of the techniques are complicated but with practice they can be mastered even if you have no prior painting experience. The golden pear design on a deep red background used here will make a luscious frame for a mirror or painting. You can choose colours that fit in with your decor and suit the picture that will eventually sit in your customized frame.

❖ YOU WILL NEED ❖

Fine grade abrasive paper

Acrylic paints in Indian red oxide, yellow oxide, Turner's yellow, pine green, moss green, warm white, burnt umber, naphthol red light

All purpose sealer

Sponge

Tracing paper

Carbon paper

Stylus

Piece of chalk

Flat paintbrush

Old toothbrush

Liner brush

Masking tape

Crackle glaze medium

Water-based satin varnish and brush

1 Lightly sand the frame and mix one part Indian red oxide with one part sealer. Apply one coat with the sponge. Sand again and apply one unmixed coat of Indian red oxide.

2 Draw the pear pattern freehand and apply it to one side of the frame with carbon paper and a stylus. Add the pattern to the opposite side, top and bottom of the frame.

3 Using a piece of chalk, draw a line to divide each side of the frame in half lengthways. With the flat brush, float burnt umber on the inside edge of this line. Then float around the edge of the pear motif with burnt umber. Double load the flat brush with pine green and moss green, and paint the leaves on either side of the pears. Do not paint the leaves in between the pears at this stage.

4 Base coat the dark pears with yellow oxide and the light pears with Turner's yellow. To shade the pears, load the flat brush with the base colour and then pick up a small amount of Indian red oxide on one corner. Blend them by brushing up and down on your palette until you have a soft graduation of colour from dark to light on the brush. Highlight the pears by loading the brush in the base colour and then picking up warm white on one corner and blending.

5 Reinforce the shading and highlighting by dry brushing some base colour and Indian red oxide over shaded areas and some base colour and warm white on highlighted areas.

6 Dry brush on napthol red light to add a blush to the light pears and add moss green to the dark pears. Use an old toothbrush to lightly spatter Indian red oxide over the pears.

7 Paint the pear stalks with the liner brush loaded with yellow oxide and Indian red oxide lightly blended but not thoroughly mixed. Add small liner brush strokes with burnt umber to the bottom of the light pears.

8 Mask off the inner half of the frame and use a sponge to apply a coat of crackle medium to the outer part, avoiding the pears. When

▲ Give the pears a rosy glow with shading.

the crackle medium is dry, use the sponge to apply another coat of Indian red oxide. Remove the tape, allow the cracking to dry and then apply two or three coats of satin varnish with the varnish brush.

HINTS AND TIPS

Folk art paint techniques will enable you to create exquisite paint finishes:

• Loading: Stroke the brush through the paint on the palette and then stroke the brush on a clean part of the palette until the paint has worked through the brush.

• Double loading: Load the brush fully with one paint colour, then stroke the brush through the second colour.

• Floating: Allows you to add shading to your design. Dip the brush in water and then dip one corner of the brush into the paint. Stroke the brush along your palette so that the paint gradually fades out across the bristles.

For further frame projects see:
Porphyry picture frame pp106–7; Gilded mirror frame pp119–21; Limed picture frame pp230–1; Painted frames pp232–3; Poppies picture frame pp236–7.

Poppies picture frame

POPPIES CONJURE UP the quintessential hazy feeling of a high summer's day. In this project, the combination of yellow ochre, deep purple, red and fiery orange creates a harmonious warm atmosphere. Spiky leaves, curvaceous poppy flowers with dark seductive centres, rounded seed heads, gently bending buds and bumble bees fuse to form a sympathetic union of shapes. Together the colours and shapes convey the feeling of walking through a golden field of corn, dotted with the richness of red and orange wild flowers.

❖ YOU WILL NEED ❖

All in one primer/undercoat

Yellow ochre acrylic paint

Artists' acrylic paint in burnt umber, orange, deep red and fiery orange

Acrylic glaze

Large artists' paintbrush

Paper cut-outs of poppies

Tracing paper

Manila card, acetate or plan trace

Scalpel (or cutting blade) and cutting mat

Non-permanent adhesive spray

Small household paintbrush

Clear varnish

1 Paint the frame with all-in-one primer/undercoat. Leave to dry, then paint two layers of yellow ochre acrylic paint.

2 Mix up a wash, the consistency of single cream, using a burnt umber acrylic and acrylic glaze. Gently apply the wash with big brush strokes, working across the frame to give it a hint of colour.

3 Plan the position of the stencils over the frame using paper cutouts. Move the shapes around until you are happy with the design. Apply the large poppy stencils in the corners of the frame and add the other elements in a random pattern. Start with the larger shapes to get the pattern going and fill in the gaps with the smaller ones.

4 Trace the final design for the background pattern and transfer to the stencil card. Use a scalpel to cut out the stencil. Hold in place over the frame with non-permanent adhesive spray and apply the paint.

5 For the large poppy stencil, make three seperate stencils, one for each colour used in the design. Stencil on each colour one at a time. To position the stencils accurately on the frame, slide them into position under a tracing of the whole poppy shape, then remove the tracing paper.

6 Finish the frame by painting the inner and outer edges in a rich red colour to give the sides definition. Allow the paint to dry, then apply two protective coats of varnish.

HINTS & TIPS

• When using two colours within the same shape, work from opposite ends of the stencil. Combine the colours in the middle with a different brush to keep the tones clean and clear.

For further stencilling projects see:
Stencilled balustrade pp130–2; Cups and saucers chairs pp146–7; A kitchen frieze pp148–9; Stencilled cane chair pp160–1; Frottaged and stencilled screen pp167–9; A bedroom frieze pp172–4; Cherub wardrobe pp180–3.

▲ Use paper cut-outs to plan the design.

▲ Line up the poppy stencils using a tracing.

▲ Use an artists' paintbrush to apply the paint.

Newspaper rack

THIS EVERYDAY PIECE was given a makeover in no time at all. It should take no more than a couple of hours to complete the work (plus drying time). Stencilling is used as the main technique with a little pen work added to give the design extra definition. Glued-on pieces of newspaper are added as a finishing touch to complete the overall effect. This newspaper rack is intended to be less flowery and feminine than many stencils, and would be suitable as a gift for a man or a woman. For a truly individual touch, you can choose items such as charts and headlines from newspapers that the person who will receive the gift actually reads. Of course, the same techniques could be adapted for any container.

❖ YOU WILL NEED ❖

Piece of paper

Pencil

Pile of books or design to copy

Artists' acrylic paint in colours of your choice

Household paintbrushes

Tracing paper

Manila card, acetate or plan trace

Scalpel (or cutting blade) and cutting mat

Non-permanent adhesive spray

Stencil brush

Spirit-based marker pen

Old newspapers or magazines

PVA adhesive and adhesive brush

Clear varnish

1 Plan your design on paper. Then either draw your stencil design yourself by copying a pile of real books or photocopy an image from a book or magazine, to the correct size. Colour the final photocopy as you want the stencil to look so that you can refer to this as a template as you work.

2 Use tracing paper to transfer the design on to a piece of manila card or acetate. Carefully cut out the stencil design using a scalpel on a cutting mat. Start by removing the smaller areas to keep the stencil as firm as possible. Hold the stencil in place on the newspaper rack with non-permanent adhesive spray. Apply the paint with a stencil brush in a dabbing motion. Carefully peel away the stencil.

3 Outline every section using a spirit-based marker pen to make them stand out more.

4 Cut out headlines or charts from a newspaper or magazine and glue them onto the rack.

5 Once the adhesive and paint are dry varnish the entire surface. Apply several coats to prevent the newspaper from peeling off.

HINTS & TIPS

• Make the pages look dirty by adding a little darker paint from a stiff, almost-dry, brush, on top of the white background and following the line of the pages.

• You could use a commercial stencil, but it is much cheaper and more satisfying to design one yourself.

For further stencilling projects see:
Stencilled balustrade pp130–2; A kitchen frieze pp148–9; Stencilled cane chair pp160–1; Frottaged and stencilled screen pp167–9; Children's balloon stencils pp184–5; Monogrammed box pp244–5.

▲ Cut out items from newspapers.

▲ Detail of the book stencil.

Ethnic stamped CD box

STAMPING IS AN EXCELLENT WAY of creating repeating patterns over surfaces. A block stamp is particularly well suited to a simple, rustic look. The decorative effect should come from repeating motifs, rather than from complex shapes. This CD box was customized as a gift for a friend, basing the stamp design on a piece of the fabric that was used in the living room. A stamp was made for each of the two basic elements of the fabric design, one checked with a zig-zag border and the other was a sinuous curving plant stem. The curvy part of the design was used to accent the top and sides of the box. The colours used exactly echo the dyes on the fabric and attractive little brass handles were added to each drawer as a finishing touch.

❖ YOU WILL NEED ❖

Design to copy (optional)

Tape measure

Pencil

Tracing paper

Piece of rubber

Scalpel (or cutting blade) and cutting mat

Piece of foam

Two wooden base blocks

PVA adhesive

Scrap paper

Bathroom sponge

Artists' acrylic paints in burnt sienna and black

▲ Select a simple pattern to copy.

1 You can either design your own stamp pattern, take your inspiration from a book or, as in this case, an attractive piece of fabric. Plan how large the stamp will need to be to cover the CD box. It may help if you lightly mark out the positions of the stamps with a pencil.

2 Photocopy your design to the correct size if necessary. Then make a tracing of it and transfer the pattern to a piece of rubber and cut out the design with a scalpel. Use PVA adhesive to apply a piece of foam to a wooden block. Stick the cut-out pieces of rubber on to the foam, press firmly in place and leave to dry.

3 Test each stamp on a piece of scrap paper before you use it. Use a piece of bathroom sponge to coat the stamp evenly with artists' acrylic paint, then turn the stamp over and press firmly down. Adjust if necessary. Once you are satisfied with the pattern, cut away the extra foam. Then use the same technique to stamp the box.

For further stamping projects see:
Sponge-stamped floor pp128–9; Ivy-stamped chair pp150–1.

▲ Cover the stamps evenly in paint.

▲ Detail of stamped drawer.

Stencilled mirror frame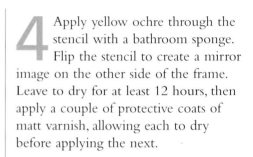

THIS MIRROR FRAME is an excellent project for beginners who have not attempted many paint effect projects before and it will delight the recipient if it is given as a gift. It is quick and easy to make. The starting point is a very simple mirror frame made of untreated pine. Before buying the mirror, check that it hasn't been treated or varnished in any way. For such a down-to-earth object, the rough finish of stencilling can be used to create a 'rustic' or 'countrified' look. The simple outline of the ivy leaf is ideal for a stencil, and the long undulating stalks perfect for decorating tall narrow areas. Mellow colours were used for a subtle effect. The position of each leaf and the regular curves of the stalk were calculated to fit in to the rectangular frame.

❖ YOU WILL NEED ❖

Fine grade abrasive paper

Tack rag

Pale stone low-sheen acrylic paint

Yellow ochre artists' acrylic paint

Paint kettle or saucer (for mixing paints)

Bathroom sponge

Pencil

Manila card, acetate or plan trace

Scalpel (or cutting blade) and cutting mat

Ruler

Non-permanent adhesive spray

Household paintbrush

Clear polyurethane varnish

1 Lightly sand the frame with the abrasive paper to remove any roughness. Remove any dust with a tack rag, then apply two coats of low-sheen acrylic paint.

2 Mix a little yellow ochre with the acrylic and apply to the frame with a sponge. When the new colour is completely dry, gently distress it by rubbing down lightly with abrasive paper to achieve a subtle clouded finish. Remove any dust with a tack rag.

3 Draw the ivy-leaf design on acetate and cut out the shape with a scalpel to form the stencil. Divide the length of the frame by the length of a leaf and stalk to calculate the number of leaves and stalks that will fit. Lay the stencil design on the mirror frame and pencil in each leaf then connect each with a curved stalk.

4 Apply yellow ochre through the stencil with a bathroom sponge. Flip the stencil to create a mirror image on the other side of the frame. Leave to dry for at least 12 hours, then apply a couple of protective coats of matt varnish, allowing each to dry before applying the next.

HINTS & TIPS

• Take care when cutting out and handling the stencil that the acetate does not tear as this could cause the paint to leak out beyond the outline of the stencil.

• Do not overload the sponge with paint when stencilling.

For further stencilling projects see:
Stencilled balustrade pp130–2; Cups and saucers chair pp146–7; A kitchen frieze pp148–9; Stencilled cane chair pp160–1; Frottaged and stencilled screen pp167–9; A bedroom frieze pp172–4; Cherub wardrobe pp180–3.

▲ Apply yellow ochre with a sponge.

▲ Draw the ivy-leaf design.

▲ Sponge yellow ochre through the stencil.

Monogrammed box

THIS IS AN IDEAL personalized present and it is particularly appropriate as a wedding gift, since the initials of the couple can be combined in the monogram. The starting point was a very ordinary little box to which a few coats of dark oak varnish had been applied. Because the box lid was quite small, simple classic letters were used, but made

more interesting by making the 'S' curve and snake around the straight lines of the 'H'. A wreathed circle of reeds and long pointed leaves was chosen for the border detail that prevents the letters from looking isolated. The masking required in such cases is time-consuming (particularly since each face can only be sprayed when the previous stencil is dry) but the effect is well worth it.

❖ YOU WILL NEED ❖

Dark oak-tinted varnish

Paintbrush

Piece of paper

Ruler

Pencil

Piece of string

Map pin

Selected capital letters for monogram, cut out from a newspaper

Tracing paper

Manila card, acetate or plan trace

Scalpel (or cutting blade) and cutting mat

Non-permanent adhesive spray

Craft spray in yellow ochre and dark umber

Pinking shears

Dark oak-tinted varnish

1 Apply two or three coats of dark oak varnish. Then make an accurate plan of the top of the box and find its midpoint by connecting the diagonals from each corner. Mark the midpoint of the box, then using a piece of string and a map pin as a simple compass, draw a circle from the midpoint of the box.

2 Take the chosen initials and enlarge them to the required size on a photocopier. Combine them on tracing paper to form a decorative monogram. Draw a wreathed circle of leaves, following the circle outlined in step one. Complete one half first and then trace it to create a mirror image.

3 Having combined the border and the monogram, transfer them to the manila card, plan trace or acetate and cut the stencil. Mask off all areas of the box that you are not spraying and lay the stencil in position, holding it in place with non-permanent adhesive spray.

▲ Spatter on some dark umber.

4 Apply a thin coat of yellow ochre craft spray and leave to dry. Then spatter on some dark umber.

5 Make a sawtooth border with pinking shears. Spray the border with yellow ochre and leave to dry.

6 Apply a final coat of dark oak tinted varnish (the same as that used to treat the box originally).

For further box projects see:
Hand-painted blanket box pp164–6.

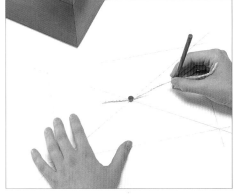
▲ Mark a circle from the centre point.

▲ Combine the initials and wreath.

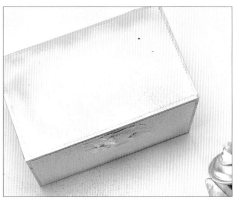
▲ Spray on the zig-zag border.

Templates

Painted decanter and glasses pp92–3
(Photocopy at 58%)

Stencilled balustrade pp130–2
(Photocopy to fit your wall)

Cups and saucers chair pp146–7
(Photocopy at 125%)

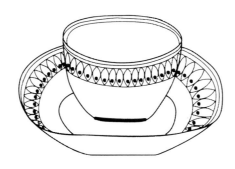

Stencilled pigs chair pp144–5
(Actual size)

Hand-painted blanket box pp164–6
(Photocopy at 74%)

Stencilled headboard pp170–1
(Photocopy at 200%)

Frottaged and stencilled screen pp167–9
(Photocopy at 200%)

Stencilled headboard pp170–1
(Photocopy at 200%)

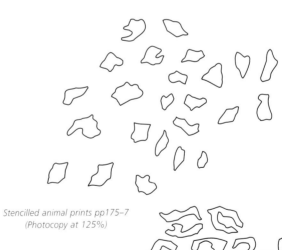

Stencilled animal prints pp175–7
(Photocopy at 125%)

Hand-painted chest pp206–7
(Photocopy at 125%)

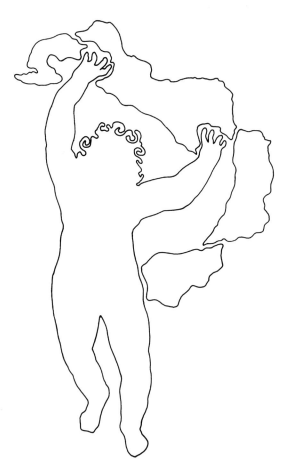

Cherub wardrobe pp180–3
(Actual size)

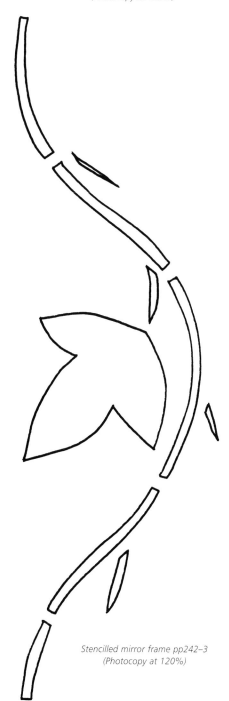

Stencilled mirror frame pp242–3
(Photocopy at 120%)

Poppies picture frame pp236–7
(Photocopy at 105%)

Monogrammed box pp244–5
(Photocopy at 110%)

Suppliers

AUSTRALIA

ACKERSLEY'S PTY LTD
525 Harris Street
Ultimo
Sydney
NSW 2000
(02) 9552 5555

GEELONG ST ANTIQUE CENTRE
2 Geelong Street
Fyshwick
ACT 2609
(02) 6280 7005

HAYMES PAINTS
25 Scott Parade
Ballarat Vic. 3350
(03) 5338 1222
(after hours enquiries)

LANGRIDGE ARTIST'S COLOURS
120 Langridge Street
Collingwood Vic. 3066
(03) 9419 4453

PADDINGHURST GALLERY
32 Oxford Street
Paddington
NSW 2021
(02) 9331 7818

PORTER'S ORIGINAL PAINTS
592 Willoughby Road
Willoughby
NSW 2068
(02) 9958 0753

UK

ARIEL PRESS
177–179 Clapham Manor Street
London
SW4 6DB
020 7720 4622

B&Q PLC
(HEAD OFFICE)
Portswood House
1 Hampshire Corporate Park
Chandlers Ford
Hampshire
SO53 3YX
023 8025 6256

BARGAIN HUNTERS
17 Fleet Street
London
EC4Y 1AA
020 7353 6606

OLIVER BONAS
113 Shepherds Bush Road
Brook Green
London
W6 7LP
020 7371 2662

BORDERLINE FABRICS
Unit 7
Second Floor
Chelsea Harbour Design Centre
London
SW10 OXE
020 7823 3567

C. BREWERS & SONS LTD
Kingston House Estate
Portsmouth Road
Surbiton
KT6 5QG
020 8398 7681

ARODIE & MIDDLETON
68 Drury Lane
London
WC2B 5SP
020 7836 3289

CHANCELLOR'S CHURCH FURNISSHINGS
Postal address:
173 Earlsfield Road
London
SW18 3DD
To view stock:
River Nook Farm
Sunnyside off Terrace Road
Walton-on-Thames
KT12 2ET
01932 252 736

COLOGNE & COTTON
791 Fulham Road
London
SW6 5HD
020 7736 9261

CREATIVE INTERIORS
20 Station Parade
Chipstead
Surrey
CR5 3TE
01737 555443

DAMASK
Broxhulme House
New Kings Road
London
SW6 4AA
020 7731 3553

H.W. DAVIES & SON LTD
Decorator's Merchants
19a Monmouth Place
Bath
BA1 2AY
01225 425638 *(tel/fax)*

E.K.A SERVICES LTD
11 & 12 Hampton Court Parade
East Molesey
Surrey
KT8 9HB
020 8979 3466

ELEPHANT
230 Tottenham Court Road
London
W1P 9AE
020 7637 7930

FOCUS DO IT ALL
(HEAD OFFICE)
Gawsworth House
Westmere Drive
Crew
Cheshire
CW1 6XB
01384 456456

FOXELL & JAMES
57 Farringdon Road
London
EC1M 3JB
020 7405 0152

GREAT MILLS RETAIL LTD
(HEAD OFFICE)
RMC House
Paulton
Bristol
BS39 7SX
01761 416034

GREEN & STONE
259 Kings Road
Chelsea
London
SW3 5EL
020 7352 0837

HIRE CENTERS

Station House
Manor Road North
Hinchley Wood
Esher
Surrey
KT10 0SP
020 8398 9169

HOMEBASE LTD

(HEAD OFFICE)
Beddington House
Wallington
Surrey
SN6 0HB
020 8784 7200

HSS HIRE SHOPS

25 Willow Lane
Mitchum
Surrey
CR4 4TS
020 8260 3100

JALI LTD

Albion Works
Church Lane
Barham
Cantebury
Kent
CT4 6QS
01227 831710

JERRY'S HOME STORE

163–167 Fulham Road
London
SW3 6SN
020 7581 0909

JOHN MYLAND LTD

80 Norwood High Street
West Norwood
London
SE27 9NW
020 8670 9161

PAPER & PAINTS

4 Park Walk
London
SW10 0AD
020 7352 8626

THE PIER

200 Tottenham Court Road
London
W1P 0AD
020 7637 7001

PLASTICOTE

PO Box 867
Pampisford
Cambridge
CB2 4XP
01223 836400

PLOTONS

273 Archway Road
London
N6 5AA
020 8348 0315

STABLE OF IMAGINATION

The Craft & Needlecraft
Centre
Squires Garden Centre
Halliford Road
Upper Halliford
Shepperton
Middlesex
TW17 8RU
01932 788052

RELICS

35 Bridge Street
Witney
Oxfordshire
OX8 6DA
01993 704611
(worldwide mail order service)

ROMANTIQUE MOSAICS

12–13 Pulteney Bridge
Bath
BA2 4AY
01225 463073

ROMO FABRICS

Lowmoor Road
Kirkby-in-Ashfield
Nottinghamshire
NG17 7DE
01623 750005

SAMPSON ASSOCIATES

Unit 1
Hobbs Court
2 Jacob Street
London
SE1 2BG
020 7394 8850

STUART STEVENSON, ARTISTS' & GILDERS' SUPPLIERS

68 Clerkenwell Road
London
EC1M 5QA
020 7253 1693

WINSOR & NEWTON

Whitefriars Avenue
Wealdstone
Harrow
Middlesex
HA3 5RH
020 8427 4343

BARBARA ISRAEL

21 East 79th Street
New York NY 10021
(212) 831 8430

CALICO CORNERS

203 Gale Lane
Kennett Square
PA 19348
(610) 444 9700

CRATE & BARREL

P.O. Box 9059
Wheeling
IL 60090–9059
(847) 215 0025

GAIL GRISI STENCILLING, INC.

P.O. Box 1263
Haddonfield
NJ 08033
(856) 354 1757

HOUSE PARTS

479 Whitehall Street SW
Atlanta GA 30303
(404) 577 5584

ADELE BISHOP STENCIL INC.

3430 South Service Road
Burlington ON L7N 3T9
Canada
(905) 3190051

Glossary

THE RANGE OF DIFFERENT materials that can be used for basic repairs and decorative techniques is vast. Whatever equipment, tool or product you plan to use, be sure to follow manufacturer's guidelines. Always wear appropriate safety equipment and work in ventilated areas.

ABRASIVE PAPER
Available in a range of fine, medium or coarse varieties, this paper is used to prepare a surface for decoration, to distress paint, and to smooth paints and varnishes. See also, silicone carbide finishing papers.

ACETATE
Used in stencilling as an alternative to oiled manila card. Designs must be traced on to acetate using a permanent marker pen.

ACRYLIC GOLDSIZE
A water-based size often used for gilding and metal leaf application. It appears milky on first application but dries to a transparent finish.

ACRYLIC PAINT
Available in matt or satin finishes, this paint has a tough, plastic waterproof finish when dry. It can be used as a paint, thinned with water to make a wash or tinted with acrylic paints, universal stainers or powder pigments to make a range of decorative colours.

ACRYLIC PRIMER
A quick-drying primer that can be used to seal wood. Some brands may also be used on metal and masonry.

ACRYLIC SCUMBLE
A slow-drying, water-based glaze medium, which can be mixed with colour and used for stippling and sponging techniques.

ANTIQUING
The act of making an object look older than it really is. There are various techniques, including the use of colour and stains, craquelure and distressing.

ARTISTS' ACRYLIC PAINT
Quick-drying and durable, these paints are suitable for many types of surface decoration, and can be used to colour acrylic glazes.

ARTISTS' BRUSHES
Finer tipped than house decorating brushes, artists' brushes can be used for intricate painting and are available in a variety of sizes and qualities.

ARTISTS' OIL COLOURS
More slow-drying than acrylics, these paints can be mixed to a range of subtle colours and are suitable for most techniques, providing the surface is oil-based. The paints can also be used to colour oil-based glazes.

BASE COAT
The initial, base application of paint to a surface.

BLACK BISON WAX
A blend of several waxes with good resistance to water and fingermarks, suitable for applying to painted furniture. It creates a seal for crackled and peeled-paint techniques, and also enhances the ageing effect.

CHINA FILLER
Used to fill missing edges, cracks and chips on china, this filler dries to a fine, hard finish on most types of chinaware.

CRACKLE GLAZE
A water-soluble glaze that is applied as a sandwich between two layers of paint or between wood and paint. It dries clear but causes the paint applied over the top to crack, giving the appearance of peeling paint.

CRAQUELURE
The French name for the fine cracks that often cover old oil paintings. The cracks are formed by the layers of paint beneath the varnish surface gradually shrinking. The effect can be imitated by using two-part craquelure varnish.

DECOUPAGE
The French art of cutting, pasting and varnishing paper or fabric images to form a decorated finish.

DISTRESSING
The action of rubbing down and battering a surface to imitate age and wear and tear.

ENAMEL PAINTS
Very smooth and fairly quick drying, these paints are suitable for projects such as barge painting. They have their own cellulose thinners to act as a solvent, but mineral turpentine can be used as an alternative.

GESSO
Made from rabbit skin size and gilders' whiting, gesso is used as a preparation before water gilding. It can also be used to fill the grain on unpainted wood, before being rubbed down to a fine, smooth finish.

GILDING
A decorative technique involving transfer leaf, gilding cream or gilding powder to imitate a metallic finish such as gold.

GILDING POWDER
Painted on to tacky size, gilding powder creates a gold, silver, bronze or copper finish. It can also be mixed with medium to make a metallic paint.

GILT CREAM
This cream can be used as a highlighting agent, or to touch up gilding on frames and furniture. It is applied either by brush or finger and then buffed to a shine, once dry.

GLASS PAINTS
Made with resins that give a brilliant, transparent and durable finish to most glass, plastic or acetate surfaces. However, test plastic surfaces to ensure they are compatible with the paint.

HOG-FITCHES
Good all-purpose brushes, hog-fitches can be used for applying paint, glue, waxes and gilt creams. They are also effective for tamping down metal leaf and painting narrow bands of colour.

HOUSEHOLD BRUSHES
Broader and coarser than artists' brushes, these brushes are suitable for painting fairly large surfaces and come in a variety of sizes.

KEY
Rubbing a surface down to make another coat of paint or varnish adhere properly is known as 'keying'. Use fine grade abrasive paper and a tack rag.

LACQUER
Available in spray or liquid form, lacquer provides a protective varnished surface. Always apply several fine coats, rather than one heavy coat, to avoid runs and a build-up of varnish.

LIMING WAX
A rich paste of clear wax and white pigment used to give a pickled-lime effect to wood. It can also be used as a finishing wax. After opening the grain of the wood with a wire brush, apply the paste with fine steel wool or a cloth. Remove the excess with a cloth and then buff up with a neutral wax to obtain a sheen.

MDF
Medium density fibreboard (often known as MDF) is made from wood fibres that have been highly compressed to create a smooth finish. It comes in different thicknesses, can be bought in various-sized sheets

and is easy to cut. Always use a protective mask when cutting or sanding MDF.

MEDIUM
A liquid in which pigment is suspended.

METHYLATED SPIRIT
Used as a solvent for acrylic paint when creating a distressed effect, methylated spirit can also be used as a thinner and a brush cleaner for shellac and French enamel varnish. It can also be used with fine steel wool for de-greasing surfaces.

MINERAL TURPENTINE
This is used as a thinner for oil-based paint and transparent oil glaze, as well as for brushes, and to clean or remove splashes and spills of oil-based paint.

OIL-BASED HOUSEHOLD PAINTS
Available in flat, semi-gloss and gloss finishes, oil-based paints give a much tougher finish than acrylic paints and are particularly useful in light-coloured, oil-based glazes. They can be tinted with artists' oil paints or universal stainers to create an even more diverse range of colours.

OIL-BASED PRIMER
A slow-drying, durable primer which is useful for surfaces that do not easily accept or grip acrylic primers, such as some metal and plastic surfaces.

OIL-BASED VARNISH
A slow-drying varnish, available in a polyurethane or alkyd formula. It comes in matt, satin and gloss finishes and is generally more durable and heat-proof than water-based varnish, although it does yellow with time. Water-soluble crackle varnish finishes should always be sealed with a protective coat of oil-based varnish.

PAINT STRIPPERS
Use these for varnished or painted surfaces that need to be taken right back to the original wood. Always work with plenty of ventilation and follow the manufacturer's guidelines.

PALETTE KNIFE
Useful for applying filler, mixing paints, or even applying paint, these knives are very flexible and available from most art shops.

PERMANENT INK PENS
Essential for marking designs on stencil film, these pens are permanent, do not smudge, and create clear outlines.

POWDERED PIGMENTS
Natural earth and mineral pigments in powder form c an be mixed with other paint colours, acrylic and PVA mediums, and wax.

PRIMER
Usually oil-based but sometimes available as acrylic, primer should be applied to all raw wood or metal surfaces before painting.

PVA & ACRYLIC MEDIUMS
These water-based mediums are coloured white but dry transparent. PVA can be used as an adhesive or varnish and, when thinned with water, as a paint medium or binder. It can also be mixed with acrylic, gouache, universal stainers or powder pigments to make paints and washes. Artists' acrylic mediums are very useful for extending acrylic paints and for mixing with pure powder pigment to make concentrated colour.

RABBIT SKIN GLUE
This is used as a preparation for gesso, a base for gilding, and as a sealant to stop varnish and water penetrating the paper.

RAGGING
This refers to a range of decorative finishes in which a scrunched cloth (ragging) or plastic bag (bagging) are used to make patterns in wet glaze.

ROTTENSTONE
A finely ground, greyish-brown limestone powder. It is usually used for polishing but can also be used as a powder pigment, especially for antiquing stains.

RUST-INHIBITING PRIMER
An essential base for any piece of metal that is to be coated in a water-based paint, or that has been cleaned and rubbed down of existing rust.

SANDING SEALER
Spirit-based, sanding sealer is useful for sealing new, stripped, dark or heavily knotted wood, before paint is applied. It is an excellent sealing base for decoupage projects and can be used before waxing to give a good base for the final wax sheen.

SCALPEL KNIFE
Needed for cutting stencils, cardboard templates and découpage cut-outs. Replace blades regularly and use in conjunction with a self-healing cutting mat.

SCUMBLE GLAZE
A medium to which paint is added to suspend the colour and delay drying time. Various decorative effects can be achieved while this glaze is wet.

SEA SPONGES
These sponges have a better absorbency and more natural structure than synthetic sponges, so are ideal for creating attractive decorative patterns.

SHELLAC
The naturally occurring resin of the lac beetle, shellac is mixed with methylated spirit to form a quick-drying varnish. It is traditionally used in furniture restoration and French polishing. Shellac is available in a variety of grades and colours and may be sold under a number of different names. Use clear shellac sanding sealer, white French polish and white button polish for sealing wood, paper and paint. Use brown French polish or garnet polish for staining, ageing and sealing. French enamel varnish is transparent shellac with added dye, and is good for ageing and sealing wood.

SILICON CARBIDE FINISHING PAPERS
Sometimes known as wet and dry papers, these papers are obtainable in much finer grades than normal abrasive sheets. They are used to give a smooth finish to varnish, or distress a painted surface without causing scratches.

SOFTENING
A term used to refer to the 'blurring' of paint, colour or glaze edges. Soft brushes or cloths are used to blend the colours and soften the division.

SOFT-HAIRED MOP BRUSHES
These round brushes are often used in gilding because they are ideal for dusting gilding powder on to goldsize. A soft squirrel paintbrush can be used as a cheap alternative.

SPONGING
A simple decorative technique involving the application of paint with a sponge. Sponges can also be used to lift off wet paint from a surface, creating an attractive, textured effect.

SPRAY PAINT
Ideal for stencilling projects, acrylic spray paints can be used on most surface types, including wood, plaster and plastic. Spray enamels for metals and glass, including pearlized finishes and polyurethane varnishes, are also available. Apply the paint in several thin coats, rather than one heavy one, to avoid paint build-up and runs.

STEEL WOOL
There are various grades of steel wool, from very fine (0000) to coarse (00). It can be used for cleaning wood, metal and glass,

for applying wax, and for distressing painted surfaces. Fine steel wool does not scratch or mark wood if it is used gently, and can help to create a very smooth finish. Soaked in mineral turpentinet or warm water, it is very useful for cleaning wooden furniture. If it is used with varnish and paint removers, wear protective gloves and always cover the surrounding area to catch the fine steel filaments that come away as the wool is rubbed.

STENCIL BRUSHES

Usually made from hog's hair, stencil brushes are round and firm-bristled, and come in a wide range of sizes for both small and large stencil work. When stencilling with acrylic paint, choose brushes that have a little 'give' in the bristles, rather than the very firm variety. A double-ended stencil brush is particularly useful when using two colours. Special stencil brushes for use on fabrics are also available; these have softer, longer bristles but are not suitable for hard surfaces.

STENCIL FILM

Made from transparent polyester sheeting, stencil film is very flexible and durable.

STENCIL PAINT AND STICKS

Water-based acrylic or oil-based stencil paint can be obtained in small pots. Stencil sticks are oil-based and wrapped in a sealed film. They are very versatile and can be blended to make different shades and colours.

STENCILLING

The technique of applying a design to a surface using thin film or card. The design is cut into the stencil card, and then paint is applied through the incisions, onto the surface.

STIPPLING

The term used for gently lifting on or off very fine speckles of paint.

STIPPLING BRUSHES

Stippling brushes have stiff, dense bristles in a squared-off shape. They are useful for merging paints and removing hard lines and edges.

STOCKINET

Ideal for polishing and mopping up, these cloths can also be used to create texture on a painted surface and for eliminating brush marks.

SWORD LINERS

These long-haired, soft brushes are tapered and angled, and are capable of producing many widths of line simply by varying the pressure applied to the brushstroke.

TACK RAGS

These are small, versatile, long-lasting oily cloths that are ideal for cleaning wood, metal, plaster or any other surface (except glass). They pick up and hold dust and dirt, leaving a completely clean surface, ready to work on.

TRADITIONAL PAINT

Containing natural pigments and chalk, traditional paints dry to a completely matt finish that appears considerably lighter than the colour in the pot. They can be easily marked, however, and so should be protected with a coat of varnish or wax. The paints can be thinned with water and tinted in the same way as acrylic paint.

TRANSFER METAL LEAF

Bronze, aluminium and copper leaf are inexpensive and a good substitute for real gold and silver leaf, when adding decorative touches to furniture. Transfer leaf, which is sold in packs of 25 sheets, is available from specialist art shops. Each sheet consists of very finely beaten metal backed with waxed paper. The metal is transferred from the paper on to tacky size. Metal leaf tarnishes in time, so it needs to be sealed with shellac or varnish.

TRANSFER PAPER

Coated with a chalky film, transfer paper is coloured red, blue, black and white. It is placed between the design to be transferred and the surface to be decorated. The outline is then transferred by tracing over it with a pen or pencil.

TWO-PART CRAQUELURE VARNISH

This consists of a slow-drying, oil-based varnish and a quick-drying, water-soluble varnish. The water-soluble varnish is brushed over a layer of very slightly tacky oil-based varnish. Later, a cracked porcelain effect appears due to the difference in drying times. This becomes clearly visible when artists' oil colour is rubbed into the surface and gets caught in the cracks.

UNDERCOAT

A layer of protective paint applied between primer and final surface paint.

UNIVERSAL STAINERS

Although universal stainers lack the range of subtle colours of oil and acrylic paints, they will mix with virtually anything, including both water-based and oil-based mediums. They come in liquid form, are extremely strong and are cheap to obtain.

VARNISH REMOVERS

A number of varnish removers are available although most paint strippers can also be used on varnished surfaces.

VERDIGRIS

A bluish-green patina which forms on copper, bronze or brass with age. The effect is associated with historic spires and domes, but can be imitated with paint and gilding cream.

WATER-BASED VARNISH

Water-based acrylic varnishes are now widely available in gloss, satin, matt and occasionally flat finishes. Although they are milky in appearance, these varnishes dry to a clear finish and are non-yellowing. However, the matt and flat versions contain chalk, which gives them a cloudy appearance when a number of coats are applied, so they are unsuitable to use for the many layers that are required in decoupage. These finishes are softer and less durable than satin or gloss varnish.

WAXES

Clear furniture wax is an effective resist (that is, it creates a block, preventing paint from reaching a surface), when creating an aged appearance to furniture. It can be used over paint or wood to prevent a new layer of paint from adhering to the surface. Clear liquid wax is particularly good for this and is obtainable from specialist suppliers. Clear wax is also used as a protective finishing wax over paint or matt varnish; it can be coloured with rottenstone and other pigments.

There is also a large variety of brown or antiquing furniture waxes that can be used for staining wood. Walnut shades are good for ageing all colours of paint, but the antiquing waxes are generally yellowing and are not suitable on blue paint. However, they give a wonderful glow to many shades of yellow and green paint.

WET AND DRY PAPER

See silicon carbide finishing paper.

WIRE BRUSHES

These are used to open up the grain on wood before liming and to remove flaking paint and rust.

WOOD FILLER

Specialist wood fillers tend to be better for wooden surfaces than ordinary, multipurpose fillers. Water-based varieties are particularly easy to use and come in a variety of wood colour finishes. They can be used to fill small holes, dents and cracks, as well as seal around bad joints and joins in wood.

Index

A

abrasive papers, 13
acetate sheets, stencils, 62
acrylic paint, 25
  stencilling, 65
acrylic varnish, 26–7
adhesive, 17, 28–9
adhesives, gilding, 68
ageing, 54
  Aged rustic chair, 212–13
  Antiqued iron bed frame, 178–9
  Antiqued table, 104–5
  Distressed chest, 198–9
  gilding, 70
  sources of inspiration, 80–1
  Verdigris mirror and door handles, 188–9
alkid paints, stencilling, 66
animal prints, Stencilled, 175–7
Antiqued table, 104–5
architecture, inspiration from, 76–7
art, inspiration from, 86–7
artists' acrylic paint, 25
  stencilling, 65
artists' brushes, 30
artists' oil crayons and pastels, 28–9
artists' oil paint, 25

B

bagging, 38
  Painted panels, 133–5
balustrade, Stencilled, 130–2
barge painting, 58–9
bathroom paint, 28–9
bathroom projects, 187–201
bedroom projects, 159–85
bed frame, Antiqued iron, 178–9
Black Bison wax, 19
blackboard paint, 28–9
boxes
  Hand-painted blanket box, 164–6
  Malachite painted box, 226–9
  Monogrammed box, 244–5
brushes, 30–1
  gilding, 68
  stencilling, 66
  wire, 13

C

carbon paper 63
CD box, Ethnic stamped, 240–1
cellulose lacquer, 18
ceramic paints, 56, 152–4
ceramics, stencilling, 63
chairs
  Aged rustic chair, 212–13
  Crackled chair, 144–5
  Cups and saucers chair, 146–7
  Gilded chair, 102–3
  Ivy-stamped chair, 150–1
  Spray-painted chairs, 204–5
  Stamped artichoke chair, 102–3
  Stencilled cane chair, 160–1
  Stencilled pigs chair, 144–5
chalking, paint problems, 33
charcoal, transferring designs, 62–3
Chequered frame, 232–3
Chequered walls, 94–7
chests
  Distressed chest, 198–9
  Hand-painted chest, 206–7
  Stencilled chest, 198–9
china, Painted, 152–4
chipboard, preparation, 21
cissing, 33
cleaning surfaces, 12
cloths, 12
colour toning, 40–1
colours, mixing, 31–2
colourwashing, 36–7
  Colourwashed oak sideboard, 98–9
  Colourwashed wall, 124–5
complementary colours, 31–2
cracking, paint problems, 33
crackle glaze 54–5
  Aged rustic chair, 212–13
  Brightly coloured pots, 216–17
  Crackled chair, 144–5
  Cups and saucers chair, 146–7
craft knives, 20
craft paint, 28–9
craquelure, 54–5
  Craquelure lamp base and shade, 116–18
cupboard, Lined clock, 142–3
cutting
  cutting tools, 20
  stamps, 73
  stencils, 63

D E

designs
  scaling up and down, 61
  transferring, 62–3
detergents, 12
dining room projects, 89–107
dragging, 38–9
  brushes, 30
    Painted panels, 133–5
  Repeating border and dragged stripes, 208–11
  Scumble-glazed table, 122–3
dressing table, Marbled, 162–3
driers, 25
dripping, paint problems, 33
Ethnic stamped CD box, 240–1

F

fabrics
  painting, 56–7, 218–21
  stencilling, 63–4, 175–7
faux stone blocks, 48
filling gaps and holes, 16
fireplace, Granite effect, 126–7
Fish stencil shower glass, 193–5
floggers, 30
floors
  Geometric starburst floor, 90–1
  Old oak woodgrained floor, 113–15
  Sponge-stamped floor, 128–9
flowers
  barge painting, 58–9
  sources of inspiration, 82–3
frames
  Chequered frame, 232–3
  Gilded mirror frame, 119–21
  Golden pear picture frame, 234–5
  Limed picture frame, 230–1
  Periwinkle frame and box, 232–3
  Poppies picture frame, 236–7
  Porphyry picture frame, 106–7
  Stencilled mirror frame, 242–3
  Verdigris mirror and door handles, 188–9
freehand painting, 57
  Colourwashed oak sideboard, 98–9
  Freehand painted tables, 110–12
  Golden pear picture frame, 234–5

Hand-painted chest, 206–7
Hand-painted blanket box, 164–6
Key holder, 140–1
Pine shelf, 138–9
Pine spice rack, 139
Pine spoon holder, 140–1
Tartan-band dining table, 100–1
friezes
  A bedroom frieze, 172–4
  A kitchen frieze, 148–9
frottage, 39–40
  Frottaged and stencilled screen, 167–9

G

garden projects, 203–21
garnet paper, 13
Geometric starburst floor, 90–1
gilding, 68–71
  Gilded chair, 102–3
  Gilded mirror frame, 119–21
glass, stencilling, 64
glass paints, 28–9, 56
  Brilliant painted glass, 155–7
  Painted decanter and glasses, 92–3
glasspaper, 13
glaze, 25, 26–7, 34–6
  Chequered walls, 94–7
  glaze ageing, 54
gloss paint, 26–7
Golden pear picture frame, 234–5
gouache, 25
granite effects, 46, 126–7
grids
  scaling designs up or down, 61
  transferring designs, 62

H

hardboard, preparation, 21
headboard, Stencilled, 170–1
hidden stencilling, 67
hog-fitch brushes, 30
holes, filling, 16
hot air guns, 14

I K

inspiration, sources of, 75–87
Ivy-stamped chair, 150–1
Key holder, 140–1
kitchen paint, 28–9
kitchen paper, 31

kitchen projects, 137–57
knives, craft, 20

L

lacquer, cellulose, 18
lamps
  Craquelure lamp base and
    shade, 116–18
  Tortoiseshell lamp base and
    shade, 224–5
lapis lazuli effects, 49
lead paint, safety, 14
leather effects, 49
leaves, inspiration, 82–3
liming wood, 51
  Limed picture frame, 230–1
  Limewashed bath panels,
    196–7
Lined clock cupboard, 142–3
living room projects, 109–35

M

mahogany finish, woodgraining,
  50
malachite effects, 45
  Malachite painted box,
    226–9
marbling, 46–7
  Marble bathroom, 200–1
  Marbled dressing table,
    162–3
  Marbled pots, 214–15
MDF, preparation, 21
melamine primer, 28–9
metal
  preparation, 21
  sources of inspiration, 78–9
metal effects, 44–5
  verdigris, 44–5, 188–9
Mexican-style bathroom, 190–2
mirror frames see frames
mops, soft-haired, 30

N O

newspaper rack, Stencilled
  238–9
oak finish, woodgraining, 50
oil-based glaze, 26–7, 36
oil-based paints, 24
  stencilling, 66
oiled manila card, stencils, 62
Old oak woodgrained floor,
  113–15

P

paint kettles, 31
paint strippers, 14–16
painted surfaces, stencilling, 63
paints, types, 24–9
panels
  Limewashed bath panels,
    196–7
  Painted panels, 133–5
pantographs, 61
pencil, transferring designs, 63
Periwinkle frame,
  232–3
picture frames see frames
pigments, 28–9, 32
Pine shelf, 138–9
Pine spice rack, 139
Pine spoon holder, 140–1
plaster, mock, 49
plastics, preparation, 21
plywood, preparation, 21
polyurethane varnish, 26–7
Poppies picture frame, 236–7
porphyry effects, 49
  Porphyry picture frame,
    106–7
pots, Decorated, 214–17
primary colours, 31
primer, 24, 26–7
priming, 16–17
problems, paint, 32–3
pumice, filling holes, 16
PVA adhesive, 28–9

R

rabbit skin glue, 17
rag rolling, 37–8
  Cherub wardrobe, 180–3
ragging, 37
  Painted panels, 133–5
reverse stencilling, 67
rollers, 31
rubber stamps, 72–3
rubbing down, 13–14

S

safety, 12, 14, 36
sagging, paint problems, 33
saws, 20
scaling designs up or down, 61
Scandinavian painting, 59
scrapers, 13–14
screen, Frottaged and
  stencilled, 167–9
Scumble-glazed table, 122–3
sealants, 17
semi-gloss paint, 26–7
shading, trompe l'oeil, 53
shellac, 18
  stripping, 15
shelves, 138–9

sideboard, Colourwashed
  oak, 98–9
size, gilding, 68
skies, trompe l'oeil, 53
small rollers, 31
spice rack, Pine, 139
sponges, 30
  stamping, 72
  stencilling, 66
sponging, 41
  Sponged pots, 214–15
spoon holder, Pine, 140–1
spray paint, 25, 28–9
  Spray-painted table and
    chairs, 204–5
  stencilling, 65–6
staining wood, 51
stamping, 72–3
  Ethnic stamped CD box,
    240–1
  Ivy-stamped chair, 150–1
  Sponge-stamped floor, 128–9
  Stamped artichoke chair,
    102–3
stencilling, 60–7
  A bedroom frieze, 172–4
  Cherub wardrobe, 180–3
  Children's balloon stencils,
    184–5
  Fish stencil shower glass,
    193–5
  Frottaged and stencilled
    screen, 167–9
  Geometric starburst floor,
    90–1
  A kitchen frieze, 148–9
  Mexican-style bathroom,
    190–2
  Monogrammed box, 244–5
  newspaper rack, Stencilled
    238–9
  Poppies picture frame, 236–7
  Repeating border and
    dragged stripes, 208–11
  Stencilled animal prints,
    175–7
  Stencilled balustrade, 130–2
  Stencilled cane chair, 160–1
  Stencilled chest, 198–9
  Stencilled headboard, 170–1
  Stencilled mirror frame, 242–3
  Stencilled pigs chair, 144–5
stippling, 39, 41
stippling brushes, 30
stone effects, 44, 45–9
  faux stone blocks, 48
  granite effects, 46, 126–7
  lapis lazuli effects, 49
  malachite effects, 45, 226–9
  marbling, 46–7
  porphyry effects, 49, 106–7
  sources of inspiration, 78–9
surfaces, preparation, 12–19, 21
sword liners, 30

T

tablecloth, Painted, 218–21
tables
  Antiqued table, 104–5
  Dragged effect table, 122–3
  Freehand painted tables,
    110–12
  Spray-painted table, 204–5
  Tartan-band dining table,
    100–1
tack rags, 12
Tartan-band dining table, 100–1
textiles, sources of inspiration,
  84–5
textured wall paint, 28–9
tortoiseshell, 45
  Tortoiseshell lamp base and
    shade, 224–5
tracing designs, 20
traditional paints, 25
transferring designs, 62–3
trompe l'oeil, 52–3

U V

undercoat, 26–7
varnishes, 17–19, 26–7
  stripping, 15
vegetable stamps, 72, 73
verdigris, 44–5
  Verdigris mirror and door
    handles, 188–9
vinyl paints, 26–7

W Y

wallpaper, stripping, 16
walls
  A bedroom frieze, 172–4
  Chequered walls, 94–7
  Children's balloon stencils,
    184–5
  Colourwashed wall, 124–5
  Marble bathroom, 200–1
  Painted panels, 133–5
  Repeating border and
    dragged stripes, 208–11
  Stencilled balustrade, 130–2
wardrobe, Cherub, 180–3
waxes, 19, 26–7
  ageing with, 54
wet and dry paper, 13
wire brushes, 13
wood
  preparation, 21
  sources of inspiration, 78–9
  stencilling, 64
wood finish effects, 50–1
woodgraining, 50
  Old oak woodgrained floor,
    113–15
woodstain, 26–7